Knitting the New Classics

60 Exquisite Sweaters from Classic Elite Yarns

Kristin Nicholas

Sterling Publishing Co., Inc. New York
A Sterling/Lark Book

Editor: Leslie Dierks
Art Director: Kathleen Holmes
Production: Elaine Thompson, Kathleen Holmes

Photography:
  Richard Babb, pp. 5, 149.
  Clint Clemens, pp. 17, 42.
  Terry Davis, RBA Studios, pp. 49, 96, 98, 121, 123.
  John Goodman, pp. 6, 11, 12, 19, 21, 33, 34, 72, 75, 114, 117, 134, 159.
  Philip Newton, pp. 4, 5, 7, 14, 29, 30, 39, 40, 45, 47, 53, 56, 63, 64, 77, 79,
      85, 87, 89, 103, 107, 108, 110, 112, 119, 125, 131, 132, 139, 141, 142,
      145, 147, 148.
  Peter Ogilvie, pp. 4, 8, 10, 23, 25, 26, 69, 71, 81, 82, 93, 94, 99, 100, 127,
      128, 137.

Illustrations:
  Sandra Montgomery, pp. 152, 153 (right side of page)
  Kay Holmes Stafford, pp. 153 (lower left), 154

Library of Congress Cataloging-in-Publication Data
  Nicholas, Kristin.
      Knitting the new classics : 60 exquisite sweaters from Elite /
  Kristin Nicholas
          p.   cm.
      "A Sterling/Lark book."
      Includes index.
      ISBN 0-8069-3172-8
          1. Knitting--United States--Patterns.   2. Sweaters--United States.
  I. Classic Elite Yarns (Firm)   II. Title
  TT819.U6N53   1995
  746.43'20432--dc20   95-6205
                                                            CIP

10 9 8 7 6 5

A Sterling/Lark Book

First paperback edition published in 1998 by
  Sterling Publishing Company, Inc.
  387 Park Avenue South, New York, N.Y. 10016

Produced by Altamont Press, Inc.
  50 College Street, Asheville, NC 28801

© 1995 by Classic Elite Yarns

Distributed in Canada by Sterling Publishing
  % Canadian Manda Group, One Atlantic Avenue, Suite 105
  Toronto, Ontario, Canada M6K 3E7

Distributed in Great Britain and Europe by Cassell PLC
  Wellington House. 125 Strand, London WC2R 0BB, England

Distributed in Australia by Capricorn Link (Australia) Pty Ltd.
  P.O. Box 6651, Baulkham Hills, Business Centre, NSW 2153, Australia

Sterling ISBN 0-8069-3172-8 Trade
               0-8069-3170-1 Paper

To the mothers, grandmothers, and friends who have tirelessly shared their knitting knowledge and expertise.

ACKNOWLEDGMENTS

This collection would not have been possible without our talented in-house designers, Gerlinde Faria, Susan Mills, Cathy Payson, Linda Pratt, and Pauline St. Germain, our freelance contributors, Norah Gaughan, Stephanie Gildersleeve, Julie Hoff, Sally Lee, Deborah Newton, Michele Rose, and Kathy Zimmerman, and our dedicated team of knitters, including Carol Moran, Peggy Desmond, Judy Goldman, Kathy Zimmerman, and Jeanne Moran. Nor would it have been possible without the support of Patricia Chew, the owner of Classic Elite Yarns, who continues to have confidence in all I do. Sincere thanks go to our pattern checkers, Dottie Ratigan, Sheila Richardson, and Carla Patrick Scott, our fashion stylists, Karen Harrison and Teresa Ginori, our photographers, especially Philip Newton, and our friend and hair stylist, Michael Tammaro. Thanks are extended to Madelaine D'Addiego, the Mohair Council of America, the American Wool Council, and David Xenakis of Golden Fleece Publications for their technical assistance. For their indispensable help with photo locations, props, and such, a hearty thank you goes to Jane Barber, Mrs. H. Laughlin Blair, Marguerite Moore Blair, Carole Campbell, Liz Crawford, Susan Eggerton, Jo Flanagan, Nancy Fry, Jane Kellogg, Grace Panciera, Mickey Pugh, Bob Sneider at Dobson's Boat Yard, and the entire staff of the Smith-McDowell House Museum. Special thanks go to the following child models (and their parents) for donating their time and personalities to our photos: Leslie, Julie, Willie, Jackson, and Andrew Barber, Hillary and Rachel Greene, Alec and Caitlin Gorski, Jeffrey and Matthew Phillips, and Trevor and Tim Utley. Thanks, too, to all the employees of Classic Elite Yarns; through their efforts, what was once a vision is now a reality.

Introduction

Easy styling and technique make this design
ideal for inexperienced knitters.

KNITTING IS A creative art form that
began thousands of years ago when
an enterprising spinner took two
sticks and began wrapping and loop-
ing yarn to produce a springy, elastic
piece of fabric for nets and garments.
In the present century, knitting has
come into its own with the emer-
gence of new techniques and
improved ways to work ancient ones.

The sweaters in this book utilize a
wide cross section of knitting techniques, including cables, intarsia,
Fair Isle, and basic knitting. They
also embrace a full range of skill levels. Some designs are easy enough
for beginners (see the chapter called
"Quick and Simple"), while others
are very challenging due to their
intricate cabling or color work. Most
designs fall well within the skill levels of experienced knitters.

All of the garments were produced by
American knitwear designers who
specialize in hand knits. The collection has its roots in the casual, sporty
look that American designers have
made their signature style. As it has
found its way into European and
Asian markets, this "American look"
has become an important influence in
fashion worldwide.

Many of the patterns in this book
feature "unisex" styling and are
equally flattering on men and
women. Some designs are given in
both cardigan and pullover versions,
and many are sized for children as
well as adults. With all the time
that is expended on one hand-knit
sweater, it is very satisfying to have
a husband and wife, brother and
sister, or boyfriend and girlfriend
share a sweater.

Hand-knit sweaters quickly become
an integral part of anyone's
wardrobe. A classic sweater can be
worn for many years and is suitable
for most occasions. It's equally comfortable and attractive to wear to a

picnic, to work, or out to dinner. Sweaters are flattering to many figure types, and they're beautiful displays of the technical ability of the knitters who make them.

CREATING A KNITWEAR COLLECTION

For over ten years, Classic Elite Yarns has produced an annual collection of hand-knitting patterns. Beginning with input from an assortment of international fashion magazines, the silhouettes, lengths, widths, stitch ideas, textures, and colors are developed in our studio for the upcoming season's hand-knit collection. Other sources of ideas are old pattern booklets and women's magazines from the 1920s, when hand-knit designs were first published. These older books and pamphlets are valuable today because their photographs often trigger a new stitch idea or a different neckline.

Stitch books are probably the most important sources for the fabric designs in our collections. These books, some of which have been in print for over 20 years, can continue to inspire a designer for countless seasons. Each year, as fashions change, the same book can be a source of fresh, "new" stitch ideas.

Classic Elite also works with a few select outside designers to produce sweater patterns. Designers such as Deborah Newton, Michele Rose, Sally Lee, and Norah Gaughan design knitwear to fit the Classic Elite style.

In the end, the individual hand knitter is the strongest influence on the development of our collection. We know that knitters are always looking for a new idea, stitch, or technique as they work their next project. Hand knitters also want to be wearing the colors and textures that are important in the current fashion cycle. We choose classic designs that will be wearable for many seasons while still projecting a fashion image; this book is a collection of 60 of our favorites.

WITH THEIR ELABORATE CABLING PATTERNS, THESE SWEATERS OFFER GREATER CHALLENGES.

Quick & Simple

SIZES

Small(Medium,Large,Extra Large)
Finished measurements: 36(40,44,48)"
(91.5,101.5,112,122 cm)

MATERIALS

La Gran (74% mohair, 13% wool, 13% nylon; 1½ oz. = approx. 90 yards):
10(11,11,12) balls
Equivalent yarn: 900(990,990,1080) yards/823(905,905,988) meters of bulky brushed mohair
Knitting needles in sizes 7 and 9 U.S. (4.5 and 5.5 mm)
Cable needle (cn)
¾" (2 cm) buttons for cardigan (8)
16" (40.5 cm) circular needle in size 7 U.S. (4.5 mm) for pullover

GAUGE

Stockinette stitch on larger needles: 16 sts and 20 rows = 4" (10 cm)
Cable over 10 sts = 2" (5 cm)
Take time to save time—check your gauge.

PATTERN STITCHES

1 x 1 RIB

(over even number of sts)
All rows: K1, p1.

STOCKINETTE STITCH

Row 1: (RS) K all sts.
Row 2: P all sts.

CABLE PATTERN

(over 10 sts)
Rows 1, 5, and 7: (RS) P2, k6, p2.
Rows 2, 4, 6, and 8: K2, p6, k2.
Row 3: P2, sl 3 sts to cn and hold in front, k3, k3 from cn, p2.
Repeat rows 1-8.

PULLOVER

BACK

With smaller needles, c.o. 68(76,84,92) sts.
Work 1 x 1 rib for 3" (7.5. cm) inc 14 sts evenly across last row to give 82(90, 98,106) sts.
Change to larger needles and est cable patt as foll: Work 4(6,8,10) sts in St st, * work cable over 10 sts, work 6(7,8,9) sts in St st, *; rep bet *'s 3 more times, work cable over 10 sts, work 4(6,8,10) sts in St st.
When piece meas 23(24,25,26)" (58.5,61,63.5,66 cm), b.o. all sts.

FRONT

Work as for back until piece meas 21(22,23,24)" (53.5,56,58.5,61 cm).
Shape neck as foll: Work across 1st 33(37,40,44) sts, join a 2nd ball of yarn and b.o. center 16(16,18,18) sts, work to end.
Cont working each side sep and b.o. 2 sts at each neck edge 1(2,2,2) times, then 1 st every other row 3(2,3,3) times to give 28(31,33,37) sts on each side.
When piece meas same as back, b.o. all sts.

SLEEVES

With smaller needles c.o. 30(32,34,36) sts.
Work 1 x 1 rib for 3" (7.5 cm).
Change to larger needles and est cable patt as foll: K0(1,2,3), p2, work 8 sts St st, cable 10, work 8 sts in St st, p2, k0(1,2,3) sts.
At the same time, inc 1 st each end every 3rd row 22(23,24,24) times to give 74(78,82,84) sts.
Work inc sts into cable when there are sufficient sts.
When piece meas 17(17,17½,18)" (43,43,44.5,45.5 cm), b.o. all sts.

FINISHING

Sew shoulder seams.
With circular needle, p.u. and k 68(72,76,80) sts around neck edge.
Work in 1 x 1 rib for 1" (2.5 cm).
B.o. all sts.
Meas down 8½(9,9¾,9¾)" (21.5,23, 25,25 cm) from shoulder seam on front and back.
Sew in sleeves bet points.
Sew side and underarm seams.

Beginners who want a challenge will be fascinated by the easy crossing of stitches that form the simple rope cable on these cardigan and pullover sweaters. The use of brushed mohair adds a sophisticated look to this basic, flattering design. Beginner's note: Avoid dark colors, since they make it more difficult to examine stitches, especially in poorly lit circumstances.

Design: CATHY PAYSON
Knitting rating: BEGINNER

CARDIGAN

BACK

Work as for pullover back.

RIGHT FRONT

With smaller needles, c.o. 41(45,49,53) sts.
Work 1st 5 sts in garter st (knit all sts, all rows), pm, work in 1 x 1 rib to end.
Work as est for 3" (7.5 cm) placing a buttonhole when piece meas 1" (2.5 cm).
For buttonhole: K3, yo, k2tog, work to end of row.
Next row: Work garter st in yo to complete buttonhole.
When piece meas 3" (7.5 cm) and you are on WS, inc 4 sts evenly across to give 45(49,53,57) sts.
Change to larger needles and est cable patt as foll: Work 5 sts in garter st, * work 10(11,12,13) sts in St st, work cable over 10 sts, *; rep bet *'s once more, end with 4(6,8,10) sts in St st.
Work as est in patt placing 5 more buttonholes evenly spaced as before every 3¼(3¼,3½,3¾)" (8.5,8.5,9,9.5 cm).
When piece meas 20(21,22,23)" (51,53.5,56,58.5 cm), **shape neck:**

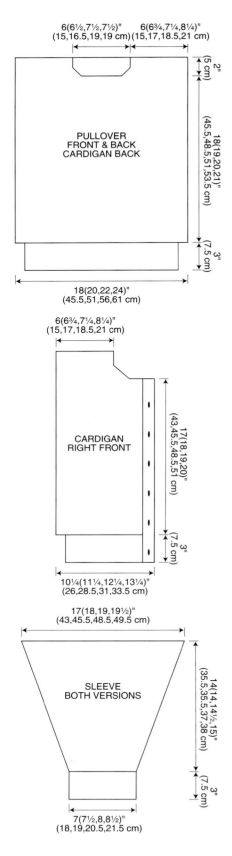

6(6½,7½,7½)"
(15,16.5,19,19 cm)　6(6¾,7¼,8¼)"
(15,17,18.5,21 cm)

2"
(5 cm)

PULLOVER
FRONT & BACK
CARDIGAN BACK

18(19,20,21)"
(45.5,48.5,51,53.5 cm)

3"
(7.5 cm)

18(20,22,24)"
(45.5,51,56,61 cm)

6(6¾,7¼,8¼)"
(15,17,18.5,21 cm)

CARDIGAN
RIGHT FRONT

17(18,19,20)"
(43,45.5,48.5,51 cm)

3"
(7.5 cm)

10¼(11¼,12¼,13¼)"
(26,28.5,31,33.5 cm)

17(18,19,19½)"
(43,45.5,48.5,49.5 cm)

SLEEVE
BOTH VERSIONS

14(14,14½,15)"
(35,35.5,37,38 cm)

3"
(7.5 cm)

7(7½,8,8½)"
(18,19,20.5,21.5 cm)

On RS, b.o. 12(12,13,13) sts, then every other row on RS b.o. 2 sts 1(2,2,2) times, then 1 st 3(2,3,3) times to give 28(31,33,37) sts.

When piece meas same as back, b.o. all sts.

LEFT FRONT

Work as for right front, omitting buttonholes and reversing shaping and cable positions.

FINISHING

Sew shoulder seams.

With smaller needles p.u. and k 68(72, 76,80) sts around neck edges and work in 1 x 1 rib for 1" (2.5 cm) making 7th buttonhole on right front in third row.

B.o. all sts.

Meas down 8½(9,9½,9¾)" (21.5,23, 24,25 cm) from shoulder seam on front and back and sew sleeve bet points.

Sew side and underarm seams.

Sew on buttons.

SIZES

Small(Medium,Large,Extra Large)
Finished measurements at bust: 36(40,44,48)" (91.5,101.5,112,122 cm)

MATERIALS

Applause (33% mohair, 14% silk, 41% rayon, 6% wool, 6% nylon; 50 grams = approx. 70 yards): 11(12,12,13) hanks; OR La Gran (74% mohair, 13% wool, 13% nylon, 1½ oz. = approx. 90 yards): 9(10,10,11) balls
Equivalent yarn: 810(900,900,990) yards/741(823,823,905) meters of bulky brushed novelty mohair
24" (61 cm) circular needles in sizes 8 and 10½ U.S. (5 and 6.5 mm)
Double-pointed needles (dpn) in sizes 8 and 10½ U.S. (5 and 6.5 mm)
Stitch holders (4)

GAUGE

St st worked in round: 3½ sts and 4½ rows = 1" (2.5 cm)
Take time to save time—check your gauge.

Knitting in the round is a favorite method for many beginners. The sleeves and body of this pullover are worked on circular needles, and the underarm stitches are slipped to holders; then all pieces are joined, and the shaping of the raglan sleeves is worked in the round. This technique goes rapidly, and there are no seams to sew when the knitting is finished. Many knitters will want to work up multiples of this simple design, which is shown here in a space-dyed novelty mohair/silk blend.

Design: **Kristin Nicholas**
Knitting rating: **BEGINNER**

PATTERN STITCHES

1 x 1 TWISTED RIB

Row 1: (RS) * K1 into back of st, p1 *, rep bet *'s.
Row 2: * K1, p1 *, rep bet *'s.
Repeat rows 1 and 2.

STOCKINETTE STITCH

(in round)
All rnds: K all sts.

SSK

Sl as if to knit, sl as if to knit, insert the left needle into the front of the two sts (from left to right), and knit them tog as if they were one.

BODY

Using smaller circular needle, c.o. 108(118,130,142) sts.
Join sts taking care not to twist.
Work in 1 x 1 twisted rib for 3½" (9 cm).

11

In last row of rib, inc 20(22,22,26) sts evenly around to give 128(140,152, 168) sts.

Mark side seams bet 1st and last sts and 64th and 65th(70th and 71st,76th and 77th,84th and 85th) sts.

Change to larger needles and beg working in St st.

Work until piece meas 14½(15,15½, 16)" (37,38,39.5,40.5 cm) or desired length at underarm.

Sl centered 10(12,12,14) sts at sides onto holder for underarm join— 5(6,6,7) sts on each side of marker.

Stop at one of seam lines.

Set aside.

SLEEVES

On smaller dpn, c.o. 28(28,30,32) sts.

Join sts onto 3 needles taking care not to twist. Use the 4th needle to knit with.

You may want to work a few rows in 1 x 1 twisted rib back and forth to make joining easier.

Then join and work in round and use tail of yarn to sew little seam.

Work in 1 x 1 twisted rib for 3" (7.5 cm).

Mark underam point 1 st after 1st st and 1 st before last st in round. These will become the underarm increase points.

In last row of rib, inc 8 sts evenly around to give 36(36,38,40) sts.

Beg working in St st using larger needles.

Inc 2 sts at underarm point 14(15,16, 17) times every 4th round.

To do this, k1 st, m1, work to mark at end of round, m1 k last st.

You will have 64(66,70,74) sts when inc are complete.

Work until sleeve meas 17(17½,18, 18½)" (43,44.5,45.5,47 cm) or desired length at underam stopping at under-arm mark.

Sl centered 10(12,12,14) sts at seam to holder for underam join—5(6,6,7) sts at each side of "seam line."

Set aside.

FINISHING

Join sleeves and body onto circular nee-dle by knitting the sleeves in between

back and front to give 216(224,244, 260) sts on needle, placing markers as you go between the body sts and the sleeve sts. These points will be shaping points for the raglan sleeves.

Work 5 rounds in St st.

First dec round: Beg at 1st body mark-er (which will become back), sl marker, k1, ssk, * knit to within 3 sts of next marker, k2tog, k1, sl marker, k1, ssk *, rep at each marker ending last (eighth) dec—knit to within 3 sts of next mark-er, k2tog, k1. Eight sts are dec each round.

It is necessary in the beginning rounds to eliminate the sleeve sts faster than the body back and front sts. Therefore, for the 1st 12(8,6,6) rounds, dec 1 st inside the sleeve markers **every round** and at the same time dec 1 st inside body markers **every other round.**

136(168,200,236) sts rem on needle.

Now dec at all points every other round 8(12,16,18) times to give 72 sts rem.

Next round: Sl center front 14 sts to holder for front neck and continue

working back and forth on rem 58 sts as follows: At each neck edge, dec 1 st every other round for side neck shap-ing, and at the same time, cont to dec at raglan points every other row as before.

When all front sts and all sleeve sts have been decreased, there should be 12(12,12,14) sts rem on back.

Next row: (RS facing) Change to larger dpn; then p.u. and knit 11 sts along side neck shaping, 14 sts from front holder, 11 sts along side neck shaping, work across 12(12,12,14) sts on back, giving 48(48,48,50) sts on needle.

Work St st for 4" (10 cm) for roll collar.

B.o. loosely.

Allow collar to roll naturally to outside.

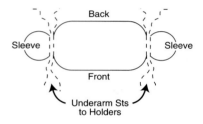

JOINING BODY & SLEEVES

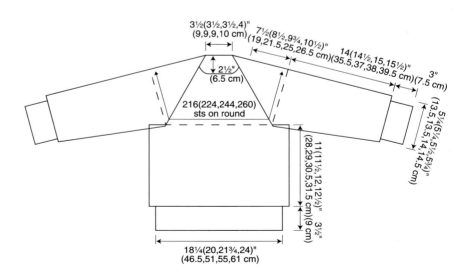

3½(3½,3½,4)" (9,9,9,10 cm)

7½(8½,9¾,10½)" (19,21.5,25,26.5 cm)

14(14½,15,15½)" (35.5,37,38,39.5 cm)

3" (7.5 cm)

2½" (6.5 cm)

216(224,244,260) sts on round

5¼(5¼,5½,5¾)" (13.5,13.5,14,14.5 cm)

11(11½,12,12½)" (28,29,30.5,31.5 cm)

3½" (9 cm)

18¼(20,21¾,24)" (46.5,51,55,61 cm)

SIZES

Small(Medium,Large)

Finished measurements: 44½(48½, 52½)" (113,123,133.5 cm)

MATERIALS

Sharon (74% mohair, 13% wool, 13% nylon; 1½ oz. = approx. 90 yards): 11(12,12) balls of main color (MC)—#2597 Woodland; 1 ball each of colors A—#2555 Tomato and B—#2598 Sunflower

Equivalent yarn: 990(1080,1080) yards/905(988,988) meters of looped mohair for main color and 90 yards/83 meters each of 2 contrasting colors

Knitting needles in size 8 U.S. (5 mm)

16" (40.5 cm) circular needle in size 8 U.S. (5 mm)

GAUGE

Stockinette stitch on larger needles: 16 sts and 24 rows = 4" (10 cm)

Take time to save time—check your gauge.

PATTERN STITCHES

REVERSE STOCKINETTE STITCH

Row 1: (RS) P all sts.

Row 2: K all sts.

BACK

With color A, c.o. 89(97,105) sts.

Work in rev St st for 2½" (6.5 cm).

Change to MC and work in rev St st until piece meas 25½(26½,27½)" (64.5,67.5,70 cm), incl color band.

B.o. all sts.

FRONT

Work same as for back.

When piece meas 15½(16½,17½)" (39.5,42,44.5 cm), **shape neck:** Work 44(48,52) sts, join a second ball of yarn and b.o. center st, work to end.

Working each side sep, b.o. 1 st at neck edge every 4th row 15(16,16) times, then every 5th row 1(0,2) times to give 28(32,34) sts at shoulder.

When piece meas same as back at shoulders, b.o. all sts.

SLEEVES

With color B, c.o. 34(36,36) sts.

Work in rev St st for 2½" (6.5 cm).

Change to MC and work in rev St st, inc 1 st each end every 5th row 2(1,2) times, then every 4th row 19(21,20) times to give 76(80,80) sts.

When piece meas 17(17½,18)" (43,44.5,45.5 cm), b.o. all sts.

FINISHING

Sew shoulder seams.

With MC, p.u. center b.o. st, then 39(39,41) sts evenly to shoulder, 32(32,36) sts around back of neck, and 40(40,42) sts to bottom of V-neck.

Work back and forth in rev St st for 3" (7.5 cm), end on WSR.

Begin color band: Work first 56(56, 60) sts in color A and work rem sts in color B.

Cont working both colors in rev St st until band meas 2½" (6.5 cm).

B.o. all sts.

Mark underarm points 9½(10,10)" (24,25.5,25.5 cm) down in front and back from shoulder.

COUNTRY CONTRASTS

Probably the easiest design in this collection, this entire sweater is knit in reverse stockinette stitch and edged with contrasting autumn shades. Looped mohair yarn adds texture to the otherwise simple design, and two contrasting colors at the V-neck provide the knitter's only challenge.

Design: **KRISTIN NICHOLAS**
Knitting rating: **BEGINNER**

Sew sleeve bet points.

Sew underarm and side seams.

Turn 2" (5 cm) of color bands on hem, sleeve, and neckline to inside and sew in place.

Overlap V-neck fronts and sew.

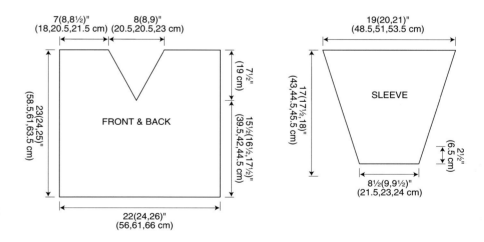

FRONT & BACK

7(8,8½)" (18,20.5,21.5 cm)   8(8,9)" (20.5,20.5,23 cm)

23(24,25)" (58.5,61,63.5 cm)

7½" (19 cm)

15½(16½,17½)" (39.5,42,44.5 cm)

22(24,26)" (56,61,66 cm)

SLEEVE

19(20,21)" (48.5,51,53.5 cm)

17(17½,18)" (43,44.5,45.5 cm)

2½" (6.5 cm)

8½(9,9½)" (21.5,23,24 cm)

Ribbed Mohair Trio

One simple-to-knit reversible rib stitch makes this trio great for beginners. Three unisex shape and style variations are given: a cardigan with pockets, a mock turtleneck, and a placketed pullover that can be worn open or closed. Mohair is one of the lightest and warmest fibers you will ever own, and a sweater in this design is sure to become a favorite.

Design: **Kristin Nicholas**
Knitting rating (all sweaters): **Beginner**

SIZES

Small(Medium,Large,Extra Large)
Finished measurements at underarm: 38 (42,46,49½)" (96.5,106.5,117,125.5 cm)

MATERIALS

La Gran (74% mohair, 13% wool, 13% nylon; 1½ oz. = approx. 90 yards): 10(11,11,12) balls for cardigan; 11(12,12,13) balls for placket pullover or mock turtleneck
Equivalent yarn: 900(990,990,1080) yards/823(905,905,988) meters of bulky brushed mohair for cardigan, 990 (1080,1080,1170) yards/905(988, 988,1070) meters of bulky brushed mohair for placket pullover and mock turtleneck
Knitting needles in sizes 7 and 10 U.S. (4.5 and 6 mm)
16" (40.5 cm) circular needle in size 7 U.S. (4.5 mm) for both pullovers
Stitch holders
1" (2.5 cm) buttons for cardigan (6)
⅝" (1.5 cm) buttons for pullover (5)

GAUGE

Farrow rib stitch on larger needles: 4 sts and 5 rows = 1" (2.5 cm)
Take time to save time—check your gauge.

PATTERN STITCHES

1 x 1 Twisted Rib

Row 1: (RS) K1-b (k1 into back of st), p1.
Row 2: Work all sts as they appear but do not twist sts.
Repeat rows 1 and 2.

Farrow Rib Stitch

(over multiple of 3 sts)
Row 1: * K2, p1 *, rep bet *'s.
Row 2: Work same as row 1.
Knitting Tip: To make edge of garment and band neat, on each last st of every row, sl last st as if to purl, ending with yarn in front of work. On 1st st of next row, knit the stitch.

CARDIGAN

BACK

Using smaller needles, c.o. 64(72,80, 85) sts and work in 1 x 1 twisted rib for 2½" (6.5 cm).
In last row of rib, inc 11(12,13,14) sts evenly across to give 75(84,93,99) sts.
Change to larger needles.
Work in farrow rib stitch.
When piece meas 19(20,21,22)" (48.5,51,53.5,56 cm) including rib, work 25(29,33,36) sts; join a 2nd ball of yarn and b.o. center 25(26,27,27) sts; work to end.
Working both sides at same time, b.o. 1 st each neck edge 2 times to give 23(27,31,34) sts at each shoulder.
When piece meas 20(21,22,23)" (51, 53.5,56,58.5 cm), b.o. all shoulder sts.

POCKET BACKS

Make 2.
Using larger needles, c.o. 24 sts.
Work in farrow rib for 5" (12.5 cm).
Sl sts to holder.

RIGHT FRONT

Using smaller needles, c.o. 42(44,46, 48) sts.
Work in 1 x 1 twisted rib for 2½" (6.5 cm).
In 5th row, work buttonhole.

To work buttonhole: On RS, work 4 sts, b.o. next st and work to end.
On next row, work across rib and where b.o. st is, m1 to replace st.
When rib meas 2½" (6.5 cm) and you are on RS, sl 1st 9 sts to st holder to be worked later for band.
Inc 6(7,8,9) sts evenly across rem sts to give 39(42,45,48) sts.
Change to larger needles.
Work in farrow rib st.
When piece meas 6" (15 cm), insert pocket back as foll: Beg at center front, work 9 sts, sl next 24 sts to holder, work to end.
Next row, work across and replace sl sts with pocket back.
When piece meas 8(9,10,11)" (20.5,23,25.5,28 cm), beg shaping right front.
B.o. 1 st every 2nd row 3(2,1,0) times, then every 4th row 13 times to give 23(27,31,35) sts at shoulder.
When piece meas same as back, b.o. all shoulder sts.
Note: For man's sweater, work buttonholes on left side.

LEFT FRONT

Work same as right front, omitting buttonholes on band and reversing neckline shaping.

SLEEVES

Using smaller needles, c.o. 28(30,32, 34) sts.
Work in 1 x 1 twisted rib for 2½" (6.5 cm).
In last row of rib, inc 5(6,4,5) sts evenly across to give 33(36,36,39) sts.
Change to larger needles and beg farrow rib.
Inc 1 st each end every 3rd row 20(20, 22,22) times to give 73(76,80, 83) sts.
When sleeve meas 17(18,19,20)" (43,45.5,48.5,51 cm), b.o. all sts.

FINISHING

Pocket ribs: Using smaller needles, p.u. 24 sts on holder at body of sweater.
Work in 1 x 1 twisted rib for 1" (2.5 cm).

B.o. all sts neatly.

Sew inside pocket and ribs down neatly.

Sew shoulder seams.

For buttonhole band: P.u. 9 sts on holder.

Work a buttonhole every 1½" (4 cm) as done before.

When piece meas 8(9,10,11)" (20.5,23, 25.5,28 cm) including bottom rib, work band without buttonholes.

Cont working rib piece until it meas to center back of neck; then b.o.

On left side, p.u. the 9 sts held and work in 1 x 1 twisted rib until piece meets other rib at back of neck.

For neat band, remember to sl last stitch as given in knitting tip.

Sew down band neatly around cardigan opening.

Meas down 9(9½,10,10⅜)" (23,24, 25.5, 26.4 cm) on each side of shoulder seam.

Sew in sleeve bet points.

Sew arm and side seams.

Sew buttons on left front (or right front if making man's sweater).

PLACKET PULLOVER

BACK

Work same as cardigan.

FRONT

Work same as back.

When piece meas 11(12,13,14)" (28, 30.5,33,35.5 cm), beg placket opening.

Work 34(38,42,45) sts, sl center 7(8,9,9) sts to holder, join 2nd ball of yarn and work to end.

Working each side sep, cont in farrow rib.

When piece meas 16(17,18,19)" (40.5, 43,45.5,48.5 cm), beg to shape neck.

At neck edge, b.o. 5 sts 1 time, 2 sts 2 times, 1 st 2 times to give 23(27,31,34) sts at shoulder.

When piece meas same as back, b.o. all sts.

SLEEVES

Make same as cardigan.

FINISHING

Sew shoulder seams.

At right front, p.u. 7(8,9,9) sts on holder.

Using smaller circular needle, inc 2(1,0,0) times in 1st row to give 9 sts.

Work in 1 x 1 twisted rib.

If making woman's sweater, work buttonholes every 1½" (4 cm) as instructed for cardigan; omit for man's.

When piece is equal to front, sl sts to holder.

Work left placket underside as right, eliminating buttonholes for woman's sweater but working them for man's placket.

Using circular needle, p.u. 9 sts on holder, p.u. 85(87,89,91) sts around front and back of neck, then other 9 sts on holder.

Work in 1 x 1 twisted rib, cont buttonholes as est in band every 1½" (4 cm).

When neck ribbing meas 4" (10 cm), b.o. all sts.

Sew plackets down neatly at openings.

Insert sleeves as done on cardigan.

Sew on buttons.

MOCK TURTLENECK

BACK

Work same as cardigan.

FRONT

Work same as placket pullover front, omitting placket opening.

When piece meas 16(17,18,19)" (40.5, 43,45.5,48.5 cm), beg neck shaping.

Work 29(33,37,40) sts, join 2nd ball of yarn and b.o. center 17(18,19,19) sts, work to end.

Working both sides at same time, b.o. 2 sts at neck edge 2 times, then 1 st at neck edge 2 times to give 23(27,31,34) sts.

When piece meas same as back, b.o. all sts.

SLEEVES

Work same as cardigan.

FINISHING

Sew shoulder seams.

Using circular needle, p.u. 94(96,100,104) sts evenly around neckline and work in 1 x 1 twisted rib.

When neck band meas 4" (10 cm), b.o. all sts neatly.

Insert sleeves and finish underarm seams as done on cardigan.

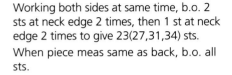

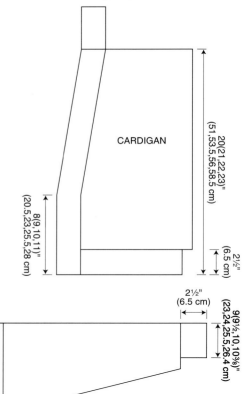

SIZES

Small(Medium,Large,Extra Large)
Finished measurements: 36(40,44,48)"
(91.5,101.5,112,122 cm)

MATERIALS

Applause (33% mohair, 14% silk, 41%
rayon, 6% wool, 6% nylon; 50 grams =
approx. 70 yards): 7(7,8,8) hanks; OR La
Gran (74% mohair, 13% wool, 13%
nylon; 1½ oz. = approx. 90 yards):
6(6,7,7) balls
Equivalent yarn: 540(540,630,630)
yards/494(494,576,576) meters of
bulky brushed mohair
Knitting needles in sizes 8 and 10½ U.S.
(5 and 6.5 mm)
Circular knitting needle in size 8 U.S. (5
mm) for V-neck
Stitch holder
Double-pointed needle (dpn)

GAUGE

Stockinette stitch on larger needles: 14
sts and 17 rows = 4" (10 cm)
*Take time to save time—check your
gauge.*

PATTERN STITCHES

ABBREVIATIONS

M: Form loop by inserting index finger
under yarn from front and turn back.
Tighten loop.

1 x 1 TWISTED RIB

(over even number of sts)
Row 1: (RS) K1-b (k1 into back of st),
p1.
Row 2: Work all sts as they appear but
do not twist sts.

STOCKINETTE STITCH

Row 1: (RS) K all sts.
Row 2: P all sts.

HARVEST HEATHER VEST

This vest will give the beginner a
slight challenge as skills progress.
Start with a 1 x 1 rib at the back
of the sweater; then work a
stockinette stitch body with
decreases at the underarms.
The front of the vest features a
simple cable that parts in two
when the V-neck is shaped.
Mohair yarn is a good choice for
a beginnner because uneven
tensions are hidden by the fluffy
texture of the yarn. Beginners
should stay away from dark
colors, though, which make
examination of the stitches
more difficult.

Design: CATHY PAYSON
Knitting rating: BEGINNER

CABLE STITCH

(over 20 sts)
Row 1: (RS) P2, k16, p2.
Row 2 and all WS rows: K2, p16, k2.
Rows 3, 7, and 9: As row 1.
Row 5: P2, sl 4 sts to dpn and hold in
back of work, k4, k4 from dpn, sl 4 sts
to dpn and hold in front of work, k4,
k4 from dpn, p2.
Repeat rows 1-10 for pattern.

BACK

With smaller needles c.o. 54(60,68,74)
sts.
Work 1 x 1 twisted rib for 3" (7.5 cm).
In last WS row of rib, inc 10 sts evenly
across to give 64(70,78,84) sts.
Change to larger needles and begin
working in St st.
Work straight until piece meas 14(14½,
15½,16)" (35.5,37,39.5,40.5 cm)
including rib.

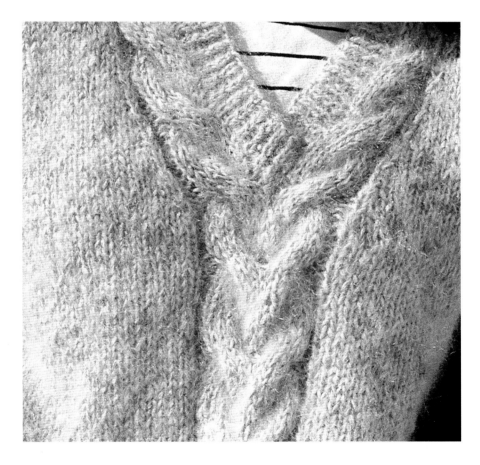

Shape armholes: B.o. 4 sts at beg of next 2 rows then 1 st at beg of next 14 rows to give 42(48,56,62) sts.

Work until piece meas 23½(24,24¾, 25½)" (59.5,61,63,64.5 cm).

B.o. all sts.

FRONT

With smaller needles c.o. 54(60,68,74) sts.

Work in 1 x 1 twisted rib for 3" (7.5 cm).

In last WS row of rib inc 14 sts evenly across to give 68(74,82,88) sts.

Change to larger needles and est cable patt.

On RS k24(27,31,34) sts, work 1st row of cable pattern over 20 sts, k24(27,31, 34) sts to end.

Continue as est.

When piece meas 12½(12½,12¾,13)" (31.5,31.5,32.5,33 cm) on RS row, shape neck.

Work 34(37,41,44) sts, inc 2 sts by M2, join 2nd ball of yarn, M2 and work to end.

Working each side separately, work cables at each side of V-neck.

Sl right side of V-neck shaping to holder.

At each RS neck edge, b.o. 1 st every other row 0(0,2,2) times, then 1 st every 4th row 11(12,11,12) times.

To do this: On RS k across until there are 2 sts rem in St st before the cable, k2tog to form right-leaning decrease, p2 and continue crossing cable in est patt, p2.

For right side of V-neck shaping, work reverse shaping to make left-leaning decreases as SSK. (Sl as if to knit, sl as if to knit, insert the left needle into the front of the 2 sts from left to right and knit them tog as if they were one.)

At the same time, when piece meas 14(14½,15¼,16)" (35.5,37,38.5,40.5 cm) shape armhole as done on back.

After all decreases for neck and shoulder, there should be 14(16,19,21) sts on each side.

When piece meas same as back, b.o. all sts.

FINISHING

Sew both shoulder seams.

Beg at center front neck with circular needle, p.u. 114(116,118,120) sts evenly spaced around neckline.

Work 1 x 1 twisted rib back and forth for 1½" (4 cm).

B.o. all sts.

Sew ribs, overlapping them at center front.

Using circular needle, p.u. 82(84,86,88) sts around each armhole and work 1 x 1 twisted rib for 1" (2.5 cm).

B.o. all sts.

Sew side seams.

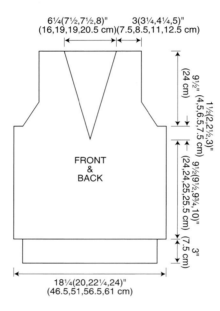

6¼(7½,7½,8)" (16,19,19,20.5 cm) 3(3¼,4¼,5)" (7.5,8.5,11,12.5 cm)

9½" (24 cm)

1½(2,2½,3)" (4.5,5,6.5,7.5 cm)

9½(9½,9¾,10)" (24,24,25,25.5 cm)

3" (7.5 cm)

FRONT & BACK

18¼(20,22¼,24)" (46.5,51,56.5,61 cm)

WINDS OF WEEKAPAUG

Two strands of novelty cotton are used to work up these designs for a pullover and cardigan that are perfect for beginning knitters. Because of the chunky gauge, either sweater can be completed in less than a week. Double stranding of novelty yarns allows for plenty of creativity; assorted textures and colors can be combined to make vastly different effects.

Design: **Cathy Payson**
Knitting rating: **Beginner**

CARDIGAN

SIZES

Small(Medium,Large)
Finished measurements: 46(48,50)"
(117,122,127 cm)

MATERIALS

Boda (68% cotton, 12% linen, 9% acetate, 11% polyester; 100 grams = approx. 158 yards): 8(9,10) skeins
Equivalent yarn: 650(720,790) yards/ 595(659,723) meters each of two different novelty worsted-weight cotton yarns
Knitting needles in sizes 10 and 11 U.S. (6 and 8 mm)
1" (2.5 cm) buttons (6)

GAUGE

Stockinette stitch on larger needles: 12 sts and 13 rows = 4" (10 cm)
Take time to save time—check your gauge.

PATTERN STITCHES

1 x 1 Rib
Row 1: K1, p1 across row.
Row 2: Work sts as they appear.

Stockinette Stitch
Row 1: (RS) K all sts.
Row 2: P all sts.
Note: Two strands of yarn are held together throughout.

BACK

With smaller needles and 2 strands, c.o. 66(69,72) sts.
Work in 1 x 1 rib for 2" (5 cm), inc 3 sts evenly spaced across last row to give 69(72,75) sts.
Change to larger needles and work in St st until piece meas 22(23,24)" (56,58.5,61 cm) incl rib.
B.o. all sts.

LEFT FRONT

Wtih smaller needles and 2 strands, c.o. 30(32,34) sts.
Work 1 x 1 rib for 2" (5 cm), inc 2 sts across to give 32(34,36) sts.
Change to larger needles and work in St st until piece meas 20(21,22)" (51,53.5,56 cm).
Shape neck: B.o. 3 sts at next neck edge, then 2 sts every other row 2(3,3) times, then 1 st 1(0,1) time.
When piece meas same as back, b.o. all sts.

RIGHT FRONT

Work as for left front but reverse shaping.

SLEEVES

With smaller needles and 2 strands, c.o. 25(26,27) sts.
Work in 1 x 1 rib for 2" (5 cm).
Change to larger needles and work in St st, inc 1 st each end every other row 13(14,15) times to give 51(54,57) sts.
Cont evenly until piece meas 16(17, 18)" (40.5,43,45.5 cm).
B.o. all sts.

FINISHING

Sew shoulder seams.
With smaller needles, p.u. 43(45,47) sts around neck edges.
Work in 1 x 1 rib for 1½" (4 cm).
B.o. all sts.

P.u. 73(75,77) sts along right front.
Work 2 rows 1 x 1 rib.
In 3rd row, make 6 buttonholes evenly spaced by yo, k2tog.
Work 2 more rows in 1 x 1 rib.
B.o. all sts.
Work left front button band as for right but omitting buttonholes.
Sew buttons in place opposite buttonholes.
Sew in sleeves.
Sew side and sleeve seams.

PULLOVER

SIZES

Same as for cardigan

MATERIALS

Dakota (80% cotton, 20% linen; 100 grams = approx. 240 yards): 3(4,4) hanks of color A
Dunes (100% cotton; 100 grams = approx. 205 yards): 4(5,5) hanks of color B
Equivalent yarn: 750(950,950) yards/ 686(869,869) meters each of two different novelty worsted-weight cotton yarns
Knitting needles in sizes 10 and 11 U.S. (6 and 8 mm)
Circular needle in size 10 U.S. (6 mm)

GAUGE

Stockinette stitch on larger needles: 13 sts and 16 rows = 4" (10 cm)
Take time to save time—check your gauge.

PATTERN STITCHES

1 x 1 Twisted Rib
Row 1: (RS) K1-b (k1 into back of st), p1.
Row 2: Work all sts as they appear but do not twist sts.
Note: Sweater is worked with 1 strand each of Dakota and Dunes held tog throughout.

BACK

With smaller needles and 2 strands, c.o. 70(74,78) sts.

Work in 1 x 1 twisted rib for 2" (5 cm), inc 4 sts evenly across last row to give 74(78,82) sts.

Change to larger needles and work in St st until piece meas 22(23,24)" (56,58.5,61 cm).

B.o. all sts.

FRONT

Work same as back until piece meas 20(21,22)" (51,53.5,56 cm).

Shape neck: Work across 1st 30(31,32) sts, join 2nd ball of yarn and b.o. center 14(16,18) sts and work to end.

Working both sides sep, b.o. 2 sts at each neck edge once, then 1 st every other row 2 times to give 26(27,28) sts each side.

When piece meas same as back, b.o. all sts.

SLEEVES

With smaller needles, c.o. 26(28,30) sts.

Work 1 x 1 twisted rib for 2" (5 cm).

Change to larger needles and begin working St st, inc 1 st each end every 4th row 15(16,18) times to give 56(60, 66) sts.

When piece meas 17(18,19)" (43,45.5, 48.5 cm), b.o. all sts.

FINISHING

Sew shoulder seams.

With circular needle with RS facing, p.u. 72(77,80) sts evenly around neck edge and work in St st for 4" (10 cm).

B.o. all sts.

Sew in sleeves.

Sew side and sleeve seams.

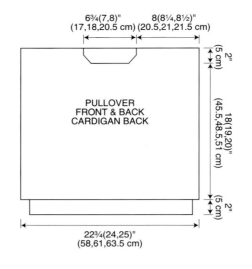

6¾(7,8)"
(17,18,20.5 cm)
8(8¼,8½)"
(20.5,21,21.5 cm)

2"
(5 cm)

PULLOVER
FRONT & BACK
CARDIGAN BACK

18(19,20)"
(45.5,48.5,51 cm)

2"
(5 cm)

22¾(24,25)"
(58,61,63.5 cm)

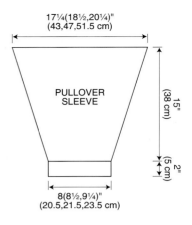

17¼(18½,20¼)"
(43,47,51.5 cm)

PULLOVER
SLEEVE

15"
(38 cm)

2"
(5 cm)

8(8½,9¼)"
(20.5,21.5,23.5 cm)

8(8¼,8½)"
(20.5,21,21.5 cm)

2"
(5 cm)

CARDIGAN
FRONT

18(19,20)"
(45.5,48.5,51 cm)

2"
(5 cm)

10¾(11¼,12)"
(27.5,28.5,30.5 cm)

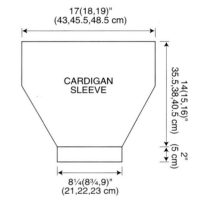

17(18,19)"
(43,45.5,48.5 cm)

CARDIGAN
SLEEVE

14(15,16)"
(35.5,38,40.5 cm)

2"
(5 cm)

8¼(8¾,9)"
(21,22,23 cm)

SIZES

Adult's Small(Medium,Large)
<Child's 2(4,6,8)>
Finished measurements: 42(44,46)"
(106.5,112,117 cm), <26(28,30,32)"
(66,71,76,81.5 cm)>

MATERIALS

La Gran (74% mohair, 13% wool, 13% nylon; 1½ oz. = approx. 90 yards): 10(10, 11) balls for long version and 8(9,10) balls for cropped version, <3(4,4,5) balls> for child's pullover or cardigan (not shown)

Equivalent yarn: 900(900,990) yards/823 (823,905) meters of bulky brushed mohair for adult's long version of pullover or cardigan, 720(810,900) yards/659 (741,823) meters for adult's cropped version of pullover or cardigan, <270(360, 360,450) yards/247(330,330, 412) meters> for child's pullover or cardigan

Knitting needles in sizes 8 and 10 U.S. (5 and 6 mm)

16" (40.5 cm) circular needle in size 8 U.S. (5 mm)

¾" (2 cm) buttons for adult's cardigan (5 or 7)

Buttons for child's cardigan <5>

Notes: Figures in < > are for child's version.

Instructions are written for longer versions of both cardigan and turtleneck.

Figures in [ ] are for cropped versions.

Instructions are also given for child's cardigan, which is not pictured.

GAUGE

Stockinette stitch on larger needles: 14 sts and 18 rows = 4" (10 cm)

Take time to save time—check your gauge.

This is a great project for beginners; it's so easy that even a child could learn to knit with this pattern! Instructions are given to make both the cardigan and pullover for every member in the family. It's a practical and versatile design for all ages.

Design: **CAThY PAYSON**
Knitting rating (all sweaters): **BEGINNER**

PATTERN STITCHES

1 x 1 RIB

Row 1: K1, p1 across row.
Row 2: K the k sts and p the p sts.

STOCKINETTE STITCH

Row 1: (RS) K all sts.
Row 2: P all sts.

BACK

With smaller needles, c.o. 68(72,76) <40(44,46,50)> sts.

Work 1 x 1 rib for 1½" (4 cm), inc 6 sts in last row to give 74(78,82) <46(50,52, 56)> sts.

Change to larger needles and work in St st until piece meas 18(18½,19)" (45.5,47,48.5 cm) incl rib [12,12½,13" (30.5,31.5,33 cm)].

<For child's version, b.o. all sts when piece meas 15(16,17,18)" (38,40.5,43, 45.5 cm).>

Shape adult armhole: B.o 2 sts at beg of next 2 rows, then 1 st each side every other row 2 times to give 66(70, 74) sts.

Cont until piece meas 8(8½,9)" (20.5, 21.5,23 cm) and total length is 26(27, 28)" (66,68.5,71 cm) [20(21,22)" (51, 53.5,56 cm)].

B.o. all sts.

PULLOVER FRONT

Work as for back until piece meas 24(25,26)" (61,63.5,66 cm) [18 (19,20)" (45.5,48.5,51 cm)] <13(14, 15,16)" (33,35.5,38,40.5 cm)>.

Neck shaping: Work across 25(26,27)

<17(18,19,20)> sts, join second ball of yarn and b.o. center 16(18,20) <12(14,14,16)> sts, work to end.

Working each side sep, b.o. at neck edge 2 sts once, then 1 st every other row twice to give 21(22,23) <13(14,15,16)> sts at shoulder.

CARDIGAN RIGHT FRONT

With smaller needles, c.o. 38(40,42) <21(23,25,27)> sts.

For adults' sizes: Work 1 x 1 rib for 1½" (4 cm).

In 5th row, work buttonhole on RS by k4 sts, b.o. next st and work to end.

In next row, work across above b.o. st and m1 to replace st.

When rib meas same as back and you are on WSR, inc 3 sts evenly across first 30(32,34) sts to give 33(35,37) sts.

Sl rem 8 sts to holder for buttonhole band.

Change to larger needles and work St st until piece meas same as back to underarm.

Shape armhole as for back and work until piece meas 24(25,26)" (61,63.5, 66 cm) [18,19,20" (45.5,48.5,51 cm)].

Shape neck by b.o. 4 sts at next neck edge, then 2 sts every other row 2(2,3) times, then 1 st 0(1,0) times to give 21(22,23) sts.

When piece meas same as back, b.o. all sts.

For children's sizes: Work 1 x 1 rib for 1½" (4 cm).

In 3rd row, work buttonhole on RS by working 3 sts, b.o. 1 st, and work to end.

In next row, work across and m1 above b.o. st to replace it.

When rib meas same as back and you are on WSR, inc 3 sts across first 15(17, 19,21) sts to give 18(20,22,24) sts.

Sl rem 6 sts to holder; these will become the buttonhole band.

Change to larger needles and work St st until piece meas 13(14,15,16)" (33, 35.5,38,40.5 cm).

Shape neck: B.o. 3(2,3,4) sts at beg of next neck edge, then 2 sts at neck edge 0(1,1,1) times, then 1 st at neck edge twice to give 13(14,15,16) sts at shoulder.

When front meas same as back to shoulders, b.o. all sts.

CARDIGAN LEFT FRONT

Work as for right front but reverse shapings and omit buttonholes.

SLEEVES

With smaller needles, c.o. 30(32,34) <20(22,24,26)> sts.

Work 1 x 1 rib for 1½" (4 cm) <1" (2.5 cm)>.

Change to larger needles and work St st, inc 1 st each end every 5th <6th> row 13(14,15) <7(8,9,10)> times to give 56(60,64) <34(38,42,46)> sts.

For adults' sizes: When piece meas 16(17,18)" (40.5,43,45.5 cm) incl rib, **shape cap.**

B.o. 2 sts at beg of next 2 rows, then 1 st each end every other row twice.

B.o. rem 48(52,56) sts.

For children's sizes: When piece meas 11(12,13,14)" (28,30.5,33,35.5 cm) incl rib, b.o. all sts.

FINISHING FOR PULLOVER

Sew shoulder seams.

With circular needle, p.u. 60(64,68) <52(54,56,58)> sts around neck edge.

Work 1 x 1 rib for 4" (10 cm) <3" (6.5 cm)>.

B.o. all sts.

Sew in sleeves.

Sew side and underarm seams.

FINISHING FOR CARDIGAN

Sew shoulder seams.

With circular needle, p.u. 52(56,60) <46(48,50,52)> sts around right front, back, and left front edges.

Work 1 x 1 rib for 1½" (6.5 cm).

B.o. all sts.

P.u. 8 <6> sts from holder on right front and work 1 x 1 rib, making buttonholes evenly spaced (approx. every 3"/6.5 cm) until band meas to top of neck edge when slightly stretched.

Work left band as for right band, but omit buttonholes.

Sew bands neatly along cardigan openings.

Sew in sleeves.

Sew side and underarm seams.

Sew on buttons.

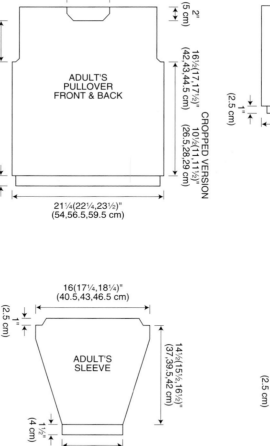

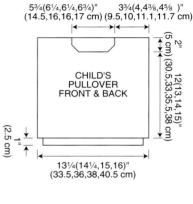

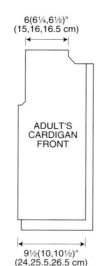

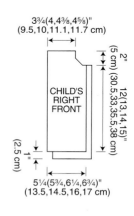

Decorative Stitchery

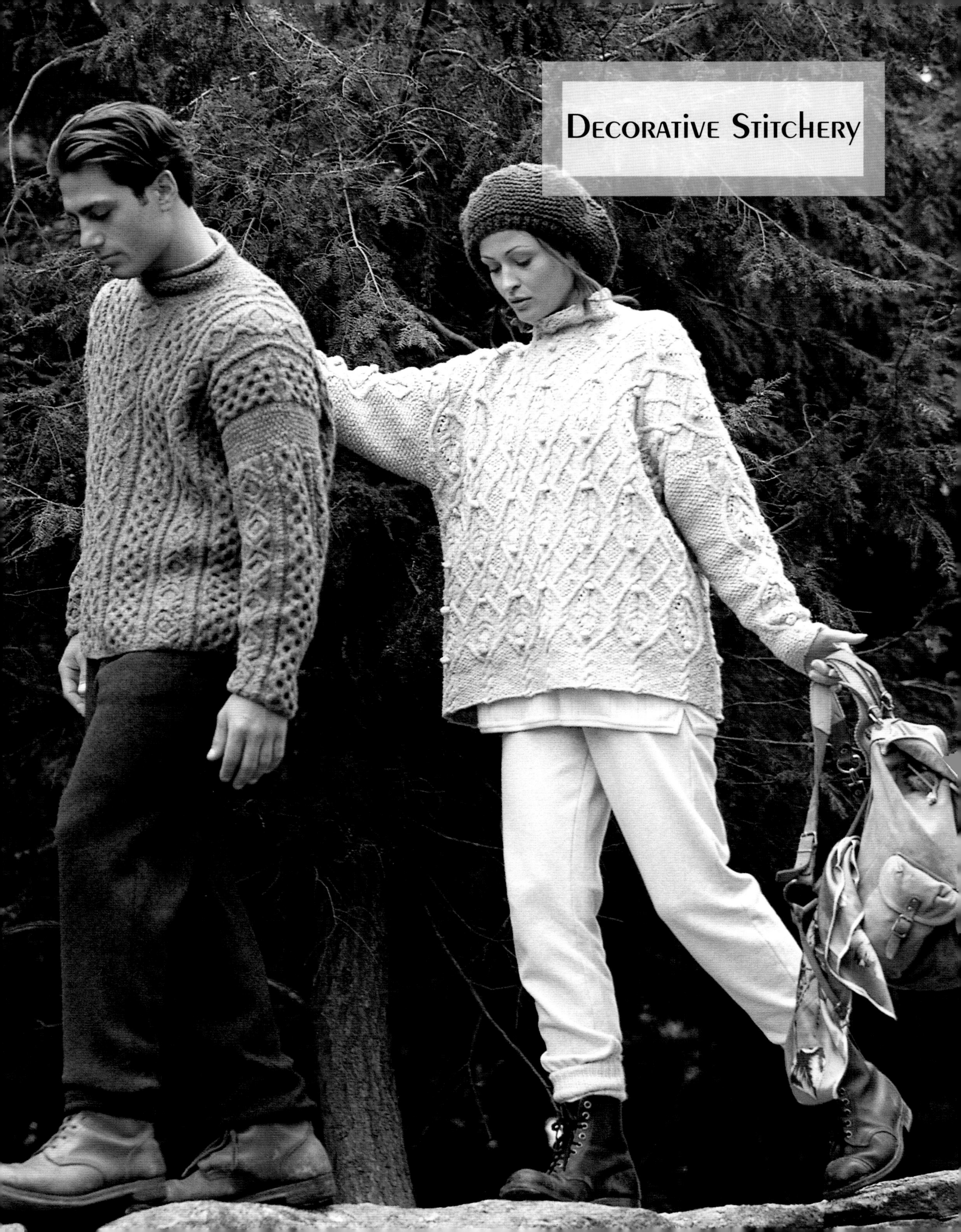

EVERGREEN ARANS

The man's sweater (which looks equally spectacular on a woman) is composed of very traditional Aran stitches, including moss stitch, honeycomb cables, and larger X and O cables. The woman's sweater, which is a bit more challenging to knit, begins with a simple border of moss stitch and cables, then grows into a complex cable pattern with bobbles. Both sweaters feature unusual neck and edge treatments.

Design: **Kristin Nicholas**
Man's sweater: **Experienced**
Woman's sweater: **Very challenging**

MAN'S ARAN

SIZES
Small(Medium,Large)
Finished measurements: 46(50,54)" (117,127,137 cm)

MATERIALS
Evergreen recycled yarn (45% cashmere, 45% wool, 10% unidentified fibers; 100 grams = approx. 226 yards): 7(7,8) hanks

Equivalent yarn: 1582(1582,1808) yards/1447(1447,1653) meters of worsted-weight wool

Knitting needles in sizes 3 and 5 U.S. (3.25 and 3.75 mm)

16" (40.5 cm) circular needle in size 3 U.S. (3.25 mm)

Cable needle (cn)

GAUGE
Moss stitch on larger needles: 16 sts and 27 rows = 4" (10 cm)
Honeycomb cable = 2½" (6.5 cm)
XOXOX cable = 2" (5 cm)
Twist stitch column = 1" (2.5 cm)

Take time to save time—check your gauge.

PATTERN STITCHES

ABBREVIATIONS
FC: Sl 2 sts to cn, hold in front, k2, k2 from cn.
BC: Sl 2 sts to cn, hold in back, k2, k2 from cn.

MOSS STITCH
(over odd number of sts)
All rows: K1, p1.

XOXOX CABLE
(over 12 sts)

Row 1: (WS) K2, p8, k2.
Row 2: P2, BC, FC, p2.
Row 3 and all WS rows: Work all sts as they appear.
Row 4: BC, k4, FC.
Row 6: K2, BC, FC, k2.
Row 8: BC, k4, FC.
Row 10: K12.
Row 12: FC, k4, BC.
Row 14: K2, FC, BC, k2.
Row 16: FC, k4, BC.
Row 18: P2, FC, BC, p2.
Repeat rows 1-18.

HONEYCOMB CABLE

(over 16 sts)

Row 1: (WS) P16.

Row 2: BC, FC, BC, FC.

Row 3 and all WS rows: P16.

Rows 4 and 8: K16.

Row 6: FC, BC, FC, BC.

Repeat rows 1-8.

TWIST ST COLUMN

(over 6 sts)

Row 1: K2, p2, k2.

Row 2: P2, k the 2nd st but do not take off needle, k the 1st st and remove both sts at same time, p2.

BACK

With smaller needles, c.o. 105(111,115) sts.

Work in moss st for 4 rows, inc 45(47,51) sts evenly across last row to give 150(158,166) sts.

Change to larger needles.

Est pattern as foll: Work 5(9,13) sts in moss st, work 2 sts in rev St st, * work honeycomb cable over 16 sts, work twist st column over 6 sts, work XOXOX cable over 12 sts, work twist st column over 6 sts *, rep bet *'s 2 more times, end with honeycomb cable over 16 sts, work 2 sts in rev St st, work 5(9,13) sts in moss st.

Work as est in patt until piece meas 25(26,27)" (63.5,66,68.5 cm).

B.o. all sts.

FRONT

Work as for back until piece meas 23(24,25)" (58.5,61,63.5 cm).

Shape neck: Work 61(64,67) sts, join 2nd ball of yarn and b.o. center 28(30,32) sts, work to end.

Working each side sep, b.o. 1 st at neck edge every other row 6 times to give 55(58,61) sts at shoulder.

When piece meas same as back, b.o. all sts.

SLEEVES

With smaller needles, c.o. 41(43,47) sts.

Work in moss st for 4 rows, inc 17(19, 19) sts evenly across last row to give 58(62,66) sts.

Change to larger needles.

Est patt as foll: Work moss st over 1(3,5) sts, work 2 in Rev St st, work XOXOX cable over 12 sts, work twist st column over 6 sts, work honeycomb cable over 16 sts, work twist st column over 6 sts, work XOXOX cable over 12 sts, work 2 sts in rev St st, work moss st over 1(3,5) sts.

Work as est in patt, inc 1 st each end in moss st every 6th row 18(15,11) times, then every 8th row 0(3,7) times to give 94(98,102) sts.

When piece meas 16½(17½,18½)" (42,44.5,47 cm), b.o. all sts.

FINISHING

Sew shoulder seams.

With circular needle, p.u. 69(73,77) sts evenly around neckline.

Work in moss st for 3" (7.5 cm).

Work 8 rows of St st.

B.o. all sts.

Meas down 9(9½,10)" (23,24,25.5 cm) from shoulder seam in front and back.

Sew sleeve bet points.

Sew underarm and side seams.

WOMAN'S ARAN

SIZES

Small/Medium(Medium/Large)

Finished measurements: 46(52)" (117,132 cm)

MATERIALS

Evergreen: 8(9) hanks

Equivalent yarn: 1808(2034) yards/1653(1860) meters of worsted-weight wool

Knitting needles in sizes 3 and 5 U.S. (3.25 and 3.75 mm)

16" (40.5 cm) circular needle in size 3 U.S. (3.25 mm)

Cable needle (cn)

GAUGE

Pattern stitch on larger needles: 23 sts and 25 rows = 4" (10 cm)

Moss stitch on larger needles: 19 sts = 4" (10 cm)

Take time to save time—check your gauge.

PATTERN STITCHES

ABBREVIATIONS

3-st RC: Sl 1 st to cn and hold in back, k2, k1 from cn.

3-st LC: Sl 2 sts to cn and hold in front, k1, k2 from cn.

3-st RPC: Sl 1 st to cn and hold in back, k2, p1 from cn.

3-st LPC: Sl 2 sts to cn and hold in front, p1, k2 from cn.

4-st RC: Sl 2 sts to cn and hold in back, k2, k2 from cn.

4-st LC: Sl 2 sts to cn and hold in front, k2, k2 from cn.

4-st RPC: Sl 2 sts to cn and hold in back, k2, p2 from cn.

4-st LPC: Sl 2 sts to cn and hold in front, p2, k2 from cn.

5-st RPC: Sl 3 sts to cn and hold in back, k2, sl p st from cn to left needle and p it, k2 from cn.

BOBBLE

K in front, back, front, and back of st, (turn, p4, turn) twice, pass the 2nd, 3rd, and 4th sts over the 1st st.

MOSS STITCH

Row 1: (WS) * P1, k1 *, rep bet *'s.

Row 2: K the p sts and p the k sts.

Repeat row 2 for moss st.

CABLE/MOSS RIB

Row 1: (WS) Work 9 sts in moss st, * p2, k1, p2, work 12 sts in moss st *, rep bet *'s, end with 9 sts in moss st.

Row 2: Work 9 sts in moss st, * 5-st RPC, 12 sts in moss st *, rep bet *'s, end with 9 sts in moss st.

Row 3: Repeat row 1.

Row 4: Work 9 sts in moss st, * k2, p1, k2, work 12 sts in moss st *, rep bet *'s, end with 9 sts in moss st.

Rows 5-8: Repeat rows 3 and 4 twice.

BACK

With smaller needles, c.o. 108(125) sts.

Work rows 1-8 of cable/moss rib 3 times; then work rows 1-3 once more.

Work 1 row of chart to give 132(153) sts.

Change to larger needles and cont in chart patt through row 54.

Rep rows 7-54 until piece meas 27(28)" (68.5,71 cm).

B.o. all sts.

FRONT

Work as for back until piece meas

25(26)" (63.5,66 cm).

Shape neck: Work 49(59) sts, join 2nd ball of yarn and b.o. center 34(35) sts, work to end.

Working each side sep, b.o. 1 st at neck edge every other row 4 times to give 45(55) sts at shoulder.

When piece meas same as back, b.o. all sts.

SLEEVES

With smaller needles, c.o. 40 sts.

Work rows 1-8 of cable/moss rib twice; then work rows 1-3 once more.

Work row 1 of chart patt to give 48 sts.

Change to larger needles and cont in chart patt as for back.

At the same time, inc 1 st ea end (working inc sts in moss st) every 2nd row 9(12) times and every 4th row 15 times to give 96(102) sts.

When piece meas 16(17)" (40.5,43 cm) or desired length, b.o. all sts.

FINISHING

Sew shoulder seams.

With circular needle, p.u. 99 sts evenly around neckline.

Est cable/moss rib as foll: * Work 6 sts in moss st, k2, p1, k2, (for 5-st cable) *, rep around.

Work 8 rows of rib 3 times; then work rows 1-3 once more.

B.o. all sts.

Meas down 9½(10)" (24,25.5 cm) from shoulder seam on front and back.

Set in sleeves at marks.

Sew underarm and side seams.

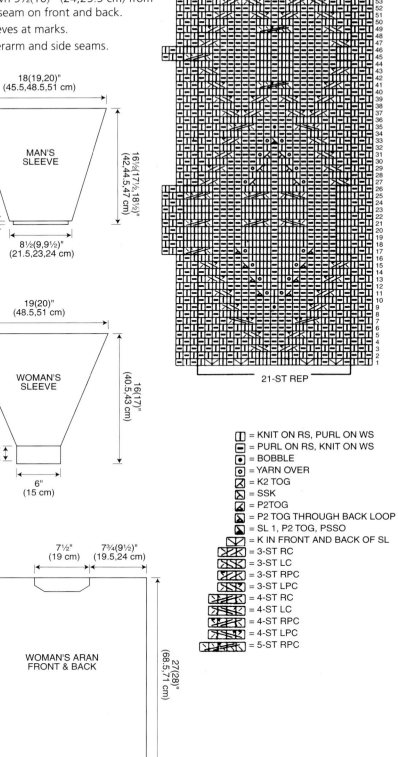

21-ST REP

▯	= KNIT ON RS, PURL ON WS
▬	= PURL ON RS, KNIT ON WS
⊙	= BOBBLE
○	= YARN OVER
⧄	= K2 TOG
⧅	= SSK
◩	= P2TOG
◪	= P2 TOG THROUGH BACK LOOP
⬒	= SL 1, P2 TOG, PSSO
⟋⟍	= K IN FRONT AND BACK OF SL
	= 3-ST RC
	= 3-ST LC
	= 3-ST RPC
	= 3-ST LPC
	= 4-ST RC
	= 4-ST LC
	= 4-ST RPC
	= 4-ST LPC
	= 5-ST RPC

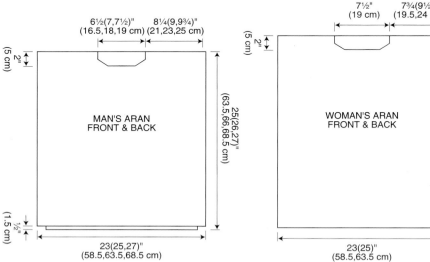

18(19,20)"
(45.5,48.5,51 cm)

MAN'S
SLEEVE

16½(17½,18½)"
(42,44.5,47 cm)

½"
(1.5 cm)

8½(9,9½)"
(21.5,23,24 cm)

19(20)"
(48.5,51 cm)

WOMAN'S
SLEEVE

16(17)"
(40.5,43 cm)

2½"
(6.5 cm)

6"
(15 cm)

6½(7,7½)"
(16.5,18,19 cm)
8¼(9,9¾)"
(21,23,25 cm)

2"
(5 cm)

MAN'S ARAN
FRONT & BACK

25(26,27)"
(63.5,66,68.5 cm)

½"
(1.5 cm)

23(25,27)"
(58.5,63.5,68.5 cm)

7½"
(19 cm)
7¾(9½)"
(19.5,24 cm)

2"
(5 cm)

WOMAN'S ARAN
FRONT & BACK

27(28)"
(68.5,71 cm)

23(25)"
(58.5,63.5 cm)

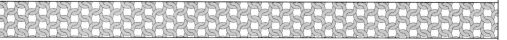

ARAN FAMILY

The cables chosen for this trio of sweaters work up beautifully in these traditionally styled, saddle shoulder sweaters for men and women. The knotted rib and rolled edges will add a different technique to an Aran knitter's repetoire. The child's sweater has drop shoulders and a hat to match.

Design: **Kristin Nicholas**
Knitting rating (all sweaters):
Experienced

MOCK TURTLENECK

SIZES

Small(Medium,Large,Extra Large)
Finished measurements at chest:
40(44,48,52)" (101.5,112,122,132 cm)
Length: 24¾(25¾,26¾,27¾)" (63,65.5, 68,70.5 cm)

MATERIALS

Cambridge (70% cotton, 30% wool; 50 grams = approx. 85 yards):
21(22,23,25) skeins
Equivalent yarn: 1785(1870,1955,2050) yards/1632(1710,1787,1874) meters of worsted-weight yarn
Knitting needles in sizes 4 and 6 U.S. (3.5 and 4 mm)
Double-pointed needle (dpn)

GAUGE

Moss stitch on larger needles: 19 sts and 28 rows = 4" (10 cm)
Basket cable = 4½" (11.5 cm)
Six knot cable = 3¾" (9.5 cm)
Take time to save time—check your gauge.

PATTERN STITCHES

STOCKINETTE STITCH

Row 1: (RS) K all sts.
Row 2: P all sts.

REVERSE STOCKINETTE STITCH

Row 1: (RS) P all sts.
Row 2: K all sts.

KNOTTED RIB

(multiple of 3 + 2)

Row 1: (RS) P2, * k into front and back of next st, p2, rep from *.
Row 2: K2, * p2tog, k2, rep from *.

GARTER RIDGE

Row 1: (RS) K all sts.
Row 2: K all sts.
Row 3: P all sts.
Row 4: K all sts.

MOSS STITCH

(over even number)
Rows 1 and 2: * K1, p1, rep from *.
Rows 3 and 4: * P1, k1, rep from *.

ABBREVIATIONS:

SBC: Sl 1 st to dpn and hold in back, k1, then k1 from dpn.
PFC: Sl 2 sts to dpn and hold in front, p2, then k2 from dpn.
FC: Sl 2 sts to dpn and hold in front, k2, then k2 from dpn.
PBC: Sl 2 sts to dpn and hold in back, k2, then p2 from dpn.
BC: Sl 2 sts to dpn and hold in back, k2, then k2 from dpn.

SIX KNOT CABLE

(over 24 sts)
Row 1: (WS) K2, (p2, k2) twice, p4, (k2, p2) twice, k2.
Row 2: P2, SBC, p2, PFC, FC, PBC, p2, SBC, p2.

Row 3 and WS rows: Work all sts as they appear.

Row 4: P2, k2, p4, BC, BC, p4, k2, p2.

Row 6: P2, SBC, p2, PBC, FC, PFC, p2, SBC, p2

Row 8: P2, k2, PBC, p2, k4, p2, PFC, k2, p2.

Row 10: P2, FC, p4, k4, p4, FC, p2.

Row 12: P2, k4, p4, FC, p4, k4, p2.

Row 14: P2, FC, p4, k4, p4, FC, p2.

Row 16: P2, k2, PFC, p2, k4, p2, PBC, k2, p2.

Repeat rows 1-16.

BANDED CABLE

(over 6 sts)

Row 1: (WS) P6.

Row 2: Sl 3 sts to dpn and hold in front, k3, k3 from dpn.

Rows 3 and 7: P6.

Rows 4 and 8: K6.

Row 5: P1, k4, p1.

Row 6: K1, p4, k1.

Repeat rows 1-8.

BASKET CABLE

(multiple of 8 sts + 4)

Rows 1, 3, and 5: (WS) K2, p to last 2 sts, k2.

Rows 2 and 4: P2, k to last 2 sts, p2.

Row 6: P2, * sl next 4 sts to dpn and hold in back, k4, then k4 from dpn; rep from *, end p2.

Rows 7, 9, and 11: K2, p to last 2 sts, k2.

Rows 8 and 10: As rows 2 and 4.

Row 12: P2, k4, * sl next 4 sts to dpn and hold in front, k4, then k4 from dpn, rep from *, end p2, k4.

Repeat rows 1-12.

BACK

With smaller needles, c.o. 89(98,107, 116) sts.

Work 10 rows in St st to form rolled hem.

Beg working knotted rib.

Work for 3½" (9 cm) ending with WSR.

Work garter ridge over 4 rows.

Next row (RS): Knit all sts, inc 35(38,37, 40) sts evenly across to give 124(136, 144,156) sts.

Change to larger needles and est pat-

tern as foll: Work 14(20,24,30) sts in moss stitch, work row 1 of six knot cable (24 sts), work 1 banded cable (6 sts), work basket cable (36 sts), work 1 banded cable (6 sts), work six knot cable (24 sts), work 14(20,24,30) sts of moss stitch.

Work until piece meas 21¾(22¾,23¾, 24¾)" (55,58,60.5,63 cm) inc rib, shape shoulders.

At beg of next 4 rows, b.o. 9(11,12,13) sts.

Then at beg of next 4 rows, b.o. 10(11, 12,13) sts.

B.o. rem sts.

FRONT

Work same as for back.

When piece meas 21¾(22¾,23¾, 24¾)" (55,58,60.5,63 cm), b.o. center 24(24,24,28) sts.

You should have 50(56,60,64) sts at each side for shoulders and neck.

For shoulder and neck shaping: Beg at shoulder edge, b.o. 9(11,12,13) sts at shoulder, work to end.

Turn, b.o. 3 sts at neck edge, work to end.

Rep these 2 rows once more.

Then b.o. 10(11,12,13) sts at shoulder edge, work to end.

Turn, b.o. 3 neck edge sts, work to end.

Repeat these 2 rows to dec all sts.

Work other shoulder the same.

SLEEVES

Using smaller needles, c.o. 41(41,44, 44) sts.

Work 10 rows of St st.

Beg working knotted rib.

Work for 3" (7.5 cm).

Work garter ridge.

Change to larger needles and knit 1 row inc 19(19,16,20) sts evenly across to give 60(60,60,64) sts.

Est patterns as foll: Work 4(4,4,6) sts in moss stitch, k2, work row 1 of banded cable (6 sts), work basket cable over 36 sts, work row 1 of banded cable (6 sts), k2, work 4(4,4,6) sts in moss st.

Cont working as est, inc 1 st each end every 4th row 21(22,24,24) times to give 102(104,108,112) sts.

When piece meas 16(16½,17,18)"

(40.5,42,43,45.5 cm), shape shoulders.

B.o. 8(9,9,9) sts at beg of next 2 rows.

B.o. 8(9,9,9) sts at beg of next 4 rows.

Then b.o. 8(8,8,10) sts at beg of next 2 rows.

Cont working basket cable in center of sleeve for saddle shoulder.

You will have 1 extra st at each side for seaming.

Work until center extension meas 6½(7½,8½,9¼)" (16.5,19,21.5,23.5 cm).

B.o. all sts.

FINISHING

Sew in sleeves leaving one of the back shoulder seams open.

Using smaller needles, p.u. 89(92,95, 98) sts evenly around neckline (multiple of 3 plus 2).

Work garter ridge.

Work knotted rib for 3" (7.5 cm).

Work 10 rows of St st to form rolled edge.

B.o.

Sew remaining shoulder seam.

Sew underarm and side seams.

CARDIGAN

SIZES, MATERIALS, AND GAUGE

Same as mock turtleneck

⅞" (2.2 cm) buttons (9)

BACK AND SLEEVES

Work same as mock turtleneck.

RIGHT FRONT

Using smaller needles, c.o. 53(59,65, 73) sts.

Work 10 rows in St st to form rolled hems.

Work in knotted rib for 3½" (9 cm) ending with WSR.

Work garter ridge over 4 rows.

Next row (RS): Knit all sts, inc 13(13,13, 11) sts evenly across to give 66(72,78,84) sts.

Change to larger needles and est pattern on WS row.

Work 8(14,20,26) sts in moss st, work 1 six knot cable (24 sts), work 1 banded cable (6 sts), work 1 basket cable over 28 sts.

Work as est in pattern.

When piece meas 21¾(22¾,23¾, 24¾)" (55,58,60.5,63 cm), shape neck and shoulders.

At neck edge, b.o. 19(19,21,20) sts and work to end.

Turn and b.o. 9(11,12,13) sts at shoulder and work to end.

Turn and b.o. 3(3,3,4) neck sts and work to end.

Turn and b.o. 9(11,12,13) shoulder sts and work to end.

Turn and b.o. 3(3,3,4) neck sts and work to end.

Turn and b.o. 10(11,12,13) shoulder sts and work to end.

Turn and b.o. 3(3,3,4) neck sts and work to end.

Turn and b.o. rem 10(11,12,13) shoulder sts.

LEFT FRONT

Work same as right front, rev shaping and placement of cables.

Est cable pattern on WS as foll: Work 1 basket cable (28 sts), work 1 banded cable (6 sts), work 1 six knot cable (24 sts), work 8(14,20,26) sts in moss stitch.

BUTTON BANDS

Right band: With smaller needles, c.o. 11 sts.

Work in knotted rib as foll:

Row 1: K1, * knit into front and back of next st, p2, *; rep bet *'s 3 times, end by slipping last st as if to purl.

Row 2: K1,* k2, p2tog, *; rep bet *'s 3 times, end by slipping last st as if to purl.

Work buttonhole on RS when piece meas ¾" (2 cm) as foll:

Work 6 sts, p2tog, work to end.

Next row: Make 1 st where 2 sts were purled tog.

Work buttonholes every 2" (5 cm).

When piece meas 20¼(21¼,22¼, 23¼)" (51.5,54,56.5,59 cm), slip sts to holder.

Left band: With smaller needles c.o. 11 sts and work in knotted rib as foll:

Row 1: K1, * p2, knit into front and back of st, *; rep bet *'s 3 times, end by slipping last st as if to purl.

Row 2: K1, * p2tog, k2, *; rep bet *'s 3 times, slip last st as if to purl.

Work as est until piece meas same as other band and slip all sts to holder.

FINISHING

Sew shoulder/armhole seam.

Sew underarm seam.

Sew on button bands, stretching band to fit fronts of cardigan.

Using smaller needles and having RS facing you, p.u. 10 sts on holder (11th disappeared into seam), p.u. 99(102, 105,108) sts evenly around neckline, p.u. 10 sts rem at left holder.

Work in knotted rib for 1½" (4 cm) working buttonhole in right side as est in band.

Then dec at neck on RS by p2tog in the knotted rib.

Then cont working the p2 sequence as p1.

Work 2" (5 cm) and b.o. on WS.

Sew on buttons opposite buttonholes.

CHILD'S PULLOVER

SIZES

2(4,6,8,10)

Finished measurements at chest: 25(27,29,31,33)" (63.5,68.5,73.5,78.5, 84 cm)

MATERIALS

Cambridge: 8(8,9,10,12) skeins

Equivalent yarn: 680(680,765,850, 1020) yards/622(622,700,777,933) meters of worsted-weight yarn

Knitting needles: same as for adult sweaters

GAUGE AND STITCHES

Same as for adult sweaters

BACK

With smaller needles, c.o. 62(65,70,80, 86) sts.

Work 8 rows in St st to form rolled hem.

Beg working in knotted rib.

Work for 2" (5 cm) ending with WSR.

Work garter ridge over 4 rows.

Change to larger needles.

Next row (RS): Knit all sts, inc 14(15, 18,16,18) sts evenly across to give 76(80,88,96,104) sts.

Est pattern as foll: Work 12(14,18,14, 18) sts in moss stitch, k2, work 1 banded cable over 6 sts, k0(0,0,2,2), work 0(0,0,1,1) banded cable over 6 sts, work basket cable over 36 sts, work banded cable over 6 sts, k2, work 0(0,0,1,1) banded cable over 6 sts, k0(0,0,2,2), work 12(14,18,14,18) sts in moss st.

Work until piece meas 14(14½,15,15½, 16½)" (35.5,37,38,39.5,42 cm) or desired length.

B.o. all sts.

FRONT

Work same as back until piece meas 12(12½,13,13½,14½)" 30.5,31.5,33, 34,37 cm).

Shape neck: Work 20(22,26,30,34) sts, join second ball of yarn and b.o. center 36 sts; work to end.

Working both sides at same time separately b.o. 2 sts every 2nd row 3(3,4,5, 6) times to give 14(16,18,20, 22) sts at each shoulder.

When piece meas same as back, b.o. all sts.

SLEEVES

Using smaller needles, c.o. 26(26,29, 29,29) sts.

Work 8 rows in St st.

Beg knotted rib.

Work for 2" (5 cm).

Work garter ridge.

Change to larger needles and knit 1 row, inc 22(22,23,23,27) sts evenly across to give 48(48,52,52,52,56) sts.

Est pattern as foll: Work 6(6,8,8,10) sts in moss stitch, work row 1 of basket cable over 36 sts, work 6(6,8,8,10) sts in moss stitch.

Work as est in pattern, inc 1 st each end every 2nd row 0(1,0,3,2) times, then 1 st each end, alt every 4th and every 6th row 8(9,10,9,10) times and building out in moss stitch.

You should have 64(68,72,76,80) sts.

When piece meas 10(10½,10¾,11, 11½)" (25.5,26.5,27.5,28,29 cm), b.o. all sts.

FINISHING

Sew one shoulder seam.

Using smaller needles, p.u. 68(71,77, 83,86) sts evenly around neckline.

Work garter ridge.

Work knotted rib for 2" (5 cm).

Work 8 rows of St st to form rolled edge.

B.o.

Sew remaining shoulder seam and neck rib.

Measure down 5(5½,6,6½,7)" (12.5, 14,15,16.5,18 cm) from shoulder in both front and back and sew in sleeve between points.

Sew underarm and side seams.

CHILD'S HAT

Using smaller needles, c.o. 80 sts.

Work in St st for 11 rows.

In last row of St st, inc 10 sts evenly across to give 90 sts.

Change to larger needles and est pattern as foll: On WS, * K2 in rev St st, work 1 banded cable (6 sts), k2 in rev St st, work 8 sts in moss st, *; rep bet *'s 4 more times.

Work as est in patterns until piece meas 6" (15 cm).

Dec for crown shaping: On RS, * p2 in rev St st, work banded cable, p2 in rev St st, k2tog, work 4 sts in moss st, k2tog, *; rep 4 more times.

Work WS as est.

Dec on next RS row but instead of working 4 in middle of moss st, work 2.

Keep dec every other row until no moss sts remain.

Thread yarn through all loops to pull sts together and gather up.

Make a little wrapped tassel and attach at center of hat.

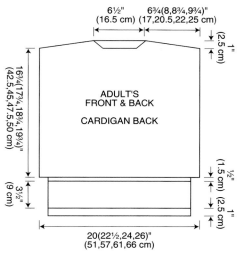

6½"
(16.5 cm)   6¾(8,8¾,9¾)"
(17,20.5,22,25 cm)

1"
(2.5 cm)

16¾(17¾,18¾,19¾)"
(42.5,45,47.5,50 cm)

ADULT'S
FRONT & BACK

CARDIGAN BACK

½"
(1.5 cm)

1"
(2.5 cm)

3½"
(9 cm)

20(22½,24,26)"
(51,57,61,66 cm)

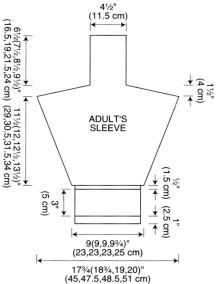

4½"
(11.5 cm)

6½(7½,8½,9½)"
(16.5,19,21.5,24 cm)

11½(12,12½,13½)"
(29,30.5,31.5,34 cm)

ADULT'S
SLEEVE

1½"
(4 cm)

3"
(5 cm)

½"
(1.5 cm)

1"
(2.5 cm)

9(9,9,9¾)"
(23,23,23,25 cm)

17¾(18¾,19,20)"
(45,47.5,48.5,51 cm)

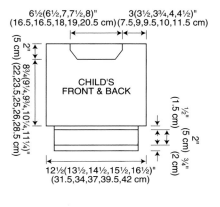

6½(6½,7,7½,8)"
(16.5,16.5,18,19,20.5 cm)   3(3½,3¾,4,4½)"
(7.5,9,9.5,10,11.5 cm)

2"
(5 cm)

8¾(9¼,9¾,10¼,11¼)"
(22,23.5,25,26,28.5 cm)

CHILD'S
FRONT & BACK

½"
(1.5 cm)

2"
(5 cm)

¾"
(2 cm)

12½(13½,14½,15½,16½)"
(31.5,34,37,39.5,42 cm)

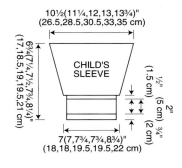

10½(11¼,12,13,13¾)"
(26.5,28.5,30.5,33,35 cm)

6¾(7¼,7½,7¾,8¼)"
(17,18.5,19,19.5,21 cm)

CHILD'S
SLEEVE

½"
(1.5 cm)

2"
(5 cm)

¾"
(2 cm)

7(7,7¾,7¾,8¾)"
(18,18,19.5,19.5,22 cm)

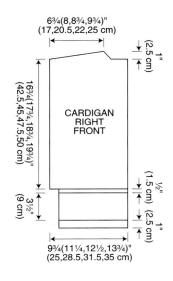

6¾(8,8¾,9¾)"
(17,20.5,22,25 cm)

1"
(2.5 cm)

16¾(17¾,18¾,19¾)"
(42.5,45,47.5,50 cm)

CARDIGAN
RIGHT
FRONT

½"
(1.5 cm)

1"
(2.5 cm)

3½"
(9 cm)

9¾(11¼,12½,13¾)"
(25,28.5,31.5,35 cm)

LAND'S END LABYRINTH

Both sweaters in this ensemble use the same combination of chunky and easy-to-knit cables. Varying the weight of the yarn and the edge finishes makes each garment look distinctly different. The woman's lighter-weight sweater is based on a fisherman's smock with Guernsey-style stockinette stitch at the bottom of the sweater. It's feminized with the addition of a fun-to-knit lacy, bobbled border. The other version, which looks equally attractive on men and women, is edged in a cabled rib stitch that gives it a more traditional "sweater look."

Design: **Kristin Nicholas**
Knitting rating (both sweaters):
Experienced

SIZES

Unisex version: Small(Medium,Large, Extra Large)

Woman's smock version: <Small (Medium,Large,Extra Large)>

Finished measurements: 40½(50½,56½, 62½)" (103,128.5,143.5,159 cm); <37 (45,53,61)" (94,114.5,134.5,155 cm)>

MATERIALS

Unisex version: Cambridge (70% cotton, 30% wool; 50 grams = approx. 85 yards): 16(16,17,17) hanks #3911 Prospect Peach.

Woman's version: <Willough (65% cotton, 35% silk; 50 grams = approx. 136 yards): 19(20,20,21) hanks #3616 Natural>

Equivalent yarn: 1360(1360,1445,1445) yards/1244(1244,1321,1321) meters of worsted-weight yarn for unisex

sweater; 2584(2720,2720,2856) yards/2362(2487,2487,2611) meters of light worsted-weight yarn for woman's sweater

Knitting needles in sizes 5 and 7 U.S. (3.75 and 4.5 cm)

16" (40.5 cm) circular needle in size 5 U.S. (3.75 mm)

GAUGE

Stockinette stitch on larger needles: 18 sts and 30 rows = 4" (10 cm) <20 sts and 30 rows = 4" (10 cm)>

Giant cable = 5¼" (13.5 cm) <4¾" (12 cm)>

X Cable = 4¼" (11 cm) <3¾" (9.5 cm)>

PATTERN STITCHES

ABBREVIATIONS

BC: Sl 3 sts to cn and hold in back, k3, k3 from cn.

FC: Sl 3 sts to cn and hold in front, k3, k3 from cn.

LBC: Sl 6 sts to cn and hold in back, k6, k6 from cn.

LFC: Sl 6 sts to cn and hold in front, k6, k6 from cn.

SBC: Sl 1 st to cn and hold in back, k3, p1 from cn.

SFC: Sl 3 sts to cn and hold in front, p1, k3 from cn.

STOCKINETTE STITCH

Row 1: (RS) K all sts.
Row 2: P all sts.

REVERSE STOCKINETTE STITCH

Row 1: (WS) K all sts.
Row 2: P all sts.

BOBBLE BORDER FOR WOMAN'S VERSION

(multiple of 10 + 1)

Row 1: (RS) P5, * (k1, p1, k1, p1) in next st before slipping from left needle, turn to WS and k4, turn to RS and k4, turn to WS and k4, turn to RS and lift 2nd, 3rd, and 4th sts, one at a time (in that order) over 1st st and off left needle, k1 (the rem st of group just worked), p9 *, rep bet *'s, end last rep p5.

Row 2 and all WSR: P all sts.

Row 3: P1, * yo, p2, p2tog, k1, p2tog, p2, yo, p1 *, rep bet *'s.

Row 5: P2, * yo, p1, p2tog, k1, p2tog, p1, yo, p3 *, rep bet *'s, end last rep p2.

Row 7: P3, * yo, p2tog, k1, p2tog, yo, p5 *, rep bet *'s, end last rep p3.

Rows 8, 9, and 10: P all sts.

TWIST STITCH (TWST)

Row 1: (WS) P1.
Row 2: K1-b (k1 into back of st) to twist.

CABLED RIB FOR UNISEX VERSION

(over multiple of 19 + 13)

Row 1: (WS) * K3, p1, k2, p1, k2, p1, k3, p6 *, rep bet *'s, end last rep omitting last p6.

Rows 2 and 6: * P3, TWST, p2, TWST, p2, TWST, p3, k6 *, rep bet *'s, end last rep omitting last k6.

Row 3 and all WSR: Repeat row 1.

Row 4: * P3, TWST, p2, TWST, p2, TWST, p3, FC *, rep bet *'s, end last rep omitting last FC.

SIMPLE CABLE

(panel of 6 sts)

Row 1: (WS) P6.
Row 2: K6.
Row 3 and all WSR: Work sts as they appear.
Row 4: FC.
Rows 6 and 8: Repeat row 2.

GIANT CABLE

(panel of 33 sts)

Row 1: (WS) K3, p5, k1, p6, k3, p6, k1, p5, k3.

Rows 2, 6, 34, and 38: P3, k5, p1, BC, p3, FC, p1, k5, p3.

Row 3 and all WSR: Work sts as they appear.

Rows 4, 8, 32, 36, and 40: P3, k5, p1, k6, p3, k6, p1, k5, p3.

Row 10: P3, LFC, p3, LBC, p3.

Rows 12, 16, 20, 24, and 28: P3, k6, p1, k5, p3, k5, p1, k6, p3.

Rows 14, 18, 22, and 26: P3, FC, p1, k5, p3, k5, p1, BC, p3.

Row 30: P3, LBC, p3, LFC, p3.

Repeat rows 1-40.

X Cable

(over panel of 26 sts)

Row 1: (WS) K3, p6, k8, p6, k3.

Row 2: P3, FC, p8, BC, p3.

Row 3 and all WSR: Work sts as they appear.

Row 4: P3, k3, SFC, p6, SBC, k3, p3.

Row 6: P3, k3, p1, SFC, p4, SBC, p1, k3, p3.

Row 8: P3, k3, p2, SFC, p2, SBC, p2, k3, p3.

Row 10: P3, k3, p3, SFC, SBC, p3, k3, p3.

Row 12: P3, k3, p4, BC, p4, k3, p3.

Row 14: P3, k3, p3, SBC, SFC, p3, k3, p3.

Row 16: P3, k3, p2, SBC, p2, SFC, p2, k3, p3.

Row 18: P3, k3, p1, SBC, p4, SFC, p1, k3, p3.

Row 20: P3, k3, SBC, p6, SFC, k3, p3.

Repeat Rows 1-20.

Bobble Neckline Trim for Woman's Version

(over 7 sts in rnd)

Rnd 1: * P6, k1 *, rep bet *'s.

Rnd 2: K all sts.

Repeat rnds 1-2.

B.o. bobble rnd: * B.o. 6 sts in p, (k1, p1, k1, p1) in next st before slipping from left needle, turn to WS and k4, turn to RS and k4, turn to WS and k4, turn to RS and lift 2nd, 3rd, and 4th sts, one at a time (in that order) over 1st st and off left needle, b.o. the rem st (of group just worked) in knit st *, rep bet *'s.

Cabled Rib

(over multiple of 19 + 13)

Row 1 and all WSR: * K3, p1, k2, p1, k2, p1, k3, p6 *, rep bet *'s, omitting last p6 in last rep.

Row 2: * P3, k1-b, p2, k1-b, p2, k1-b, p3, k6 *, rep bet *'s, omitting last k6 in last rep.

Row 4: * P3, k1-b, p2, k1-b, p2, k1-b, p3, FC *, rep bet *'s, omitting last FC in last rep.

Row 6: Repeat row 2.

Repeat rows 1-6.

Neckline

(over multiple of 19 sts in rnd)

All rnds but cable twisting rnd:
* P3, TWST, p2, TWST, p2, TWST, p3, k6 *, rep bet *'s

Rnd 4: * P3, TWST, p2, TWST, p2, TWST, p3, FC *, rep bet *'s.

Repeat rnds 1-6.

Note: When two sets of numbers are given, unisex version is shown first; woman's version is shown in brackets < >.

Back

Unisex version: With smaller needles, c.o. 108(127,146,165) sts.

Work in cabled rib for 3" (7.5 cm).

On last RSR, inc 13(20,27,34) sts evenly across to give 121(147,173,199) sts.

<Woman's version>: With smaller needles, c.o. 91(111,121,141) sts.

Work in bobble border for one com-

40

plete rep, inc 0(0,5,0) sts across last row to give 91(111,126,141) sts.

Change to larger needles.

Beg working in St st for 6" (15 cm), ending with a RSR.

(WS) K all sts.

(RS) K and inc 30(36,47,58) sts evenly across to give 121(147,173,199) sts.

Establish pattern for both versions:
[K3 in rev St st, p1 TWST, k3 in rev St st, p6 in simple cable] 0(1,2,3) times, k3 in rev St st, p1 TWST, work X-cable over 26 sts, p1 TWST, k3 in rev St st, p6 in simple cable, k3 in rev St st, p1 TWST, work large cable over 33 sts, p1 TWST, k3 in rev St st, p6 in simple cable, k3 in rev St st, p1 TWST, work X-cable over 26 sts, p1 TWST, k3 in rev St st; [p6 in simple cable, k3 in rev St st, p1 TWST, k3 in rev St st] 0(1,2,3) times.

When piece meas 25(26,27,28)" (63.5,66,68.5,71 cm) <26(27,28,29)" (66,68.5,71,73.5 cm)> from beg, b.o. all sts.

FRONT

Work as for back until piece meas 22(23,24,25)" (56,58.5,61,63.5 cm) <23(24,25,26)" (58.5,61,63.5,66 cm)>.

Shape neck: Work 44(56,69,80) <42(54,66,78)> sts, join a 2nd ball of yarn and b.o. center 33(35,35,39) <37(39,41,43)> sts, work to end.

Working each side sep, b.o. 1 st at neck edge every other row 6(6,7,7) <4(5,6,7)> times to give 38(50,62,73) <38(49,60,71)> sts at shoulder.

When piece meas same as back at shoulders, b.o. all sts.

SLEEVES

Unisex version: With smaller needles, c.o. 51 sts.

Work in cabled rib for 3" (7.5 cm).

On last RSR, inc 10 sts evenly across to give 61 sts.

Est patt on WSR as foll: * P1 TWST, k3 in rev St st, p6 in simple cable, k3 in rev St st, p1 TWST *, work large cable over 33 sts, rep bet *'s.

Work in patt as est, inc 1 st each end in rev St st every 4 rows 0(0,0,5) times, every 6 rows 12(16,22,19) times, then every 8 rows 6(4,0,0) times to give 97(101,105,109) sts.

<Woman' version>: With smaller

needles, c.o. 51 sts.

Work bobble border.

On last row, inc 5 sts evenly across to give 56 sts.

Work in St st for 3" (7.5 cm), inc 1 st each end every 4th row 5 times to give 66 sts, end with a RSR.

(WS) K all sts.

(RS) K and inc 9 sts evenly across to give 75 sts.

(WS) K all sts.

(RS) K all sts.

Est patt as foll on WSR: Work 7 sts in rev St st, * p1 TWST, k3 in rev St st, p6 in simple cable, k3 in rev St st, p1 TWST *, work large cable over 33 sts, rep bet *'s, end with 7 sts in rev St st.

Inc 1 st each end in rev St st every 6 rows 0(0,0,4) times, every 8 rows 6(8,9,12)

times, then every 10 rows 5(4,4,0) times to give 97(99,101,107) sts.

When piece meas 19(20,20½,21)" (48.5,51,52,53.5 cm) <17(18,19,20)" (43,45.5,48.5,51 cm)>, b.o. all sts.

FINISHING

Sew shoulder seams.

With circular needle, p.u. 95(95,114, 114) <105(112,119,126)> sts evenly around neckline.

Work in cabled rib <bobble rib> for 3" (7.5 cm) <1-1/4" (3 cm)>.

B.o. loosely.

Mark underarm points 9(9½,10,10½)" (23,24,25.5,26.5 cm) <9(9¼,9½,10)" (23,23.5,24,25.5 cm)> down in front and back from shoulder.

Set in sleeve bet points.

Sew underarm and side seams.

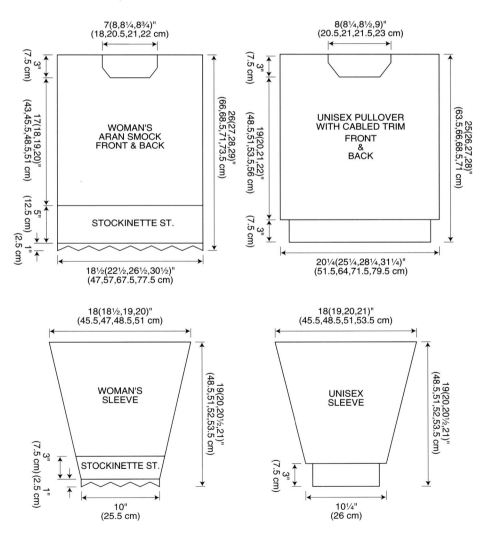

7(8,8¼,8¾)"
(18,20.5,21,22 cm)

3"
(7.5 cm)

17(18,19,20)"
(43,45.5,48.5,51 cm)

26(27,28,29)"
(66,68.5,71,73.5 cm)

WOMAN'S
ARAN SMOCK
FRONT & BACK

STOCKINETTE ST.

5"
(12.5 cm)

1"
(2.5 cm)

18½(22½,26½,30½)"
(47,57,67.5,77.5 cm)

8(8¼,8½,9)"
(20.5,21,21.5,23 cm)

3"
(7.5 cm)

19(20,21,22)"
(48.5,51,53.5,56 cm)

UNISEX PULLOVER
WITH CABLED TRIM
FRONT
&
BACK

25(26,27,28)"
(63.5,66,68.5,71 cm)

3"
(7.5 cm)

20¼(25¼,28¼,31¼)"
(51.5,64,71.5,79.5 cm)

18(18½,19,20)"
(45.5,47,48.5,51 cm)

WOMAN'S
SLEEVE

STOCKINETTE ST.

3"
(7.5 cm)

1"
(2.5 cm)

19(20,20½,21)"
(48.5,51,52,53.5 cm)

10"
(25.5 cm)

18(19,20,21)"
(45.5,48.5,51,53.5 cm)

UNISEX
SLEEVE

3"
(7.5 cm)

19(20,20½,21)"
(48.5,51,52,53.5 cm)

10¼"
(26 cm)

SIZES

Small(Medium,Large,Extra Large)
Finished measurements at underarm: 38(42,46,49)" (96.5,106.5,117,124.5 cm)

MATERIALS

Cambridge (70% cotton, 30% wool, 50 grams = approx. 85 yards): 17(19,21, 23) skeins

Equivalent yarn: 1445(1615,1785,1955) yards/1320(1476,1631,1787) meters of worsted-weight yarn

Knitting needles in sizes 5 and 6 U.S. (3.75 and 4 mm)

Cable needle (cn)

Stitch holders (4)

¾" (2 cm) buttons (4)

GAUGE

Brocade stitch on larger needles: 21 sts and 32 rows = 4" (10 cm)

Take time to save time—check your gauge.

PATTERN STITCHES

CABLE RIB

(over multiple of 4 + 2)

Row 1: (RS) * P2, k2 *, rep bet *'s, end p2.

Rows 2 and 4: Work all sts as they appear.

Row 3: * P2, sl 1 st to cn and hold in back, k1, k1 from cn *, rep bet *'s, end p2.

Repeat rows 1-4 for rib.

BROCADE PATTERN

(over 10 st rep and 16 rows)

See chart on page 44.

SEED STITCH

(over odd number of sts)

All rows: * K1, p1 *, rep bet *'s, end k1.

CENTER PANEL

See chart. Over 55(55,73,73) sts. Rep side cable 2(2,3,3) times, work center diamond panel once, rep side cable 2(2,3,3) times.

ABBREVIATIONS

FC: Sl2 to cn and hold in front, k2, k2 from cn.

F4C: Sl4 to cn and hold in front, k4, k4 from cn.

BC: Sl2 to cn and hold in back, k2, k2 from cn.

B4C: Sl4 to cn and hold in back, k4, k4 from cn.

BACK

With smaller needles, c.o. 102(110,122, 130) sts.

Use a cast-on method that makes the 1st row worked a RSR.

K 2 rows, p 2 rows.

Work cable rib for 2½" (6.5 cm), ending with WSR.

K 2 rows, p 2 rows.

On 2nd p row, dec 2(0,2,0) sts across row to give 100(110,120,130) sts.

Change to larger needles and beg brocade patt according to chart.

Work straight until piece meas 23(24,25,26)" (58.5,61,63.5,66 cm).

Shape back neck: Work 41(46,49,54) sts, join 2nd ball of yarn and b.o. center 18(18,22,22) sts.

Finish row.

B.o. at each neck edge 5 sts 2 times.

Place rem 31(36,39,44) sts at each side on holders.

FRONT

Work same as back until piece meas 12(12,13,14)" (30.5,30.5,33,35.5 cm), ending with row 6 or row 14 of brocade stitch (WSR).

Place markers after 1st 27(32,30,35) sts and after next 46(46,60,60) sts.

Est center panel as foll:

Rows 1 and 2: Work brocade patt to 1st marker, knit to next marker, work brocade patt to end.

Row 3: Work brocade patt to 1st marker, purl to next marker, work brocade patt to end.

Row 4: Work brocade patt to 1st marker, p2, * p1, P-inc1 (P into back of strand that divides sts on right-hand needle from sts on left-hand needle), p2, p1, P-inc1, p3 *, rep from * to * 1(1,2,2) times more, p7, p1, P-inc1, p9, work from * to * 2(2,3,3) times ending

with p2 instead of p3, work brocade patt to end.

You will now have 109(119,133,143) sts.

Work chart over center marked 55(55,73,73) sts working brocade on 27(32,30,35) sts at each end.

Work straight until piece meas 20½ (21½,22½,23½)" (52,54.5,57,59.5 cm).

Shape front neck: (RSR) Work 49(54, 59,64) sts, join 2nd ball of yarn and b.o. center 11(11,15,15) sts, work to end.

Work one shoulder at a time.

For right shoulder: B.o. at neck edge 4 sts once, 3 sts 2 times, 2 sts 2 times, 1 st 1(1,2,2) times to give 34(39,43,48) sts.

Work straight until piece meas same as back to shoulder.

On last row dec 3(3,4,4) sts evenly across 1st 7(7,13,13) sts of RSR.

Place rem 31(36,39,44) sts on a holder.

Left shoulder: B.o. at neck edge as for right shoulder.

When piece meas 2" (5 cm) from beg of neck shaping, dec 3(3,4,4) sts across 1st 7(7,13,13) sts of a WSR.

Place rem 31(36,39,44) sts on a holder.

You will attach button band at this shoulder.

SLEEVES

With smaller needles, c.o. 42(46,50,58) sts.

K 2 rows, p 2 rows.

SEASIDE GUERNSEY

A cabled rib adds an appropriate finish to the intricate Guernsey stitches in this classicly styled pullover. With one buttoned shoulder and a gusset at the underarm, this design is reminiscent of the true Guernsey sweaters from England.

Design: **NORAH GAUGHAN**
Knitting rating: **VERY CHALLENGING**

Work in cable rib as for back with one less rep of the 4-row patt, ending with a WSR.

K 1 row, inc 18(14,10,12) sts evenly to give 60(60,60,70) sts.

K 1 row, p 2 rows.

Change to larger needles and work in brocade patt, inc 1 st at each end every 9th(7th,8th,9th) row 12(15,15,15) times to give 84(90,90,100) sts.

Work straight until piece meas 16(16, 17,19)" (40.5,40.5,43,48.5 cm).

B.o. all sts.

UNDERARM GUSSETS

Make 2.

With larger needles, c.o. 21 sts.

Work in seed st until piece meas 4" (10 cm).

B.o. all sts.

FINISHING

Knit the right shoulder pieces tog.

Neck: With smaller needles, p.u. 82(86,90,94) sts around neck opening.

K 1 row, p 2 rows.

Work in cable rib for 2¼" (5.5 cm), ending with a WSR.

K 2 rows.

B.o. in purl.

This piece is the collar.

Button band (back left shoulder): With smaller needle, p.u. 15 sts along collar edge, k across 31(36,39,44) sts on holder to give 46(51,54,59) sts.

K 1 row, p 2 rows.

Work in K1, P1 rib for 1¼" (3 cm), ending with a WSR.

B.o. in knit for stability.

Buttonhole band (front left shoulder): With smaller needle, k across 31(36,39,44) sts on holder, p.u. 15 sts along edge of collar to give 46(51,54, 59) sts.

Work as for button band, placing buttonholes in the third rib row as foll:

Small: Work 8 sts, yo twice, work 2 tog, (work 9, yo twice, work 2 tog) 3 times, end with work 3.

Medium: (Work 10, yo twice, work 2 tog) 4 times, end with work 3.

Large: Work 10, yo twice, work 2 tog (work 11, yo twice, work 2 tog) 3 times, end with work 3.

Extra Large: (Work 12, yo twice, work 2 tog) 4 times, end with work 3.

On next row, drop one of the yo's in each double yo and rib as est to make buttonhole.

Cont in rib as est until same as button band.

B.o. in knit on a RSR.

Sew the ends of the rib bands tog, placing the front band on top.

Place markers 8(8½,8½,9½)" (20.5, 21.5,21.5,24 cm) down from each shoulder on front and back. (On the left shoulder the top of the front band is the shoulder line.)

Sew in sleeves between markers.

Place markers 4" (10 cm) from underarm on sleeves and body.

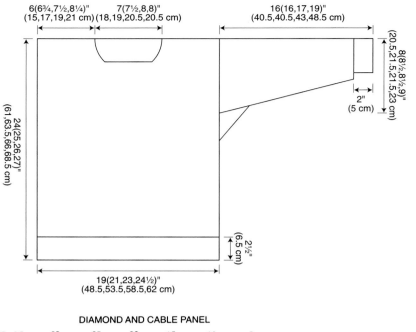

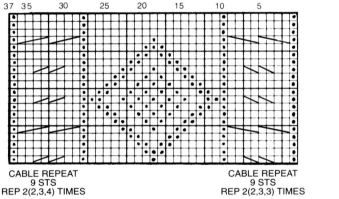

DIAMOND AND CABLE PANEL

37 35   30   25   20   15   10   5

CABLE REPEAT
9 STS
REP 2(2,3,4) TIMES

CABLE REPEAT
9 STS
REP 2(2,3,3) TIMES

| F4C |
| FC |
| B4C |
| BC |

☐ K ON RS; P ON WS
⊡ P ON RS; K ON WS

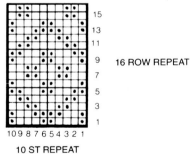

BROCADE PATTERN

15
13
11
9
7
5
3
1

10 9 8 7 6 5 4 3 2 1

16 ROW REPEAT

10 ST REPEAT

Sew in gussets between the markers.

Complete sleeve and side seams.

Place buttons on button band to correspond with buttonholes of front shoulder band.

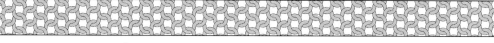

SIZES

Small(Medium,Large)

Finished measurements: 44(48,52)"
(112,122,132 cm)

MATERIALS

Tapestry (25% mohair, 75% wool; 50 grams = approx. 95 yards): 16(16,19) hanks

Equivalent yarn: 1520(1520,1805) yards/1390(1390,1650) meters of worsted-weight yarn

Knitting needles in sizes 4 and 6 U.S. (3.5 and 4 mm)

16" (40.5 cm) circular needle in size 4 U.S. (3.5 mm)

GAUGE

Stockinette stitch on larger needles: 19 sts and 25 rows = 4" (10 cm)

Take time to save time—check your gauge.

PATTERN STITCHES

2 x 2 RIB

(over even number of sts)

Row 1: K2, p2 across row.

BARNYARD GUERNSEY

This Guernsey-style sweater looks equally attractive on men and women. The rather complicated diamond pattern is formed using seed stitch. Unlike some Guernsey stitches, each side of the fabric is different, and complete concentration is necessary when knitting the yoke section. The rolled bottom edge completes the casual style of the sweater.

Design: NORAH GAUGHAN
Knitting rating: VERY CHALLENGING

Row 2: Work sts as they appear.

STOCKINETTE STITCH

Row 1: (RS) K all sts.

Row 2: P all sts.

CHEVRON BORDER

See chart A.

ALLOVER GUERNSEY PATTERN

See chart B.

RIGHT TWIST (RT)

Skip 1 st, insert needle from left to right in front loop of next st, k this st, leave on left-hand needle, k the skipped st, drop both sts from left-hand needle.

BACK

With larger needles c.o. 105(115,125) sts.

Work straight in St st for 7½(8,8½)" (19,20.5,21.5 cm), ending with a RS row (measure with the curl unrolled).

Work according to chart A over next 19 rows; then change to chart B and work until piece meas 27(28,29)" (68.5,71, 73.5 cm) from beg (unrolled).

B.o. all sts.

FRONT

Work as for back until piece meas 24(25,26)" (61,63.5,66 cm) from beg.

Shape neck: Work 47(52,56) sts, join 2nd ball of yarn and b.o. center 11(11,13) sts, work to end.

Working each side sep, b.o. at each neck edge 3 sts once, 2 sts twice, and 1 st 4(4,5) times to give 36(41,44) sts at each shoulder.

When piece meas same as back, b.o. all sts.

SLEEVES

With smaller needles, c.o. 50(54, 62) sts.

Work in 2 x 2 rib for 3" (7.5 cm), ending with a WS row.

Change to larger needles and k 1 row, inc 1 st to give 51(55,63) sts.

Work according to chart A, beg and end as indicated for sleeve.

Then work in St st inc 1 st each end every 4th row 18(20,21) times to give 87(95,105) sts.

When piece meas 18(19,20)" (45.5, 48.5,51 cm) from beg or desired length to underarm, b.o. all sts.

FINISHING

Sew shoulder seams.

With circular needle, beg at back neck, p.u. 104(104,112) sts around neckline and work rib as follows:

Rounds 1, 3, and 4: P2, k2 around.

Round 2: * P2, RT, p2, k2 *, repeat bet *'s to end.

Repeat rows 1-4 until neck meas 4" (10 cm).

B.o. all sts.

Sew side and underarm seams.

CHART A - CHEVRON BORDER
6 ST REPEAT

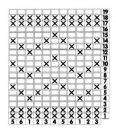

☐ K1 ON RS; P1 ON WS

☒ P1 ON RS; K1 ON WS

CHART B - GUERNSEY PATTERN

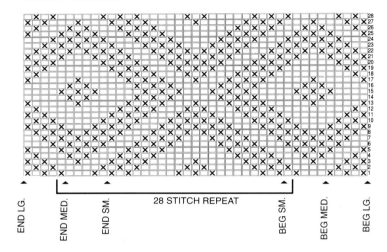

END LG. END MED. END SM. 28 STITCH REPEAT BEG SM. BEG MED. BEG LG.

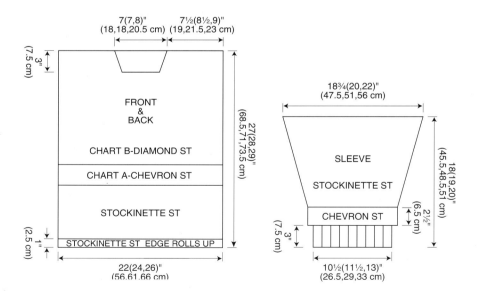

46

BLUE RIDGE INN

In this Aran-style cardigan, challenging cables are combined with simple moss stitch. The larger rib at the bottom is loosely sized and features side slits to give the feeling of a jacket, not a typical cardigan. The easy-to-knit Guernsey-style pullover combines ridges of reverse stockinette stitch, a plain stockinette stitch border, and a simple four-row texture stitch. Its rolled collar and oversized proportions make it a comfort to wear.

Cardigan: **Kristin Nicholas**
Guernsey: **Susan Mills**

Cardigan: **Experienced**
Guernsey: **Beginner**

CARDIGAN

SIZES

Small(Medium,Large,Extra Large)
Finished measurements: 45(49,53,58)" (114.5,124.5,134.5,147.5 cm)

MATERIALS

Stonington (100% superwash wool; 100 grams = approx. 137 yards): 14(15,16,17) hanks
Equivalent yarn: 1918(2055,2192,2329) yards/1754(1879,2004,2130) meters of bulky-weight wool.
Knitting needles in sizes 7 and 9 U.S. (4.5 and 5.5 mm)
36" (91.5 cm) circular needle in size 7 U.S. (4.5 mm)
Cable needle (cn)
Stitch markers if desired
1" (2.5 cm) buttons (7)

GAUGE

Moss stitch on larger needles: 15 sts and 28 rows = 4" (10 cm)
Intricate cable = 5" (12.5 cm)

Diamond cable = 4" (10 cm)
2 st twist cable = ½" (1.5 cm)
4 sts of rev St st = 1" (2.5 cm)
Take time to save time—check your gauge.
Note: This sweater is shown in size medium. Size small has no moss st at front side seams. Cables do not match at shoulders in front and back. A ridge is added at shoulders to compensate.

PATTERN STITCHES

ABBREVIATIONS

C4B: Sl 2 sts to cn and hold in back, k2, k2 from cn.
C4F: Sl 2 sts to cn and hold in front, k2, k2 from cn.
T4B: Sl 2 sts to cn and hold in back, k2, p2 from cn.
T4F: Sl 2 sts to cn and hold in front, p2, k2 from cn.
T3B: Sl next st to cn and hold in back, k2, p1 from cn.
T3F: Sl next 2 sts to cn and hold in front, p1, k2 from cn.
T4R: Sl next st to cn and hold in back, k 3, p1 from cn.
T4L: Sl next 3 sts to cn and hold in front, p1, k3 from cn.
C6B: Sl next 3 sts to cn and hold in back, k3, k3 from cn.

2 x 2 RIB

(over multiple of 4 + 2)
Row 1: (RS) * K2, p2, rep from *, end k2.
Row 2: * P2, k2, rep from *, end p2.

MOSS STITCH

(over even number of sts)
All rows: * K1, p1, rep from *.

REVERSE STOCKINETTE STITCH RIDGE

Row 1: (WS) P all sts.
Row 2: P all sts.
Row 3: K all sts.
Row 4: K all sts.

REVERSE STOCKINETTE STITCH

Row 1: (WS) K all sts.
Row 2: P all sts.

TWO-STITCH TWIST CABLE (2 ST TW)

Row 1: (WS) P2.
Row 2: Skip 1st st, k 2nd st without slipping off needle, k 1st st.

INTRICATE KNOTTED CABLE

(over 26 sts and 24 rows)
Row 1: (WS) K8, p10, k8.
Row 2: P8, C4B, k2, C4F, p8.
Row 3 and all WSR: Work all sts as they appear.
Row 4: P6, T4B, k2, C4B, T4F, p6.
Row 6: P4, T4B, p1, T3B, k2, T3F, p1, T4F, p4.
Row 8: P2, T4B, p2, T3B, p1, k2, p1, T3F, p2, T4F, p2.
Row 10: P2, k2, p3, T3B, p2, k2, p2, T3F, p3, k2, p2.
Row 12: P2, T4F, T3B, p3, k2, p3, T3F, T4B, p2.
Row 14: P4, C4B, p4, k2, p4, C4F, p4.
Row 16: P2, T4B, T4F, p2, k2, p2, T4B, T4F, p2.
Row 18: P2, k2, p4, T4F, k2, T4B, p4, k2, p2.
Row 20: P2, T4F, p4, C4F, k2, p4, T4B, p2.
Row 22: P4, T4F, p2, k2, C4B, p2, T4B, p4.
Row 24: P6, T4F, C4F, k2, T4B, p6.

DIAMOND CABLE

(over 20 sts and 24 rows)
Row 1: (WS) K7, p6, k7.
Row 2: P6, C4B, C4F, p6.
Row 3 and all WSR: Work all sts as they appear.
Row 4: P5, C4B, k2, C4F, p5.
Row 6: P4, T4R, k4, T4L, p4.
Row 8: P3, T4R, p1, C4B, p1, T4L, p3.
Row 10: P2, T4R, p2, k4, p2, T4L, p2.
Row 12: P2, k3, p3, C4B, p3, k3, p2.
Row 14: P2, T4L, p2, k4, p2, T4R, p2.
Row 16: P3, T4L, p1, C4B, p1, T4R, p3.
Row 18: P4, T4L, k4, T4R, p4.
Row 20: P5, T4L, k2, T4R, p5.
Row 22: P6, T4L, T4R, p6.
Row 24: P7, C6B, p7.

BACK

With smaller needles, c.o. 110(122,130, 142) sts.

Work 2 rows in moss st.

Work 2 sts in moss st, work 106(118, 126,138) sts in 2 x 2 rib, work 2 sts in moss st.

Work until rib meas 6" (15 cm), ending with RSR.

Work rev St st ridge, dec 8(12,12,16) sts in last row to give 102(110,118,126) sts.

Change to larger needles.

Est patt on WS as foll: Work 14(18,22, 26) sts in moss st, work 2 st TW, work diamond cable over 20 sts, work 2 st TW, work intricate knotted cable over 26 sts, work 2 st TW, work diamond cable over 20 sts, work 2 st TW, work 14(18,22,26) sts in moss st.

When piece meas 27(27,28,29)" (68.5,68.5,71,73.5 cm), end on RSR.

P 1 row (1st row of rev St st ridge), dec 10(12,14,16) across to give 92(98,104, 110) sts.

When ridge is complete, b.o. all sts.

RIGHT FRONT

C.o. 48(52,56,60) sts using smaller needles.

Work 2 rows moss st.

Then work in rib patt with moss st at side seams as foll: On RSR, work 46(50, 54,58) in 2 x 2 rib, work last 2 sts in moss st.

Work as est until piece meas 6" (15 cm), ending with RSR.

Now work rev St st ridge, inc 4(2,2,2) sts evenly across last row of rev St st ridge to give 52(54,58,62) sts.

You should be beg a WSR.

Change to larger needles.

Est patt on WS as foll: Work 0(4,8,12) sts in moss st, work 2(0,0,0) in rev St st, work 2 st TW, work diamond cable over 20 sts, work 2 st TW, work intricate knotted cable over 26 sts.

Work as est until piece meas 20(20,21, 22)" (51,51,53.5,56 cm) from beg.

Shape neck: At neck edge, b.o. 1 st now and every 4th row 7(8,9,10) times to give 45(46,49,52) sts at shoulder.

When piece meas 27(27,28,29)" (68.5,

68.5,71,73.5 cm) and you are beg a WSR, p 1 row (1st row of rev St st ridge), dec 4(5,6,7) sts across to give 41(41,43,45) sts.

When ridge is complete, b.o. all sts.

LEFT FRONT

C.o. 48(52,56,60) sts using smaller needles.

Work 2 rows moss st.

Work 2 sts in moss st, work 46(50,54, 58) sts in 2 x 2 rib.

Cont as for right front, ending with rev St st ridge.

Now est patt: On WS, work intricate knotted cable over 26 sts, work 2 st TW, work diamond cable over 20 sts, work 2 st TW, work 0(4,8,12) in moss st, work 2(0,0,0) in rev St st.

Work as for right front, rev patt placement.

SLEEVES

C.o. 30(30,34,34) sts using smaller needles.

Work 2 rows in moss st.

Work 2 x 2 rib for 3½" (9 cm).

Work rev St st ridge, inc 4(4,2,4) sts in last row to give 34(34,36,38) sts.

Change to larger needles and work in moss st, inc 1 st each end every 5th row 17(17,18,18) times to give 68(68,72, 74) sts.

When piece meas 17(17,17½,18)" (43, 43,44.5,45.5 cm), b.o. all sts.

FINISHING

Sew shoulder seams.

With circular needle, p.u. 100(100,103, 108) sts from bottom of sweater to shoulder, 46(46,48,50) sts at back of neck, 100(100,103,108) sts from shoulder to bottom of sweater.

Work 1st 2 sts in moss st, work all other sts in 2 x 2 rib, work last 2 sts in moss st.

Cont in est patt.

Mark 7 buttonholes evenly spaced from bottom of sweater to V-neck shaping.

When rib meas 1½" (4 cm), work buttonholes at markings by b.o. 3 sts.

Next row: C.o. 3 sts over b.o. sts.

When rib meas 3" (7.5 cm), work 2 rows moss st.

B.o. in moss st.

Meas down 9(9,9½,10)" (23,23,24, 25.5 cm) from shoulder seam in front and back.

Sew sleeves bet points.

Sew underarm and side seams, leaving open from rev St st ridge down at side seams.

Sew on 7 buttons.

GUERNSEY

SIZES

Small(Medium,Large,Extra Large,Jumbo)
Finished measurements: 39(43½,48, 52½,57)" (99,110.5,122,133.5,145 cm)

MATERIALS

8(9,10,10,11) hanks
Equivalent yarn: 1096(1233,1370,1370, 1507) yards/1002(1127,1253,1253, 1378) meters of bulky-weight wool
Knitting needles in sizes 9 and 10 U.S. (5.5 and 6 mm)
16" (40.5 cm) circular needle in size 9 U.S. (5.5 mm)

GAUGE

Stockinette stitch on larger needles: 14 sts and 20 rows = 4" (10 cm)
Take time to save time—check your gauge.

PATTERN STITCHES

GARTER RIDGE
Row1: (RS) P all sts.
Row 2: K all sts.
Row 3: K all sts.
Row 4: P all sts.

TEXTURE STITCH
(multiple of 4 sts)
Row 1: (RS) * K2, p2, rep from *.
Row 2: P all sts.
Row 3: * P2, k2, rep from *.
Row 4: P all sts.

1 x 1 RIB
(multiple of 2 sts)
All rows: * K1, p1, rep from *.

STOCKINETTE STITCH
Row 1: (RS) K all sts.
Row 2: P all sts.

BACK

With smaller needles, c.o. 68(76,84,92, 100) sts.

Option 1: Work garter ridge for 3(3½, 3½,4,4)" (7.5,9,9,10,10 cm).

Option 2: Work 1 x 1 rib for 2½(3,3, 3½,3½)" (6.5,7.5,7.5,9,9 cm), ending with a WSR. P 1 row, then K 1 row to form ridge.

Change to larger needles and work in St st until piece meas 8(8½,8½,9,9)" (20.5,21.5,21.5,23,23 cm), ending with a WSR.

P 1 row then k 1 row to form ridge.

Beg working in texture stitch patt and work until piece meas 24(25,26,27, 28)" (61,63.5,66,68.5,71 cm).

B.o. all sts.

FRONT

Work as for back until piece meas 22(23,24,25,26)" (56,58.5,61,63.5,66 cm).

Keeping in patt, work across 25(29,30, 34,38) sts, put center 18(18,24,24,24) sts on holder, join 2nd ball of yarn, and work across rem 25(29,30,34,38) sts.

B.o. 1 st at each neck edge every other row 4 times, leaving 21(25,26,30,34) sts rem for each shoulder.

When piece meas same length as back, b.o. all sts.

SLEEVES

With smaller needles, c.o. 28(30,30,32, 32) sts and work either **Option 1** (shown): garter ridge for 2½(3,3,3½, 3½)" (6.5, 7.5,7.5,9,9 cm) or **Option 2:** 1 x 1 rib for 2(2½,2½,3,3)" (5,6.5,6.5, 7.5,7.5 cm), then 1 garter ridge.

Change to larger needles and beg working in St st.

When sleeve meas 5(5¼,5½,5¾,6)" (12.5,13.5,14,14.5,15 cm), work garter ridge and beg texture stitch patt as for back.

At the same time, inc 1 st each edge every 3rd row 18(18,20,21,22) times to give 64(66,70,74,76) sts.

When sleeve meas 15(15¾,16½,17¼, 18)" (38,40,42,43,45.5 cm) or desired length, b.o. all sts.

FINISHING

Sew shoulder, side, and sleeve seams.

With circular needle, p.u. 60(66,72,74, 78) sts around neck and work 1 garter ridge (k 1 rnd, p 2 rnds).

Work 3½" (6.5 cm) in St st (k each rnd).

B.o. all sts **loosely.**

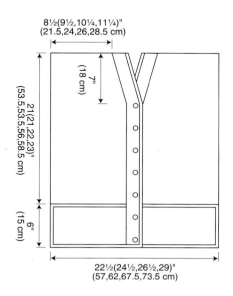

8½(9½,10¼,11¼)"
(21.5,24,26,28.5 cm)

7" (18 cm)

21(21,22,23)" (53.5,53.5,56,58.5 cm)

6" (15 cm)

22½(24½,26½,29)" (57,62,67.5,73.5 cm)

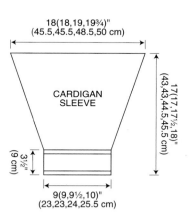

18(18,19,19¾)"
(45.5,45.5,48.5,50 cm)

CARDIGAN SLEEVE

17(17,17½,18)"
(43,43,44.5,45.5 cm)

3½" (9 cm)

9(9,9½,10)"
(23,23,24,25.5 cm)

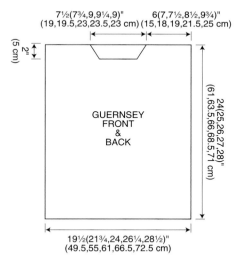

7½(7¾,9,9¼,9)" (19,19.5,23,23.5,23 cm)   6(7,7½,8½,9¾)" (15,18,19,21.5,25 cm)

2" (5 cm)

GUERNSEY FRONT & BACK

24(25,26,27,28)" (61,63.5,66,68.5,71 cm)

19½(21¾,24,26¼,28½)" (49.5,55,61,66.5,72.5 cm)

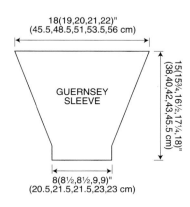

18(19,20,21,22)"
(45.5,48.5,51,53.5,56 cm)

GUERNSEY SLEEVE

15(15¾,16½,17¼,18)"
(38,40,42,43,45.5 cm)

8(8½,8½,9,9)"
(20.5,21.5,21.5,23,23 cm)

Plaits, Knots & Crosses

In this duo of casual sweaters, the woman's oversized pullover has the appeal of a loose fisherman's smock. The knit and purl stitches it uses are very easy, with a bit of concentration, and the look is quite complicated. The classic Aran sweater shown on the man employs a large array of cable stitchery, including twist stitches, braids, X-and-O cables, and sailor's rib at the sides. Instructions for both sweaters are given in unisex sizes.

Woman's Pullover: Cathy Payson
Man's Pullover: Kristin Nicholas
Knitting rating (both sweaters):
Experienced

WOMAN'S PULLOVER

SIZES

Small(Medium,Large,Extra Large)
Finished measurements: 40(44,48,52)" (101.5,112,122,132 cm)

MATERIALS

Cambridge (70% cotton, 30% wool; 50 grams = approx. 85 yards): 16(17,18, 18) hanks

Equivalent yarn: 1360(1445,1530,1530) yards/1244(1321,1399,1399) meters of worsted-weight yarn

Knitting needles in sizes 5 and 7 U.S. (3.75 and 4.5 mm)

16" (40.5 cm) circular needle in size 5 U.S. (3.75 mm)

GAUGE

Pattern stitch on larger needles: 20 sts and 28 rows = 4" (10 cm)

Take time to save time—check your gauge.

PATTERN STITCHES

DOUBLE SEED STITCH RIB

(over multiple of 9 + 4)

Row 1: (RS) P1, * k2, p1, k2, p4 *, rep bet *'s, end k2, p1.

Row 2 and all even rows: P across. (K these rnds when working in the round.)

Row 3: * P1, k2, p4, k2 *, rep bet *'s, end p1, k2, p1.

Row 5: * P4, k2, p1, k2 *, rep bet *'s, end p4.

Repeat rows 1-6 for pattern.

Note: When working neckline in the round, rep bet *'s only for patt.

CROSS AND DIAMOND PATTERN

(over multiple of 20 + 1)
See chart.

BACK

With smaller needles, c.o. 94(103,112, 121) sts.

Work in double seed st rib for 2" (5 cm), inc 7(8,9,10) sts evenly in last row to give 101(111,121,131) sts.

Change to larger needles and work chart 8½(9,9½,10) times or until piece meas 24(25,26,27)" (61,63.5,66,68.5 cm) from beg.

For sizes medium and extra large, beg chart on st 7 and end on st 16.

B.o. all sts.

FRONT

Work as for back until piece meas 22(23,24,25)" (56,58.5,61,63.5 cm) from beg.

Shape neck: Work 35(38,42,46) sts, place center 31(35,37,39) sts on holder, join 2nd ball of yarn and work to end.

Working each side sep, b.o. 1 st at neck edge every 4th row 3 times to give 32(35,39,43) sts at each shoulder.

When piece meas same as back, b.o. all sts.

SLEEVES

With smaller needles, c.o. 49(49,49,58) sts.

Work in double seed st rib for 2" (5 cm), inc 12(12,12,3) sts evenly in last row to give 61 sts.

Change to larger needles and work chart, inc 1 st each end every 4th row 0(0,0,2) times, then every 6th row 13(16,15,19) times, then every 8th row 2(1,3,0) times to give 91(95,97,103) sts.

Rep chart 5½(6,6½,7) times or until piece meas 18(20,21,22)" (45.5,51, 53.5,56 cm) from beg.

B.o. all sts.

FINISHING

Sew shoulder seams.

Beg at left shoulder seam with circular needle, k up 11(12,10,12) sts along left front neck edge, k 31(35,37,39) sts on front holder, k up 11(12,10,12) sts along right front neck edge, k up 37(40,42,45) sts at back neck to give 90(99,99,108) sts.

Join and work in double seed st rib for 2" (5 cm).

B.o. loosely.

Set in sleeves.

Sew underarm and side seams.

MAN'S PULLOVER

SIZES

Small(Medium,Large)
Finished measurements: 42(46,50)" (106.5,117,127 cm)

MATERIALS

Montera (50% llama, 50% wool; 100 grams = approx. 128 yards): 9(10,11) hanks

Equivalent yarn: 1152(1280,1408) yards/1053(1170,1287) meters of bulky-weight yarn

Knitting needles in sizes 7 and 9 U.S. (4.5 and 5.5 mm)

16" (40.5 cm) circular needle in size 7 U.S. (4.5 mm)

Cable needle (cn)

GAUGE

Sailor's rib on larger needles: 18 sts and 24 rows = 4" (10 cm)

Basket cable = 4¾" (12 cm)

OXO cable = 2" (5 cm)

Moss diamond cable = 4" (10 cm)

Take time to save time—check your gauge.

PATTERN STITCHES

KNOTTED RIB

(multiple of 8 + 7)

Set-up row: (WS) * K2, p1, k1, p1, k2, p1 *, rep bet *'s, end k2, p1, k1, p1, k2.

Row 1: (RS) * P2, k1-b (k into back of st), p1, k1-b, p2, k into front, back, and front of next st *, rep bet *'s, end p2, k1-b, p1, k1-b, p2.

Row 2: * K2, p1, k1, p1, k2, p3tog *, rep bet *'s, end k2, p1, k1, p1, k2.

SAILOR'S RIB

(multiple of 5 + 1)

Set-up row: (WS) P1, * k4, p1 *, rep bet *'s.

Row 1: (RS) K1-b, * p1, k2, p1, k1-b *, rep bet *'s.

Row 2: P1, * k1, p2, k1, p1 *, rep bet *'s.

Row 3: K1-b, * p4, k1-b *, rep bet *'s.

Row 4: P1, * k4, p1 *, rep bet *'s.

BASKET LATTICE

(over 30 sts)

BC: Sl 1 st to cn, hold in back, k2, p1 from cn.

FC: Sl next 2 sts to cn, hold in front, p1, k2 from cn.

C4R: Sl 2 sts to cn, hold in back, k2, k2 from cn.

C4L: Sl next 2 sts to cn, hold in front, k2, k2 from cn.

Set-up row: (WS) K4, * p4, k2 *, rep bet *'s, end k2.

Row 1: (RS) P4, *C4R, p2 *, rep bet *'s, end p2.

Row 2 and all WSR: Work all sts as they appear.

Row 3: P3, * BC, FC *, rep bet *'s, end p3.

Row 5: P3, k2, p2, * C4L, p2 *, rep bet *'s, end k2, p3.

Row 7: P3, * FC, BC *, rep bet *'s, end p3.

OXO CABLE

(over 12 sts)

Set-up row: (WS) K2, p8, k2.

Row 1: (RS) P2, k8, p2.

Row 2: K2, p8, k2.

Row 3: P2, C4R, C4L, p2.

Row 4: K2, p8, k2.

Row 5: P2, k8, p2.

Row 6: K2, p8, k2.

Row 7: P2, C4L, C4R, p2.

Row 8: K2, p8, k2.

Rows 9, 10, 11, 12: Rep rows 5-8.

Rows 13, 14, 15, 16: Rep rows 1-4.

KNOT STITCH

(1 st)

Set-up row: (WS) P1.

Row 1: K into front, back, and front of st.

Row 2: P3tog.

Row 3: K1.

Row 4: P1.

MOSS STITCH

Set-up row: (WS) K1, p1.

Row 1: Work sts as they appear in moss st.

Row 2: K the p sts and p the k sts as they appear.

MOSS DIAMOND CABLE

(over 20 sts)

FPC: Sl 3 sts to cn and hold in front, p1, k3 from cn.

BPC: Sl 1 st to cn and hold in back, k3, p1 from cn.

Set-up row: (WS) K2, p3, (k1, p1) 5 times in moss st, p3, k2.

Row 1: P2, FPC, work center 8 sts as they appear in moss st, BPC, p2.

Row 2 and all following WSR: Work all sts as they appear, changing the center moss sts of diamond cable to row 2 of moss st as given above.

Row 3: P3, FPC, work center 6 sts in moss st, BPC, p3.

Row 5: P4, FPC, work center 4 sts in moss st, BPC, p4.

Row 7: P5, FPC, work center 2 sts in moss st, BPC, p5.

Row 9: P6, FPC, BPC, p6.

Row 11: P7, sl 3 sts to cn, hold in front, k3, k3 from cn, p7.

Row 13: P6, BPC, FPC, p6.

Row 14: Work all sts as they appear, changing the center p sts of diamond cable to p1, k1.

Row 15: P5, BPC, work 2 sts in moss st, FPC, p5.

Row 17: P4, BPC, work 4 sts in moss st, FPC, p4.

Row 19: P3, BPC, work 6 sts in moss st, FPC, p3.

Row 21: P2, BPC, work 8 sts in moss st, FPC, p2.

BACK

With smaller needles, c.o. 87(95,103) sts.

Work in knotted rib for 3" (7.5 cm), ending with row 2.

In last RSR of rib, inc 23(25,27) sts evenly across to give 110(120,130) sts.

Change to larger needles and est set-up patt row as foll: Work 6(11,16) sts in sailor's rib, 20 sts in moss diamond, 1 knot st, 12 sts in OXO cable, 1 knot st, 30 sts in basket cable, 1 knot st, 12 sts in OXO cable, 1 knot st, 20 sts in moss diamond, 6(11,16) sts in sailor's rib.

Work as est until piece meas 25(26, 27)" (63.5,66,68.5 cm) from beg.

B.o. all sts.

FRONT

Work as for back until piece meas 22(23,24)" (56,58.5,61 cm) from beg.

Shape neck: Work 35(38,42) sts, join 2nd ball of yarn and b.o. center 40(44, 46) sts, work to end.

Working each side sep, b.o. 1 st at neck edge every other row 4 times to give 31(34,38) sts at each shoulder.

When piece meas same as back, b.o. all sts.

SLEEVES

With smaller needles, c.o. 31(31,39) sts.

Work in knotted rib for 3" (7.5 cm), ending with row 2.

In last RSR of rib, inc 15(15,19) sts evenly across to give 46(46,58) sts.

Change to larger needles and est set-up patt row as foll: Work 0(0,6) sts in sailor's rib, 12 sts in OXO cable, 1 knot st, 20 sts in moss diamond, 1 knot st, 12 sts in OXO cable, 0(0,6) sts in sailor's rib.

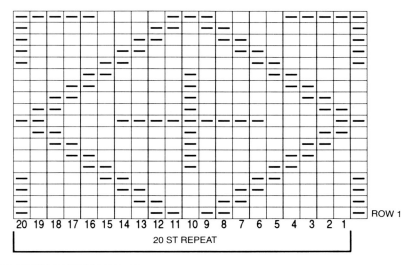

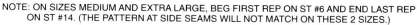

```
20  19  18  17  16  15  14  13  12  11  10  9   8   7   6   5   4   3   2   1
```
ROW 1

20 ST REPEAT

NOTE: ON SIZES MEDIUM AND EXTRA LARGE, BEG FIRST REP ON ST #6 AND END LAST REP ON ST #14. (THE PATTERN AT SIDE SEAMS WILL NOT MATCH ON THESE 2 SIZES.)

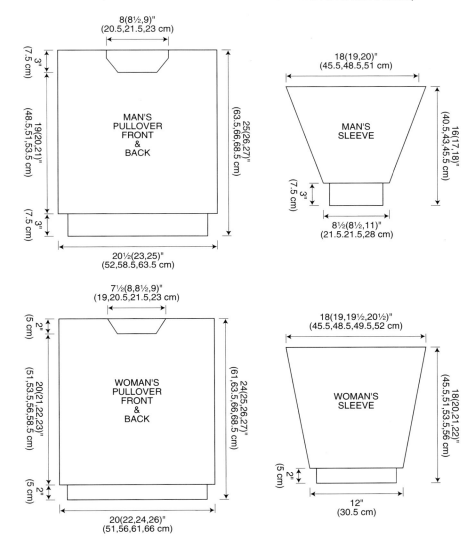

Work patt as est, inc out in sailor's rib at each side as foll: Inc 1 st each end every 2nd row 5(8,0) times, then every 4th row 16(16,21) times to give 88(94,100) sts.

When piece meas 16(17,18)" (40.5,43, 45.5 cm) from beg, b.o. all sts.

FINISHING

Sew shoulder seams.

With circular needle, p.u. 96(104,112) sts evenly around neckline.

Work in rnds as foll for knotted rib:

Rnd 1: * P2, k1-b, p1, k1-b, p2, k into front, back, and front of next st *, rep bet *'s.

Rnd 2: * P2, k1, p1, k1, p2, k3tog *, rep bet *'s.

Work for 3" (7.5 cm), b.o. loosely.

Mark underarms 9(9½,10)" (23,24,25.5 cm) down in front and back from shoulder.

Set in sleeves bet markers.

Sew underarm and side seams.

BASKET STITCH SAMPLER

SIZES

Small(Medium,Large)
Finished measurements: 42(46½,51)"
(106.5,118,129.5 cm)

MATERIALS

Denim (100% cotton; 50 grams =
approx. 95 yards): 17(17,18) hanks
Equivalent yarn: 1700(1700,1800)
yards/1554(1554,1646) meters of
worsted-weight cotton
Knitting needles in sizes 5 and 6 U.S.
(3.75 and 4 mm)
16" (40.5 cm) circular needle in size 5
U.S. (3.75 mm)

GAUGE

(on larger needles)
Basic basket stitch: 22 sts and 28 rows
= 4" (10 cm)
Woven stitch: 22 sts and 28 rows = 4"
(10 cm)
Double fleck stitch: 21 sts and 30 rows
= 4" (10 cm)
Close checks: 22 sts and 28 rows = 4"
(10 cm)
Oblong texture: 20 sts and 32 rows =
4" (10 cm)
Take time to save time—check your
gauge.
Note: Back is 4" (10 cm) longer than
front.

PATTERN STITCHES

GARTER STITCH
K all rows.

WOVEN STITCH
(on back—multiple of 4 + 2)
Row 1: (RS) K all sts.
Row 2: P all sts.
Row 3: K2, * p2, k2, rep from * to end.
Row 4: P2, * k2, p2, rep from * to end.
Row 5: K all sts.
Row 6: P all sts.
Row 7: Work as for row 4.
Row 8: Work as for row 3.
Repeat rows 1-8.

HEARTWOOD FARM

Four sweaters, all unisex sized,
make up this versatile collection
of pullovers. The shirt-tailed
pullover, with its casual look,
contains five different basket
stitches, all knit by combining
simple knit and purl stitches.
The man's pullover features a
patchwork pattern of knit and
purl stitches and a jumbo cable.
The cropped pullover is knit in
a simple cable and lace pattern,
and the guernsey, sized for adults
and children, is a combination of
moss and cable stitches.

Woman's Basket Stitch Pullover:
CATHY PAYSON
Man's Patchwork Cable Pullover:
NORAH GAUGHAN
Woman's Lace Cable Pullover:
SUSAN MILLS
Guernsey for Adults and Children:
SUSAN MILLS

Basket Stitch Pullover: INTERMEDIATE
Patchwork Cable Pullover: EXPERIENCED
Lace Cable Pullover: INTERMEDIATE
Guernsey: INTERMEDIATE

OBLONG TEXTURE STITCH
(on yoke—multiple of 10 + 1)
Row 1: (RS) K3, p5, * k5, p5, rep from
* to last 3 sts, k3.
Row 2: P3, k5, * p5, k5, rep from * to
last 3 sts, p3.
Row 3: Work as for row 2.
Row 4: Work as for row 1.
Repeat rows 1-4.

DOUBLE FLECK STITCH
(sleeve—multiple of 6 + 4)
Rows 1 and 3: (RS) K all sts.
Row 2: P4, * k2, p4, rep from * to end.

Row 4: P1, * k2, p4, rep from * to last 3 sts, k2, p1.

Repeat rows 1-4.

CLOSE CHECK PATTERN

(sleeve—multiple of 6 + 3)

Row 1: (RS) K3, * p3, k3, rep from * to end.

Row 2: P3, * k3, p3, rep from * to end.

Repeat these last 2 rows once more.

Row 5: Work as for row 2.

Row 6: Work as for row 1.

Repeat these last 2 rows once more.

Repeat rows 1-8.

BASIC BASKET STITCH

See chart on page 62.

BACK

With smaller needles, c.o. 116(128,140) sts.

Work garter st for 1" (2.5 cm).

Change to larger needles and beg patt as follows: K3, work woven st patt to last 3 sts, k3.

Keeping 1st and last 3 sts in garter st, work woven st patt until piece meas 10" (25.5 cm).

Discontinue garter st edges.

Cont to work woven st patt with 1 edge st each side until piece meas 21(22,23)" (53.5,56,58.5 cm), ending on row 2 or 6 and dec 13(15,17) sts evenly in last row to give 103(113,123) sts.

Work oblong texture patt with 1 edge st each side until piece meas 27(28, 29)" (68.5,71,73.5 cm) from beg.

B.o. all sts.

FRONT

With smaller needles, c.o. 114(126,138) sts.

Work garter st for 1" (2.5 cm).

Change to larger needles and beg patt as follows: K3, work basic basket st patt to last 3 sts, k to end.

Keeping 1st and last 3 sts in garter st, work basic basket st patt until piece meas 6" (15 cm).

Discontinue garter st edges.

Inc 1 st each side (edge sts).

Cont to work basic basket st patt with 1 edge st each side until piece meas 17(18, 19)" (43,45.5,48.5 cm), ending on row 2, 8, or 14 and dec 13(15,17) sts evenly

in last row to give 103(113, 123) sts.

Work oblong texture patt with 1 edge st each side until piece meas 21(22, 23)" (53.5,56,58.5 cm) from beg.

Shape neck: Work across 1st 41(44,47) sts, join 2nd ball of yarn and b.o. center 21(25,29) sts, work to end.

Working each side separately, b.o. 1 st at each neck edge every other row 8 times to give 33(36,39) sts at each shoulder.

When piece meas same as back, b.o. all sts.

DOUBLE FLECK SLEEVE

With smaller needles, c.o. 46(46,52) sts and work in garter stitch for 1" (2.5 cm).

Change to larger needles and beg working double fleck patt, inc 1 st each end now and every 4th row 11(16,13) times, then every 6th row 12(10,13) times to give 94(100,106) sts.

When piece meas 17(18,19)" (43,45.5,48.5 cm), b.o. all sts.

CLOSE CHECK SLEEVE

With smaller needles, c.o. 48(48,54) sts and work in garter stitch for 1" (2.5 cm).

Inc 5 sts evenly on last row.

Change to larger needles and beg working close check patt, inc 1 st each end every 4th row 15(21,17) times, then every 6th row 8(5,9) times to give 99(105,111) sts.

When piece meas 17(18,19)" (43,45.5,48.5 cm), b.o. all sts.

FINISHING

Sew shoulder seams.

With circular needle, pick up 94(100, 106) sts around neck edge and work in garter stitch for 1" (2.5 cm).

Sew on sleeves.

Sew underarm and side seams.

GUERNSEY

SIZES

Adult's Small(Medium,Large,Extra Large) <Child's 2-4(6-8,10-12)>

Finished measurements: 40(44,48,52)" (101.5,112,122,132 cm), <28(32,36)" (71,81.5,91.5 cm)>

MATERIALS

14(16,17,18) <7(9,10)> hanks

Equivalent yarn: 1400(1600,1700,1800) yards/1280(1463,1554,1646) meters <700(900,1000) yards/640(823, 914) meters> of worsted-weight cotton

Knitting needles in sizes 4 and 5 U.S. (6 and 8 mm)

16" (40.5 cm) circular needle in size 4 U.S. (6 mm)

Cable needle (cn)

GAUGE

Stockinette stitch on larger needles: 20 sts and 24 rows = 4" (10 cm)

Take time to save time—check your gauge.

PATTERN STITCHES

STOCKINETTE STITCH

Row 1: (RS) K all sts.

Row 2: P all sts.

GARTER RIDGE

Row 1: (RS) P all sts.

Row 2: K all sts.

Row 3: K all sts.

Row 4: P all sts.

GARTER LADDER

(over 6 sts)

Rows 1 and 5: (RS) P1, k4, p1.

Rows 2 and 6: K1, p4, k1.

Row 3: P6.

Row 4: K6.

CABLE

(over 6 sts)

Row 1: (RS) K6.

Row 2: P6.

Row 3: Sl 3 sts to cn and hold in back, k3, k3 from cn.

Row 4: P6.

Row 5: K6.

Row 6: P6.

DOUBLE MOSS STITCH

(multiple of 4 sts)

Rows 1 (RS) and 2: * K2, p2 *, rep bet *'s.

Rows 3 and 4: * P2, k2 *, rep bet *'s.

BACK

With smaller needles, c.o. 90(100, 110,120) <60(70,80)> sts.

Work garter ridges for 4" (10 cm) <3" (7.5 cm)>, inc 10 sts evenly across last row to give 100(110,120,130) <70(80, 90)> sts.

Change to larger needles and work in St st until piece meas 11(11½,12,12½)" (28,29,30.5,31.5 cm) <8(9,10)" (20.5, 23,25.5 cm)>.

Work 1 garter ridge, inc 6(4,6,4) <6(4, 2)> sts evenly across last row.

Next row, **est yoke patt:**

Double moss stitch over 0(0,4,8) <0> sts,

Garter ladder over 0(0,6,6) <0> sts,

Double moss over 12(16,12,12) <8(12, 12)> sts,

Garter ladder over 6 sts,

Double moss over 12 <8(8,12)> sts,

Garter ladder over 6 sts,

* Cable over 6 sts, p1 *, rep between *'s 4 <2> times, cable over 6 sts,

Garter ladder over 6 sts,

Double moss over 12 <8(8,12)> sts,

Garter ladder over 6 sts,

Double moss over 12(16,12,12) <8(12, 12)> sts,

Garter ladder over 0(0,6,6) <0> sts, and Double moss over 0(0,4,8) <0> sts.

Cont working in est patt until piece meas 24(25,26,27)" (61,63.5,66,68.5 cm) <16(18,20)" (40.5,45.5,51 cm)>.
B.o. all sts.

FRONT

Work as for back until piece meas 22(23,24,25)" (56,58.5,61,63.5 cm) <14(16,18)" (35.5,40.5,45.5 cm)> or 2" (5 cm) less than desired length.

Shape neck: Work across 38(41,46,49) <26(29,32)> sts, join 2nd ball of yarn and b.o. center 30(32,34,36) <24(26, 28)> sts.

Work rem 38(41,46,49) <26(29,32)> sts.

Dec 1 st each neck edge every other row 3 times to give 35(38,43,46) <23(26,29)> sts rem for each shoulder.

Work even until same length as back.
B.o. all sts.

SLEEVES

With smaller needles, c.o. 40(42,46,48) <30(34,38)> sts and work garter ridges

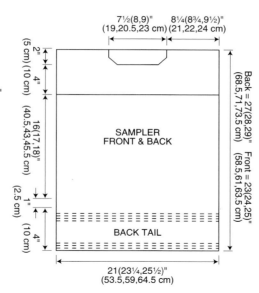

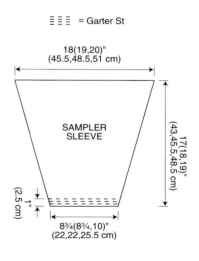

≡≡≡ = Garter St

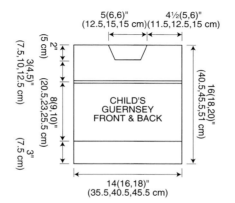

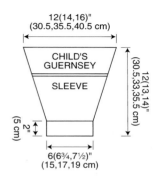

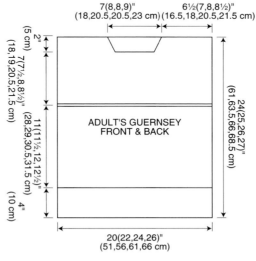

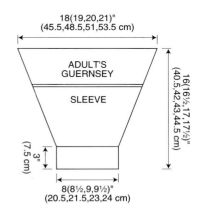

for 3" (7.5 cm) <2" (5 cm)>.

Change to larger needles and work in St st.

At the same time, inc 1 st each end every other row 26(27,27,28) <15(19, 21)> times.

When sleeve meas 10¾(11¼,11¾, 12¼)" (27.5,28.5,30,31 cm) <8½(9½, 10½)" (21.5,24,26.5 cm)>, work 1 garter ridge.

Work double moss st over 92(96,100, 104) <60(72,80)> sts for 4" (10 cm) <3" (7.5 cm)>.

Work 1 garter ridge.

Sleeve should meas 16(16½,17,17½)" (40.5,42,43,44.5 cm) <12(13,14)" (30.5,33,35.5 cm)>.

B.o. all sts.

FINISHING

Sew shoulder seams.

With circular needle, p.u. 84(88,93,98) <74(78,80)> sts around neck and work garter ridge for 2½" (6.5 cm) <2" (5 cm)>.

B.o. all sts **loosely.**

Sew in sleeves.

Sew sleeve and side seams.

EYELET CABLE PULLOVER

SIZES

Small(Medium,Large)

Finished measurements: 36(40,44)" (91.5,101.5,112 cm)

MATERIALS

15(16,16) hanks

Equivalent yarn: 1500(1600,1600) yards/1372(1463,1463) meters of worsted-weight cotton

Knitting needles in sizes 4 and 5 U.S. (3.5 and 3.75 mm)

16" (40.5 cm) circular needle in size 4 U.S. (3.5 mm)

Cable needle (cn)

GAUGE

Eyelet cable patt on larger needles: 22 sts and 28 rows = 4" (10 cm)

Take time to save time—check your gauge.

PATTERN STITCHES

ABBREVIATIONS

SSK: Sl the 1st and 2nd sts one at a time as if to knit; then insert point of left needle into fronts of these 2 sts and k them tog from this position.

EYELET CABLE

Row 1 and all WS rows: P2, * k2, p6, k2, p2 *, rep bet *'s.

Row 2: K2, * p2, k6, p2, k2 *, rep bet *'s.

Row 4: K2, * p2, sl next 3 sts to cn and hold in back, k3, then k3 from cn, p2, k2 *, rep bet *'s.

Row 6: As row 2.

Row 8: K2, * p2, ssk, yo, k4, p2, k2 *, rep bet *'s.

Row 10: K2, * p2, k1, yo, k2tog, k3, p2, k2 *, rep bet *'s.

Row 12: As row 8.

Row 14: As row 2.

Row 16: As row 4.

Row 18: As row 6.

Row 20: K2, * p2, k3, ssk, yo, k1, p2, k2 *, rep bet *'s.

Row 22: K2 * p2, k4, yo, k2tog, p2, k2 *, rep bet *'s.

Row 24: As row 20.

BACK

With smaller needles, c.o. 94(103,112) sts.

Work 4 rows St st.

For ribbing, rep the following 2 rows until cuff meas 2½" (6.5 cm), ending with a WSR.

Row 1: (RS) K2, * p2, k2, p1, k2, p2, k2 *, rep bet *'s.

Row 2: P2 * k2, p2, k1, p2, k2, p2 *, rep bet *'s.

Next row (RS): Inc 8(9,10) sts evenly across as foll: K2 * p2, k2, Pfb (purl into front and back of stitch), k2, p2, k2 *, rep bet *'s to give 102(112,122) sts.

Change to larger needles and work eyelet cable patt until back meas 20(21,22)" (51,53.5,56 cm).

B.o. all sts.

FRONT

Work as for back until piece meas 18(19,20)" (45.5,48.5,51 cm).

Shape neck: Cont in patt and work across 40(45,48) sts, put center 22(24,26) sts on holder, join 2nd ball of yarn and work across rem 37(42,48) sts.

Dec 1 st each neck edge every other row 3 times; 37(42,45) sts rem for each shoulder.

When front meas same as back, b.o. all sts.

SLEEVES

With smaller needles, c.o. 46 sts.

Work ribbing (and inc row) as for back for 2½" (6.5 cm) to give 50 sts.

Note: Place markers 2 sts in from each edge of sleeve.

Work eyelet cable patt bet markers.

Work inc sts in St st until there are enough sts to complete entire rep of eyelet cable patt.

Inc 1 st each edge every 4th row 22(24,26) times to give 94(98,102) sts.

Work in eyelet cable patt until sleeve meas 17(18,19)" (43,45.5,48.5 cm) or desired length.

B.o. all sts.

FINISHING

Sew shoulder seams.

With circular needle, p.u. 78(84,90) sts around neck including sts on holder, and k every round for 2½" (6.5 cm).

B.o. all sts **loosely.**

Sew sleeve and side seams.

PATCHWORK PULLOVER

SIZES

Small(Medium,Large)

Finished measurements: 44(48,52)" (112,122,132 cm)

MATERIALS

19(20,21) hanks

Equivalent yarn: 1900(2000,2100) yards/1737(1828,1920) meters of worsted-weight cotton

Knitting needles in sizes 5 and 8 U.S. (3.75 and 5 mm)

24" (61 cm) circular needle in size 5 U.S. (3.75 mm)

Cable needle (cn)

GAUGE

Moss stitch on larger needles: 22 sts and 26 rows = 4" (10 cm)

Cabled ladder pattern: 21 sts and 24 rows = 5" (12.5 cm)

Take time to save time—check your gauge.

PATTERN STITCHES

2 x 2 RIBBING

Row 1: K2, p2.

Row 2: Work sts as they appear.

See charts for all other pattern sts.

BACK

With smaller needles, c.o. 102(112,122) sts.

K 9 rows and change to larger needles.

Inc row WS: P8(13,18), work row 1 Chart A, row 1 Chart B, row 1 Chart A, p28, row 1 Chart A, p8(13,18) to give 123(133,143) sts.

*Set up patterns: Work 8(13,18) sts in moss st, work 15 sts Chart A, 28 sts Chart C, 15 sts Chart A, 34 sts Chart B, 15 sts Chart A, 8(13,18) sts Chart C.

Work straight in patt as est until completion of row 45 of Chart B.

Next row (RS): K8(13,18), Chart A, k28, Chart A, work row 46 of Chart B, Chart A, k8(13,18).

Work 4 rows garter ridges bet cables.

K8(13,18), Chart A, [k28, Chart A] twice, k8(13,18).

**(WS row) P8(13,18), Chart A, p28, Chart A, work row 1 of Chart B, Chart A, p8(13,18).

Set up for new pattern blocks: Work 8(13,18) sts Chart C, Chart A, Chart B, Chart A, 28 Chart C, Chart A, work 8(13,18) moss st.

Work straight in patt as est* until completion of row 45 of Chart B.

Next RS row: K8(13,18), Chart A, row 46 of Chart B, Chart A, k28, Chart A, k8(13,18).

Work 4 rows garter ridges bet cables.

K8(13,18), Chart A, [k28, Chart A] twice, k8(13,18).

P8(13,18), Chart A, row 1 Chart B, Chart A, p28, Chart A, p8(13,18).

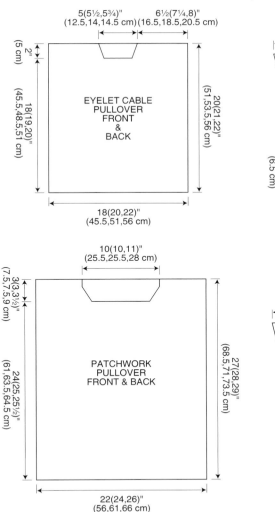

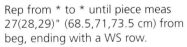

Rep from * to * until piece meas 27(28,29)" (68.5,71,73.5 cm) from beg, ending with a WS row.

K, working 5 dec across each Chart A and working 6 dec across cable in pattern B.

K 2 more rows.

B.o. in purl.

FRONT

Work same as back to 2nd time at **.

P1 row.

Set up patt as foll: 8(13,18) Chart C, Chart A, 28 moss st, Chart A, 28 Chart C, Chart A, 8(13,18) moss st.

Work straight in patt as est until 24(25,25½)" (61,63.5,64.5 cm) from the beg.

There should be 123(133,143) sts.

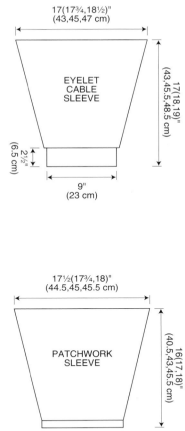

Shape front neck: Work 51(56,61) sts, join 2nd ball of yarn and b.o. center 21 sts.

Complete row.

Working each side sep, b.o. at each neck edge 3 sts 2 times, 2 sts 3(3,4) times, 1 st 2(2,3) times.

Work straight 23(28,32) sts on each side until piece meas 26½(27½,28½)" (67.5,70,72.5 cm) from the beg, ending with a WSR.

K 3 rows.

B.o. in purl.

SLEEVES

With smaller needles, c.o. 42 sts.

K 9 rows.

Change to larger needles and p 6, work row 1 of Chart A 3 times, purl 6.

Set up patt: K2, 19 Chart C, Chart A, 19 moss st, K2.

Cont in patt as est for 44 rows and, **at the same time,** inc 1 st at each end every 6th row 17(18,19) times.

Inc by working 2 times into the 2nd and 3rd to last sts.

Keeping the 1st and last 2 sts in St st, work the new sts in patt.

[When 44 rows of patt have been completed, work garter rows (knit to cable, Chart A, knit to end, keeping 1st and last 2 sts in St st) 5 times. P1 row.]

Set up new patt: K2, moss st to cable, Chart A, Chart C to last 2, K2.

Work in patt as est, cont inc.

Work from [to].

Set up new patt: K2, Chart C to cable, Chart A, moss st to last 2, K2.

Cont in patt until inc have been completed and sleeve meas 16(17,18)" (40.5,43,45.5 cm) from the beg.

B.o. all 91(93,95) sts.

FINISHING

Sew shoulder seams.

Neck band: With circular needle, p.u. 108(108,124) sts around neck opening.

Work in 2 x 2 rib for 6 rounds.

(K 1 rnd, p 1 rnd) 2 times, k 1 rnd.

Work in 1 x 1 rib for 4 rnds.

B.o.

Sew sleeve and underarm seams.

BASIC BASKET STITCH (FRONT)
FOR SAMPLER PATTERN

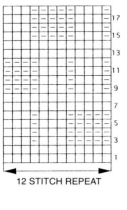

12 STITCH REPEAT

☐ K ON RS; P ON WS
⊟ P ON RS; K ON WS

CHART A — LARGE CABLE

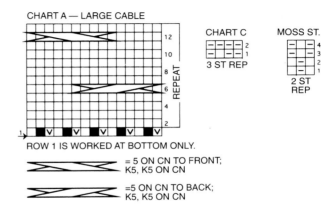

ROW 1 IS WORKED AT BOTTOM ONLY.

= 5 ON CN TO FRONT;
K5, K5 ON CN

= 5 ON CN TO BACK;
K5, K5 ON CN

CHART B

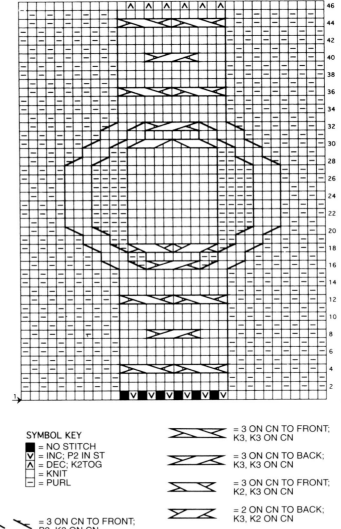

SYMBOL KEY
■ = NO STITCH
Ⅴ = INC; P2 IN ST
Λ = DEC; K2TOG
☐ = KNIT
⊟ = PURL

= 3 ON CN TO FRONT;
P2, K3 ON CN

= 2 ON CN TO BACK;
K3, P2 ON CN

= 3 ON CN TO FRONT;
K3, K3 ON CN

= 3 ON CN TO BACK;
K3, K3 ON CN

= 3 ON CN TO FRONT;
K2, K3 ON CN

= 2 ON CN TO BACK;
K3, K2 ON CN

V-Neck Pullover

Sizes

Small(Medium,Large)
Finished measurements: 42(44,46)"
(106.5,112,117 cm)

Materials

Paisley Light (50% wool, 50% rayon;
50 grams = approx. 130 yards):
16(16,17) hanks
Equivalent yarn: 2080(2210,2340)
yards/1902(2020,2139) meters of light
worsted-weight yarn
Knitting needles in sizes 5 and 6 U.S.
(3.75 and 4 mm)
24" (61 cm) circular needle in size 5
U.S. (3.75 mm)

Gauge

Cabled hexagon on larger needles: 24
sts and 30 rows = 4" (10 cm)
*Take time to save time—check your
gauge.*

Pattern Stitches

Baby Cable Rib

(over multiple of 4 + 2)
Rows 1 and 3: (WS) K2, * p2, k2 *, rep
bet *'s.
Row 2: P2, * k2, p2 *, rep bet *'s.
Row 4: P2, * k2tog but leave on needle, insert right-hand needle bet 2 sts
just knitted tog and k the 1st st again,
sl both sts from needle, p2 *, rep bet
*'s.

Abbreviations

C2R: K into front of 2nd st on needle, k
1st st, sl both sts off needle at same time.
C2L: K into back of 2nd st on needle, k
1st st, sl both sts off needle at same time.
T2F: P into back of 2nd st on needle, k
1st st, sl both sts off needle at same time.
T2B: K into front of 2nd st on needle, p
1st st, sl both sts off needle at same time.

Cabled Hexagon Pattern

(over multiple of 8 + 4)

Dobson's Boat Yard

Here are three sweaters for knitters who enjoy making cables.
The gold sweater with a deep
V-shaped neckline is composed of
very easy cable stitches for which
you needn't use a cable needle.
The beige unisex pullover features an untraditional cable that
is made by crossing the cables on
a stockinette stitch fabric. This is
unlike most other cable stitches,
which cross on a fabric of reverse
stockinette stitch. The man's
green pullover displays two fun-
to-knit designs—banjo cables and
double cables—juxtaposed with a
subtle rib pattern.

V-neck pullover:
Cathy Payson
Windowpane pullover:
Kristin Nicholas
Banjo cable pullover:
Kathy Zimmerman

V-neck: **Experienced**
Windowpane: **Experienced**
Banjo: **Very challenging**

Rows 1 and 3: (WS) K1, p2, * k6, p2 *,
rep bet *'s to last st, k1.
Row 2: P1, C2R, * p6, C2R *, rep bet
*'s to last st, p1.
Row 4: P1, k2, * p6, k2 *, rep bet *'s to
last st, p1.
Rep the last 4 rows once more, then 1st
3 rows again.
Row 12: P2, * T2F, p4, T2B *, rep bet
*'s to last 2 sts, p2.
Rows 13 and 31: K3, p1, k4, p1, * k2,
p1, k4, p1 *, rep bet *'s to last 3 sts,
k3.
Row 14: P3, * T2F, p2, T2B, p2 *, rep
bet *'s to last st, p1.

Rows 15 and 29: K4, * p1, k2, p1, k4 *, rep bet *'s to end.

Row 16: P4, * T2F, T2B, p4 *, rep bet *'s to end.

Rows 17 and 19: K5, p2, * k6, p2 *, rep bet *'s to last 5 sts, k5.

Row 18: P5, C2L, * p6, C2L *, rep bet *'s to last 5 sts, p5.

Row 20: P5, k2, * p6, k2 *, rep bet *'s to last 5 sts, p5.

Rep the last 4 rows once more, then rows 17, 18 and 19 again.

Row 28: P4, * T2B, T2F, p4 *, rep bet *'s to end.

Row 30: P3, * T2B, p2, T2F, p2 *, rep bet *'s to last st, p1.

Row 32: P2, * T2B, p4, T2F *, rep bet *'s to last 2 sts, p2.

BACK

With smaller needles, c.o. 122(126, 134) sts.

Work baby cable rib for 2" (5 cm), inc 2(6,6) sts in last row to give 124(132,140) sts.

Change to larger needles and work in cabled hexagon patt until piece meas 26(27,28)" (66,68.5,71 cm).

B.o. all sts.

FRONT

Work as for back until piece meas 10(11,12)" (25.5,28,30.5 cm).

Shape neck: Work across first 62(66, 70) sts, join 2nd skein of yarn, work to end.

Working each side sep, b.o. 1 st each neck edge every 6th row 20 times to give 42(46,50) sts each side.

When piece meas same as back, b.o. all sts.

SLEEVES

With smaller needles, c.o. 50(54,54) sts.

Work baby cable rib for 2" (5 cm), inc 10(8,10) sts in last row to give 60(62, 64) sts.

Change to larger needles and work cabled hexagon patt, inc 1 st each end every 4th row 30(32,34) times to give 120(126,132) sts.

When piece meas 18(19,20)" (45.5, 48.5,51 cm), b.o. all sts.

FINISHING

Sew shoulder seams.

With RS facing and circular needle, p.u. 230(234,242) sts evenly around neckline.

Work back and forth in baby cable rib for 1½" (4 cm).

B.o. loosely.

Stitch down ends to overlap at center of V-neck.

Set in sleeves.

Sew underarm and side seams.

WINDOWPANE PULLOVER

SIZES

Small(Medium,Large,Extra Large)
Finished measurements: 40(44,48,52)" (101.5,112,122,132 cm)

MATERIALS

Cambridge (70% cotton, 30% wool; 50 grams = approx. 85 yards), 13(14,14,15) hanks

Equivalent yarn: 1105(1190,1190,1275) yards/1010(1088,1088,1166) meters of worsted-weight yarn

Knitting needles in sizes 6 and 8 U.S. (4 and 5 mm)

16" (40.5 cm) circular needle in size 6 U.S. (4 mm)

Cable needle (cn)

GAUGE

Stockinette stitch on larger needles: 16 sts and 20 rows = 4" (10 cm)

Take time to save time—check your gauge.

PATTERN STITCHES

2 x 4 RIB

(multiple of 6 + 2)

Row 1: (WS) * P2, k4 *, rep bet *'s, end p2.

Row 2: (RS) * K2, p4 *, rep bet *'s, end k2.

Note: Rep bet *'s only when working in rnd.

REVERSE STOCKINETTE STITCH

Row 1: (WS) K all sts.

Row 2: P all sts.

ABBREVIATIONS

BKC (Back Knit Cross): Sl 1 st to cn, hold in back, k2, k1 from cn.

FKC (Front Knit Cross): Sl 2 sts to cn, hold in front, k1, k2 from cn.

BPC (Back Purl Cross): Sl 1 st to cn, hold in back, k2, p1 from cn.

FPC (Front Purl Cross): Sl 2 sts to cn, hold in front, p1, k2 from cn.

DIAMOND WINDOW PATTERN

(multiple of 26)

Row 1: (WS) * K5, p16, k5 *, rep bet *'s.

Row 2: * P4, BKC, k12, FKC, p4 *, rep bet *'s.

Row 3 and all WSR: Work all sts as they appear.

Row 4: * P3, BKC, k4, BPC, FPC, k4, FKC, p3 *, rep bet *'s.

Row 6: * P2, BKC, k4, BPC, p2, FPC, k4, FKC, p2 *, rep bet *'s.

Row 8: * P1, BKC, k4, BPC, p4, FPC, k4, FKC, p1 *, rep bet *'s.

Row 10: * BKC, k4, BPC, p6, FPC, k4, FKC *, rep bet *'s.

Row 12: * K6, BPC, p8, FPC, k6 *, rep bet *'s.

Row 14: * K6, FKC, p8, BKC, k6 *, rep bet *'s.

Row 16: * FPC, k4, FKC, p6, BKC, k4, BPC *, rep bet *'s.

Row 18: * P1, FPC, k4, FKC, p4, BKC, k4, PBC, p1 *, rep bet *'s.

Row 20: * P2, FPC, k4, FKC, p2, BKC, k4, BPC, p2 *, rep bet *'s.

Row 22: * P3, FPC, k4, FKC, BKC, k4, BPC, p3 *, rep bet *'s.

Row 24: * P4, FPC, k12, BPC, p4 *, rep bet *'s.

BACK

With smaller needles, c.o. 80(86,98, 104) sts.

Beg 1st rev St st ridge (3 rows) as foll:

Row 1: (RS) P across.

Rows 2 and 3: K across.

Work 2 x 4 rib for 3" (7.5 cm), ending with a RSR.

Work 2nd rev St st ridge (4 rows) as foll:

Rows 1 and 2: P across.

Row 3: K across.

Row 4: K across, inc 14(18,14,18) sts evenly to give 94(104,112,122) sts.

Change to larger needles and est patt on WS as foll: Work 8(13,17,22) sts in rev St st, work 3 repeats of diamond window patt over center 78 sts, work 8(13,17,22) sts in rev St st.

Work in est patt for 24(25,26,27)" (61,63.5,66,68.5 cm).

B.o. all sts.

FRONT

Work as for back.

When piece meas 21(22,23,24)" (53.5,56,58.5,61 cm), shape neck.

Work 35(38,41,45) sts, join 2nd ball of yarn and b.o. center 24(28,30,32) sts, work to end.

Working each side sep, b.o. 1 st at neck edge every other row 5 times to give 30(33,36,40) sts at shoulder.

When piece meas same as back at shoulders, b.o. all sts.

SLEEVES

With smaller needles, c.o. 44 sts.

Work 1st rev St st ridge as for body, work 2" (5 cm) of 2 x 4 rib, work 2nd rev St st ridge.

In 4th row of 2nd rev St st ridge, inc 0(0,0,2) sts evenly across to give 44(44,44,46) sts.

Change to larger needles.

Est patt as foll: Work 9(9,9,10) sts in rev St st, work 26 in diamond window patt, work 9(9,9,10) sts in rev St st.

At the same time, inc 1 st each end in rev St st every 4th row 18(24,23,24) times, then 1 st each end every 6th row 3(0,1,1) times to give 86(92, 92, 96) sts.

When piece meas 17(18,18½,19)" (43,45.5,47,48.5 cm), b.o. all sts.

FINISHING

Sew shoulder seams.

With circular needle, p.u. in k st 84(90, 96,102) sts evenly around neckline.

P 2 rnds, k 1 rnd.

Work 2" (5 cm) of 2 x 4 rib in rnd.

K 1 rnd, p 1 rnd.

B.o. in purl.

Mark underarm points 9¾(10½,10½, 11)" (25,26.5,26.5,28 cm) down from shoulder in front and back.

Set in sleeves bet points.

Sew underarm and side seams.

Banjo Cable Pullover

Sizes

Medium(Large,Extra Large)

Finished measurements: 44(48,52)" (112,122,132 cm)

Materials

Cambridge: 22(24,26) hanks

Equivalent yarn: 1870(2040,2210) yards/1710(1865,2020) meters of worsted-weight yarn

Knitting needles in sizes 4 and 7 U.S. (3.5 and 4.5 mm)

16" (40.5 cm) circular needle in size 4 (3.5 mm)

Cable needle (cn)

Stitch markers

Stitch holders

Gauge

Shadow rib on larger needles: 24 sts and 28 rows = 4" (10 cm)

Double cable = 2¼" (5.5 cm)

Take time to save time—check your gauge.

Pattern Stitches

Shadow Rib

(over multiple of 3 + 2)

Row 1: (WS) K2, * p1, k2 *, rep bet *'s.

Row 2: P all sts.

Banjo Cable

(multiple of 10)

Rows 1 and 3: (WS) K3, p4, k3.

Rows 2 and 4: P3, k4, p3.

Row 5: K3, p1, sl2 with yarn in front (wyif), p1, k3.

Row 6: P1, sl next 3 sts to cn, hold in back, k1, (p1, k1, p1) from cn, sl next st to cn, hold in front, k1, p1, k1, k1 from cn, p1.

Rows 7, 9, and 11: K1, (p1, k1) 3 times, p2, k1.

Rows 8, 10, and 12: P1, (k1, p1) 3 times, k2, p1.

Row 13: K1, sl1 wyif, (k1, p1) 3 times, sl1 wyif, k1.

Row 14: P1, sl next st to cn, hold in front, p1, k1, k1 from cn, sl next 3 sts to cn, hold in back, k1, k1, p2 from cn, p1.

Rows 15 and 16: Repeat rows 1 and 2.

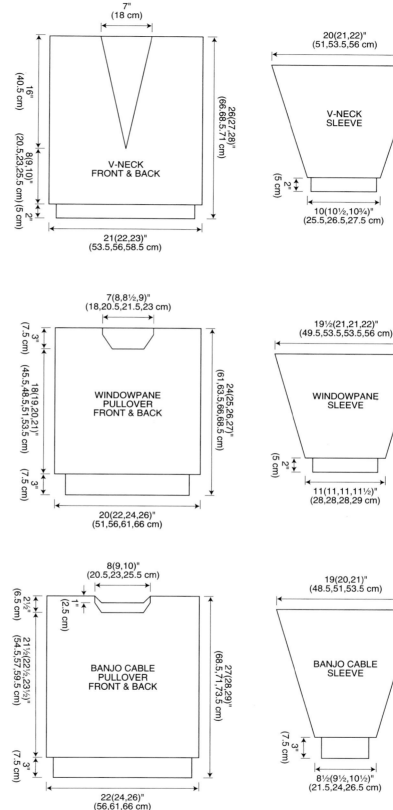

Double Cable

(multiple of 16)

Row 1: (WS foundation row only) K2, p12, k2.

Row 2: P2, sl next 3 sts to cn, hold in back, k3, (k1, p1, k1) from cn, sl next 3 sts to cn, hold in front, (p1, k1, p1) from cn, k3, p2.

Rows 3, 5, 7, 9, and 11: K2, p3, (p1, k1) 3 times, p3, k2.

Rows 4, 6, 8, and 10: P2, k3, (k1, p1) 3 times, k3, p2.

Row 12: P2, sl next 3 sts to cn, hold in back, (k1, p1, k1), k3 from cn, sl next 3 sts to cn, hold in front, k3, (p1, k1, p1) from cn, p2.

Rows 13, 15, 17, 19, and 21: K2, p1, k1, p7, k1, p1, k3.

Rows 14, 16, 18, and 20: P2, k1, p1, k7, p1, k1, p3.

Repeat rows 2-21 for pattern.

Back

With smaller needles, c.o. 140(152,164) sts.

Work in rev St st for ¾" (2 cm).

Work in shadow rib for 3" (7.5 cm), ending with RSR.

Change to larger needles.

Foundation row: (WS) Work row 1 of shadow rib across 35(41,47) sts, k1, pm, work row 1 of banjo cable over next 10 sts, pm, work row 1 of double cable (k2, p12, k2) 3 times over 48 sts, pm, work row 1 of banjo cable over next 10 sts, pm, k1, work row 1 of shadow rib over rem 35(41,47) sts.

Work in patt as est: shadow rib over 35(41,47) sts, rev St st over next st, banjo cable over next 10 sts, double cable over 48 sts, banjo cable over next 10 sts, rev St st over next st, shadow rib over rem 35(41,47) sts.

Work in est patt until piece meas 26(27, 28)" (66,68.5,71 cm) from beg.

Shape back neck: Work 46(49,53) sts in est patt, b.o. center 48(54,58) sts, working p2tog on each side of each double cable, work rem 46(49,53) sts in est patt.

Dec 1 st at each neck edge 3 times to give 43(46,50) sts.

Work until piece meas 27(28,29)" (68.5,71,73.5 cm) from beg.

Place rem sts on holders for shoulders.

Front

Work as for back until piece meas 24½(25½,16½)" (62,64.5,67.5 cm).

Shape neck: Work 50(53,57) sts in patt, join 2nd ball of yarn, and b.o. center 40(46,50) sts for front neck, working p2tog at each side of each double cable, work to end.

Working each side sep, b.o. 1 st at each neck edge every other row 7 times to give 43(46,50) sts at shoulder.

When piece meas same as back at shoulders, place rem sts on holders for shoulders.

Sleeves

With smaller needles, c.o. 56(62,68) sts.

Work in rev St st for ¾" (2 cm).

Work in shadow rib until piece meas 3" (7.5 cm), ending with RSR.

Change to larger needles.

Work foundation row: Work row 1 of shadow rib over 8(11,14) sts, k2, pm, work row 1 of banjo cable over next 10 sts, pm, work row 1 of double cable over next 16 sts, pm, work row 1 of banjo cable over next 10 sts, pm, k2, work shadow rib over rem 8(11,14) sts.

Inc 1 st each side every 4th row 31(27, 25) times, then every 6th row 0(4,6) times to give 118(124,130) sts.

Work all inc sts in shadow rib.

When piece meas 21(22,23)" (53.5,56, 58.5 cm), b.o. all sts.

Finishing

Join shoulder seams.

With circular needle and RS facing, p.u. 123 sts evenly around neckline.

Place marker and join.

Work in shadow rib as foll:

Rnd 1: * K1, p2 *, rep bet *'s around.

Rnd 2: P all sts.

Rep for 1½" (4 cm).

Knit every rnd for ¾" (2 cm) for rev St st roll.

B.o. all sts loosely.

Mark underarm points 9½(10,10½)" (24,25.5,26.5 cm) down in front and back from shoulder.

Set in sleeve bet points.

Sew underarm and side seams.

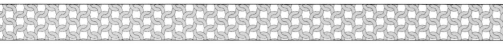

ZICKZACK

Combinations of knit and purl stitches are the favorite choices of knitters who like to make garments that look difficult but actually are quite easy to work. An all-over chevron stitch is featured on the body of these pullovers, and a clever rib pattern decorates the saddle shoulders, neckline, cuffs, and bottom edge. The child's sweater mimics the adult's version but uses a slightly smaller chevron to keep the pattern in scale.

Design: Linda Pratt
Knitting rating (all sweaters):
Intermediate

ADULT'S PULLOVER
SIZES
Small(Medium,Large,Extra Large)
Finished measurements: 38(42,46,49)" (96.5,106.5,117,124.5 cm)

MATERIALS
Paisley (50% wool, 50% rayon; 50 grams = approx. 95 yards): 13(14,15, 16) hanks; OR Newport (100% pima cotton; 50 grams = 70 yards): 16(17,18, 19) skeins
Equivalent yarn: 1235(1330,1425,1520) yards/1129(1216,1303,1390) meters of bulky worsted-weight for woman's sweater, 1120(1190,1260,1330) yards/ 1024(1888,1152,1216) meters for man's sweater
Knitting needles in sizes 7 and 8 U.S. (4.5 and 5 mm)

GAUGE
Chevron pattern on larger needles: 17 sts and 24 rows = 4" (10 cm)
Take time to save time—check your gauge.

PATTERN STITCHES
MOIRÉ RIB
(multiple of 6 + 2)
Row 1 (WS): K2, * p4, k2; rep from *.
Row 2: P2, * [with yarn in back sl1 purl-wise, k1, wind yarn around needle to m1, psso the last 2 sts (the k1 and m1)] twice, p2; rep from *.

REVERSE STOCKINETTE STITCH
Row 1 (RS): P all sts.
Row 2: K all sts.

FRONT AND BACK
With smaller needles, c.o. 84(92,98, 104) sts (preferably using a cable or chain c.o.).
Work 2 rows in rev St st.
Work in moiré rib for 3¼" (8.5 cm) ending with a WSR.
Work 2 rows rev St st, inc 1 st in last row to give 85(93,99,105) sts.
Beg chevron patt where indicated on chart and work until piece meas 21½(22½,23½,24½)" (54.5,57,59.5,62 cm) from beg.
Shape shoulders: B.o. at beg of row 14(16,17,19) sts twice, then 13(15,17, 18) sts twice, leaving 30 sts rem for each shoulder.
Place sts on holder.

SLEEVES
With smaller needles c.o. 38(44,44,50) sts (preferably using a cable or chain c.o.).
Work 2 rows rev St st, then moiré rib for 2¾" (7 cm), then 2 rows rev St st.
Change to larger needles and beg chevron patt where indicated on chart.
Inc 1 st each side every 4th row 19(18, 19,17) times to give 76(80,82,84) sts.
When piece meas 15¼(15¾,16¼,16¾)" (38.5,40,41.5,42.5 cm), **beg armhole dec:**
B.o. at the beg of each row 7(8,8,8) sts 6 times, then 4(3,4,5) sts twice to give 26 sts.
Change to smaller needles and work saddle shoulder extension in moiré rib for 6(7½,8,9)" (15,19,20.5,23 cm).
Place sts on holder.

FINISHING
Sew all but one shoulder seam, easing saddle shoulder extensions into place.
Sew sleeve and side seams.
With smaller needles, p.u. 30 sts from both front and back holders, 26 sts from each of the shoulders, and 1 st for each seam for a total of 116 sts.
Work 2 rows in rev St st then 2¼" (5.5 cm) in moiré rib.
Work 2 more rows in rev St st then k 1 row.
B.o. all sts with a knit row.
Sew rem shoulder and neck seam.

CHILD'S PULLOVER
SIZES
4(6,8,10)
Finished measurements: 21(23,25,28)" (53.5,58.5,63.5,71 cm)

MATERIALS
Boston (100% wool; 50 grams = 90 yards): 5(6,6,7) hanks
Equivalent yarn: 450(540,540,630) yards/412(494,494,576) meters of worsted-weight wool

Knitting needles same as for adult's sweater

GAUGE

Same as for adult's sweater

PATTERN STITCHES

2 x 4 RIB

(multiple of 6 + 2)

Row 1 (WS): K2, * p4, k2; rep from *.

Row 2: P2, * k4, p2; rep from *.

FRONT AND BACK

With smaller needles, c.o. 50(50,56,62) sts and work 2 rows rev St st.

Work in 2 x 4 rib for 2" (5 cm), inc 1(5,3,1) sts evenly across last WSR to give 51(55,59,63) sts.

Work 2 more rows in rev St st and beg chevron chart where indicated.

Work until piece meas 12½(13,13½, 14)" (31.5,33,34,35.5 cm).

Place center 21 sts on holder.

Working each side sep, b.o. 1 st at neck edge every other row twice.

When piece meas 14(14½,15,15½)" (35.5,37,38,39.5 cm), b.o. all sts in patt.

SLEEVES

With smaller needles, c.o. 32(32,38,38) sts and work 2 rows in rev St st.

Work 2 x 4 rib for 2" (5 cm), inc 3(3,1,1) sts evenly across last WSR to give 35(35,39,39) sts.

Work 2 more rows in rev St st.

Change to larger needles and beg chevron patt where indicated on chart.

When sleeve meas 10(10½,10¾,11)" (25.5,26.5,27.5,28 cm), b.o. all sts in patt.

FINISHING

Sew one shoulder seam.

With smaller needles, p.u. 21 sts from back holder, 9 sts from neck edge, 21 sts from front holder, and 9 st from neck edge for a total of 60 sts.

Work 2 x 4 rib for 12" (30.5 cm), ending on row 2.

B.o. all sts with a knit row.

Sew shoulder, neck, side, and sleeve seams.

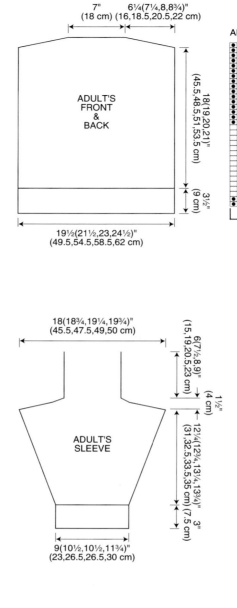

7" (18 cm)   6¼(7¼,8,8¾)" (16,18.5,20.5,22 cm)

ADULT'S FRONT & BACK

18(19,20,21)" (45.5,48,51,53.5 cm)

3½" (9 cm)

19½(21½,23,24½)" (49.5,54.5,58.5,62 cm)

18(18¾,19¼,19¾)" (45.5,47.5,49,50 cm)

6(7½,8,8.9)" (15,19,20.5,23 cm)

1½" (4 cm)

ADULT'S SLEEVE

12¼(12¾,13¼,13¾)" (31,32.5,33.5,35 cm)

3" (7.5 cm)

9(10½,10½,11¾)" (23,26.5,26.5,30 cm)

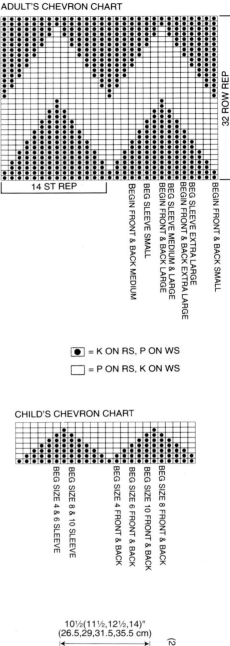

ADULT'S CHEVRON CHART

32 ROW REP

14 ST REP

BEGIN FRONT & BACK MEDIUM
BEGIN SLEEVE SMALL
BEGIN FRONT & BACK LARGE
BEGIN SLEEVE MEDIUM & LARGE
BEGIN FRONT & BACK EXTRA LARGE
BEGIN SLEEVE EXTRA LARGE
BEGIN FRONT & BACK SMALL

⬛ = K ON RS, P ON WS

⬜ = P ON RS, K ON WS

CHILD'S CHEVRON CHART

BEG SIZE 4 & 6 SLEEVE
BEG SIZE 8 & 10 SLEEVE
BEG SIZE 4 FRONT & BACK
BEG SIZE 6 FRONT & BACK
BEG SIZE 10 FRONT & BACK
BEG SIZE 8 FRONT & BACK

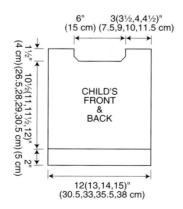

6" (15 cm)   3(3½,4,4½)" (7.5,9,10,11.5 cm)

1½" (4 cm)

CHILD'S FRONT & BACK

10½(11,11½,12)" (26.5,28,29,30.5 cm)

2" (5 cm)

12(13,14,15)" (30.5,33,35.5,38 cm)

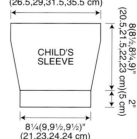

10½(11½,12½,14)" (26.5,29,31.5,35.5 cm)

CHILD'S SLEEVE

8(8½,8¾,9)" (20.5,21.5,22,23 cm)

2" (5 cm)

8¼(9,9½,9½)" (21,23,24,24 cm)

Designing
with Color

Adult's Pullover

Sizes

Small(Medium,Large,Extra Large)
Finished measurements at chest:
36(40,44,48)" (91.5,101.5,112,122 cm)

Materials

La Gran (74% mohair, 13% wool, 13% nylon, 1½ oz. = approx. 90 yards): 7(7,8,8) balls of main color (MC) for woman's pullover or 8(8,9,9) balls for man's pullover or woman's turtleneck, 1 ball of color A, 2 balls of color B, and 1 ball of color C

Equivalent yarn: 630(630,720,720) yards/576(576,659,659) meters of bulky brushed mohair in main color for pullover, 720(720,810,810) yards/659 (659,741,741) meters in main color for turtleneck, 90 yards/83 meters of color A, 180 yards/165 meters of color B, and 90 yards/83 meters of color C

29" (73.5 cm) circular knitting needles in sizes 8 and 10½ U.S. (5 and 6.5 mm)

Double-pointed needles (dpn) in sizes 8 and 10½ U.S. (5 and 6.5 mm)

16" (40.5 cm) circular needle in size 9 U.S. (5.5 mm)

Stitch markers

Note: The body is worked in the round on circular needles. The sleeves are worked in the round on 4 dpn. The body and sleeves are then joined at yoke onto the circular needle.

Gauge

Stockinette stitch on larger needles in round: 14 sts and 18 rows = 4" (10 cm)
Take time to save time—check your gauge.

Note: When working patt st, you may find it necessary to change to a larger size needle to obtain same gauge. Make sure you carry the unused color of yarn very loosely behind knitting so that it does not draw in work.

Pattern Stitches

1 x 1 Twisted Rib
(in the round)
Rnd 1: * K1-b (k1 into back of st), p1 *, rep bet *'s.
Rnd 2: * K1, p1 *, rep bet *'s.

Stockinette Stitch
(in the round)
All rnds: K all sts.

Body

With smaller circular needle and MC, c.o. 108(120,132,144) sts.

Join sts in round, taking care not to twist sts.

Work 1 x 1 twisted rib for 4½" (11.5 cm).

In last row of rib, inc 18(22,22,26) sts evenly around to give 126(142,154, 170) sts.

Place markers between 1st and last and 63rd and 64th (71st and 72nd,77th and 78th,85th and 86th) sts to mark for sides.

Change to larger needle and work St st in round until piece meas 14(15,16, 17)" (35.5,38,40.5,43 cm) including rib, 15(16,17,18)" (38,40.5,43,45.5 cm) for man's sweater, or desired length to underarm.

Sl centered 10(12,12,14) sts at sides onto scrap yarn to hold for underarm joint, taking 5(6,6,7) sts on each side of each marker.

Sleeves

Using smaller dpn, c.o. 28(30,30,32) sts.

Divide sts evenly onto 3 needles and join sts, placing markers after 1st st and before last st to mark seam line.

Work 1 x 1 twisted rib using 4th needle to knit.

If you are worried about twisting sts when joining, work a few rows back and forth in rib, then join.

Work in rib for 2½" (6.5 cm).

In last round, inc 8 sts evenly around to give 36(38,38,40) sts.

Change to larger needles and beg working St st.

At the same time, inc 1 st before 1st marked st and after last marked st every 4th round 12(13,14,15) times to give 60(64,66,70) sts.

Icelandic-style pullovers are great projects for novices. By the time the yoke is reached, the beginning knitter has become proficient and can then enjoy the challenge of knitting in two colors. The key to working in two colors is to make sure that the yarn not being used is carried very loosely behind the work. This prevents the sweater from drawing in as you knit. Icelandic-style pullovers are normally made with coarse, loosely spun wools; this one is shown in mohair, which makes it look luxurious. Mixing off-beat colors together in each design creates an out-of-the-ordinary pullover.

Design: **Kristin Nicholas**
Knitting rating: **Beginner**

When sleeve meas 15½(16,16½,17)" (39.5,40.5,42,43 cm), sl center 9(11,11, 13) sts onto holder for underarm join.

Yoke

Work 53(59,65,71) sts from front, 51(53, 55,59) sts from one sleeve, 53(59, 65,71) sts from back, 51(53,55, 59) sts from 2nd sleeve, placing markers as you go between the body sts and the sleeve sts.

There will be 208(224,240,256) sts on large circular needle.

Work 2 rounds in MC.

Work Chart 1 over 4 st repeat for 12 rounds.

Decrease round 1: Cont in color B and work as foll:

Small: K3, k2tog, (k3, k2tog, k4, k2tog) 18 times, k3, k2tog = 38 sts dec.

Medium: * (k3, k2tog) 10 times, (k4, k2tog) once *, rep from * to * 4 times = 44 sts dec.

Large: * (k3, k2tog) 4 times, (k2, k2tog) once *, rep from * to * 10 times = 50 sts dec.

Extra Large: * (k3, k2tog, k2, k2tog) 6 times, (k3, k2tog) twice *, rep from * to * 4 times = 56 sts dec.

You should have 170(180,190,200) sts rem.

Work Chart 2 over 10 st repeat for 12 rounds.

Decrease round 2: In color B work as foll:

Small: K1, k2tog, * (k1, k2tog) 13 times, k2tog *, rep from * to * 4 times, ending k1, k2tog = 58 sts dec.

Medium: (k1, k2tog) 60 times = 60 sts dec.

Large: * (k1, k2tog) 14 times, (k2, k2tog) once *, rep from * to * 4 times, then (k1, k2tog) twice = 62 sts dec.

Extra Large: * (k1, k2tog) 7 times, (k2, k2tog) once *, rep from * to * 8 times = 64 sts dec.

This gives 112(120,128,136) sts on needle.

Work Chart 3 (see page 76) over 8 st repeat for 12 rounds.

Decrease round 3: In color B work as foll:

Small: K2tog, (k1, k2tog) 36 times, k2tog = 36 sts dec.

Medium: (k1, k2tog) 40 times = 40 sts dec.

Large: * (k1, k2tog) 3 times, k2tog *, rep from * to * 10 times, then (k1, k2tog) 6 times = 46 sts dec.

Extra Large: * (k1, k2tog) 3 times, (k2tog) twice *, rep from * to * 10 times, then (k1, k2tog) twice = 52 sts dec.

You should have 74(80,82,84) sts on needle.

Neckline: With middle-size circular needle and color B for woman's sweater or MC for man's, work 1 x 1 twisted rib for 4" (10 cm).

Sew down neck sts loosely to inside, folding neckband in half.

Weave underarm sts together.

Turtleneck: With middle-size circular needle and color B, work twisted rib for 3" (7.5 cm).

Reverse work so that inside of work folds over and becomes the outside.

Using smallest dpn, work in twisted rib until turtleneck meas 8" (20.5 cm).

B.o. all sts loosely.

Child's Pullover

Sizes

2(4,6,8,10,12)

Finished measurements at chest: 24(26, 28,30,32,36)" (61,66,71,76,81.5,91.5 cm)

Materials

3(3,4,4,5,5) balls of main color (MC) and 1 ball each of colors A, B, and C.

Equivalent yarn: 270(270,360,360,450, 450) yards/247(247,330,330,412,412) meters of bulky brushed mohair in main color and 90 yards/83 meters each of colors A, B, and C

Double-pointed needles (dpn) in sizes 8 and 10½ U.S. (5 and 6.5 mm)

24" (61 cm) circular needles in sizes 8 and 10½ U.S. (5 and 6.5 mm)

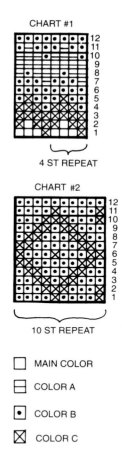

CHART #1

4 ST REPEAT

CHART #2

10 ST REPEAT

☐ MAIN COLOR

⊟ COLOR A

⊡ COLOR B

⊠ COLOR C

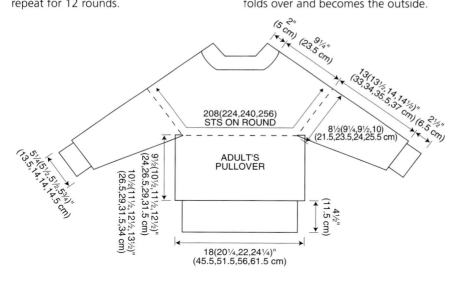

208(224,240,256) STS ON ROUND

ADULT'S PULLOVER

13(13½,14,14½)" (33,34,35.5,37 cm)

2½" (6.5 cm)

8½(9¼,9½,10)" (21.5,23.5,24,25.5 cm)

2" (5 cm)

9¼" (23.5 cm)

5¼(5½,5½,5¾)" (13.5,14,14,14.5 cm)

9½(10½,11½,12½)" (24,26.5,29,31.5 cm)

10½(11½,12½,13½)" (26.5,29,31.5,34 cm)

4½" (11.5 cm)

18(20¼,22,24¼)" (45.5,51.5,56,61.5 cm)

JOINING BODY & SLEEVES

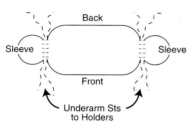

Back

Sleeve

Sleeve

Front

Underarm Sts to Holders

Gauge and Pattern Stitches

Same as for adult's sweater

Body

With smaller circular needle and MC, c.o. 84(92,100,108,116,128) sts.

Join sts in round, placing markers bet 1st and last sts and bet 42nd and 43rd(46th and 47th, 50th and 51st, 54th and 55th, 58th and 59th, 64th and 65th) sts to mark sides.

Work in 1 x 1 twisted rib for 1½" (4 cm).

Change to larger needle and work in St st until piece meas 10½(11,11½,12, 12½,13½)" (26.5,28,29,30.5,31.5,34 cm), including rib.

Sl centered 6(8,8,8,10,10) sts at sides onto scrap yarn to hold for underarm joint, taking 3(4,4,4,5,5) sts on each side of each marker.

Sleeves

With smaller dpn and MC, c.o. 28(28,30,30,32,36) sts.

Divide sts evenly onto 3 needles and join sts into round, placing markers after 1st st and before last st and taking care not to twist sts.

If desired, work a few rows back and forth; then join into round.

Work in 1 x 1 twisted rib for 1½" (4 cm).

In last round, inc 4(4,6,6,8,10) sts evenly around to give 32(32,36,36,40,46) sts.

Change to larger dpn and beg St st.

At the same time, inc 1 st after 1st st on 1st needle at marker and before last st on last needle to inc 2 sts every 5th round.

Work 2(3,3,5,5,5) inc rounds to give 36(42,46,50,56) sts.

When sleeve meas 10½(11,11½,12, 12½,13)" (26.5,28,29,30.5,31.5,33 cm) including rib, or desired length to underarm, sl centered 6(8,8,8,10,10) sts at underarm (centered over incs) for underarm join.

Yoke

With larger circular needle, work 36(38, 42,46,48,54) sts from front, 30(30,34, 38,40,46) sts from one sleeve, 36(38, 42,46,48,54) sts from back, 30(30,34, 38,40,46) sts from 2nd sleeve.

There will be 132(136,152,168,176, 200) sts on circular needle.

With MC, work 3(3,4,6,7,9) rounds in St st.

Work Chart 1 over 4 st rep for 12 rounds.

Carry yarn loosely across back of work to avoid pulling in of yoke. (You may find it necessary to inc needle size to size 11 U.S. (8 mm) to make it easier.)

Dec round 1: In color B (last color worked of Chart 1), work as foll:

Size 2: (K1, k2tog) 44 times = 44 sts dec.

Size 4: * K2, k2tog, (k1, k2tog) 3 times, k2, k2tog *, rep from * to * 8 times = 40 sts dec.

Size 6: * (K1, k2tog) 5 times, k2, k2tog *, rep from * to * 8 times = 48 sts dec.

Size 8: (K1, k2tog) 56 times = 56 sts dec.

Size 10: * (K1, k2tog) 6 times, k2, k2tog *, rep from * to * 8 times = 56 sts dec.

Size 12: (K1, k2tog) 66 times, k2 = 66 sts dec.

You should have 88(96,104,112,120, 136) sts rem.

Work Chart 4 over 8 st rep for 9 rounds.

Dec round 2: In color B, work as foll:

Size 2: * K2tog, (k1, k2tog) 3 times *, rep from * to * 8 times = 32 sts dec.

Size 4: (K1, k2tog) 32 times = 32 sts dec.

Size 6: * (K1, k2tog) 3 times, (k2, k2tog) once *, rep from * to * 8 times = 32 sts dec.

Size 8: * (k1, k2tog) 8 times, (K2, k2tog) once *, rep from * to * 4 times = 36 sts dec.

Size 10: (K1, k2tog) 40 times = 40 sts dec.

Size 12: * K2tog, (k1, k2tog) 5 times *, rep from * to * 8 times = 48 sts dec

You should have 56(64,72,76,80,88) sts rem.

If necessary at this point, change back to dpn.

Work Chart 5 over 4 st repeat for 4(6,8,10,12,14) rounds.

For Chart 5, add colors used in body to please your own taste, rep the small block patt using leftovers from sweater.

Dec round 3: In C or any color desired, dec 0(2,6,8,10,10) sts evenly around to give 56(60,66,68,70,78) sts for neck.

Change to smaller dpn and, using color C, work twisted rib for 3" (7.5 cm).

Do not b.o. but turn to inside and stitch down loosely so sweater will fit easily over child's head.

Weave underarm seams.

CHILD'S HAT

MATERIALS
1 ball of main color (MC) and scraps of A, B, and C

INSTRUCTIONS
Using large dpn, c.o. 60 sts.

Join, taking care not to twist, and work in St st for 2" (5 cm) to form rolled cuff.

Work in 1 x 1 rib for 4 rnds.

Work in St st for 2 rnds in MC.

Then work Chart 1.

After 12 rnds of chart have been completed, k 1 rnd, dec 4 sts evenly around.

Beg hat shaping as foll: * K6, k2tog *, 7 times.

K 1 rnd.

* K5, k2tog *, 7 times.

K 1 rnd.

* K4, k2tog *, 7 times.

K 1 rnd.

* K3, k2tog *, 7 times.

K 1 rnd.

* K2, k2tog *, 7 times.

K 1 rnd.

There should be 21 sts left.

Pull yarn through these sts with a tapestry needle and gather tog.

Make a pompom and attach to center of top.

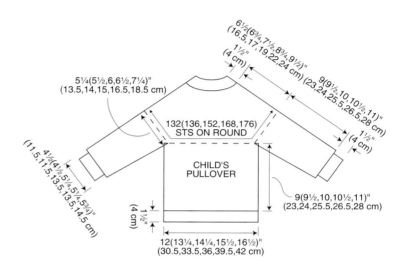

5¼(5½,6,6½,7¼)"
(13.5,14,15,16.5,18.5 cm)

6½(6¾,7½,8¾,9½)"
(16.5,17,19,22,24 cm)

1½"
(4 cm)

9(9½,10,10½,11)"
(23,24,25.5,26.5,28 cm)

1½"
(4 cm)

132(136,152,168,176)
STS ON ROUND

CHILD'S
PULLOVER

4½(4½,5¼,5½,5¾)"
(11.5,11.5,13.5,13.5,14.5 cm)

9(9½,10,10½,11)"
(23,24,25.5,26.5,28 cm)

1½"
(4 cm)

12(13¼,14¼,15½,16½)"
(30.5,33.5,36,39.5,42 cm)

CHART #3

12 11 10 9 8 7 6 5 4 3 2 1

8 ST REPEAT

CHART #4

9 8 7 6 5 4 3 2 1

8 ST REPEAT
OMIT ROUNDS 3 AND 7
FOR SIZES 2(4,6)

CHART #5

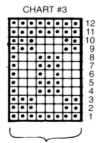

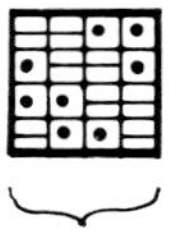

4 ST REPEAT

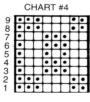

☐ MAIN COLOR

⊟ COLOR A

⊠ COLOR C

• COLOR B

SIZES

Small(Medium,Large)

Finished measurements: 44(48,52)" (112,122,132 cm)

MATERIALS

Regatta (100% cotton; 50 grams = approx. 123 yards): 3(3,4) hanks of colors A—#3052, B—#3046, C—#3032, and F—#3023; 2(2,3) hanks of color D—#3044; 4(4,4) hanks of color E—#3086

Equivalent yarn: 369(369,492) yards/338(338,450) meters of light worsted-weight cotton in colors A, B, C, and F; 246(246,369) yards/225(225, 338) meters of color D; 492(492,492) yards/450(450,450) meters of color E

Knitting needles in sizes 5, 6 and 7 U.S. (3.75, 4, and 4.5 mm)

16" (40.5 cm) circular needles in sizes 5, 6 and 7 U.S. (3.75, 4, and 4.5 mm)

GAUGE

21 sts and 27 rows = 4" (10 cm) for the following patterns and needle sizes: size 6 needles for all plain 1-color rows; size 7 needles for 2-color rows; size 5 needles for lace rows 33-41.

Take time to save time—check your gauge.

PATTERN STITCHES

See chart and key for patterns.

All color changes are listed at side of chart.

For colorwork sections of chart, knit the RS rows and purl the WS rows, loosely carrying unused yarn along WS, twisting when necessary to avoid long floats.

1 x 1 RIB

(over odd number of sts)

Row 1: (WS) K1, * p1, k1 *, rep bet *'s.

Row 2: P1, * k1, p1 *, rep bet *'s.

Repeat rows 1-2.

BACK

With smallest needles and color B, c.o. 113(125,135) sts.

Rib 1 row, change to color E and rib 2 rows, change to C and work ribbing until piece meas 1½" (4 cm), end with a WS row, inc 4 sts to give 117(129,139) sts.

Change to larger needles and work row 1 of chart, beg and end as indicated.

Work as est until piece meas 27(28, 29)" (68.5,71,73.5 cm), ending with a RS row.

Back neck and shoulder shaping:
Mark center 19(21,23) sts.

B.o. 13(15,16) sts, work to center sts, join 2nd ball of yarn, b.o. center sts, work to end.

Working each side sep, b.o. 13(15,16) sts from the next 3 shoulder edges and **at the same time,** b.o. 5 sts from each neck edge twice.

FRONT

Work as for back until piece meas 25(26,27)" (63.5,66,68.5 cm), end with a RS row.

OTTOMAN ILLUSION

A simple chevron design echoes throughout this striped pullover in a masterful variety of stitches. Knit and purl brocade stitches, lace, and two-color Fair Isle are all worked in a selection of rich tones reminiscent of a Turkish kilim. The result is an easy fitting pullover that's perfect for any occasion.

Design: DEBORAH NEWTON
Knitting rating: EXPERIENCED

Shape neck: Mark center 17(19,21) sts.

Next row (WS) work to center sts, join 2nd ball of yarn, b.o. center sts, work to end.

Working each side sep, b.o. from each neck edge 3 sts once, 2 sts 3 times, and 1 st every RS row twice to give 39(44, 48) sts each side.

Work even until front meas same as back to shoulder, b.o. 13(15,16) sts from each shoulder edge twice and 13(14,16) sts once.

SLEEVES

With smaller needles and color B, c.o. 43(45,47) sts and work rib as for back, inc 6(4,4) sts in last row to give 49(49, 51) sts.

Change to larger needles.

Next row (RS), work row 1 of chart, beg and end as indicated.

Work 3 more rows.

Work in patt as est, inc 1 st each end of next row, then every 4th row, for a total inc of 21(24,26) sts each side to give 91(97,103) sts.

Work even until sleeve meas 16(17,18)" (40.5,43,45.5 cm), ending with a WS row.

B.o. all sts.

FINISHING

Steam pieces lightly.

Sew shoulder seams.

Note: When working collar in the rnd, read all chart rows (rnds) from right to left.

Collar: With RS facing, color E, and medium circular needle, beg at right shoulder and p.u. 108 sts evenly around neck edge.

Beg with row 2 where indicated, using color A for contrast color, work even in rnds until row 4 of chart is complete.

Change to color B and work rows 19-27 in the rnd.

With colors D and C, work rows 15-18 in the rnd, dec 12 sts on last rnd to give 96 sts.

With color F and smaller circular needle, work rows 32-42 in the rnd, inc 8(12, 16) sts on last rnd to give 104(108,112) sts.

With color E, k 1 rnd, then work 1 x 1 rib for 1 rnd.

Change to color C, rib for 2" (5 cm), b.o. in ribbing.

Weave in ends.

Place markers 8½(9,9½)" (21.5,23,24 cm) down on front and back.

Set in sleeves bet markers.

Sew underarm and side seams.

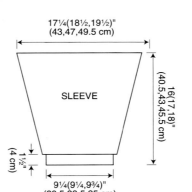

SLEEVE

17¼(18½,19½)"
(43,47,49.5 cm)

16(17,18)"
(40.5,43,45.5 cm)

1½"
(4 cm)

9¼(9¼,9¾)"
(23.5,23.5,25 cm)

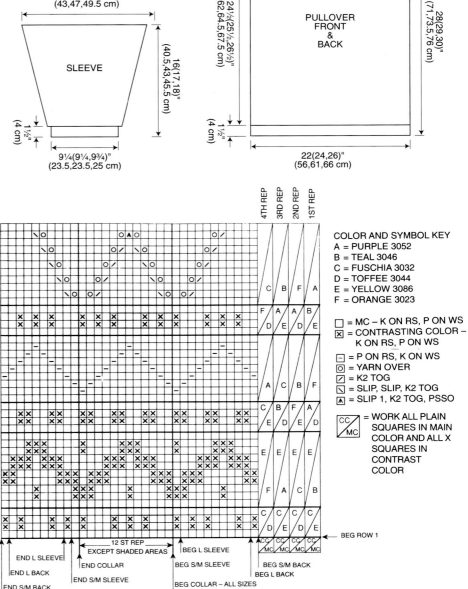

PULLOVER
FRONT
&
BACK

7½(7¾,8¼)"
(19,19.5,21 cm)

1"
(2.5 cm)

2"
(5 cm)

24½(25½,26½)"
(62,64.5,67.5 cm)

28(29,30)"
(71,73.5,76 cm)

1½"
(4 cm)

22(24,26)"
(56,61,66 cm)

4TH REP
3RD REP
2ND REP
1ST REP

COLOR AND SYMBOL KEY
A = PURPLE 3052
B = TEAL 3046
C = FUSCHIA 3032
D = TOFFEE 3044
E = YELLOW 3086
F = ORANGE 3023

□ = MC – K ON RS, P ON WS
⊠ = CONTRASTING COLOR – K ON RS, P ON WS
⊟ = P ON RS, K ON WS
◯ = YARN OVER
⧄ = K2 TOG
◺ = SLIP, SLIP, K2 TOG
▲ = SLIP 1, K2 TOG, PSSO

CC/MC = WORK ALL PLAIN SQUARES IN MAIN COLOR AND ALL X SQUARES IN CONTRAST COLOR

C B F A
F A A B
D E D E

A C B F

C B F A
E D E D

E E E E

F A C B

C C C C
D E D E

BEG ROW 1

12 ST REP EXCEPT SHADED AREAS

END L SLEEVE
END L BACK
END S/M BACK
END COLLAR
END S/M SLEEVE
BEG L SLEEVE
BEG S/M SLEEVE
BEG S/M BACK
BEG L BACK
BEG COLLAR – ALL SIZES

NOTES:
1. WORK COLORWORK BANDS WITH NEEDLE 1 SIZE LARGER THAN FOR KNIT/PURL AND LACE BANDS
2. COLOR CHANGES ARE NOTED AT SIDE OF CHART.
3. BEGIN AND END PATTERNS WHERE INDICATED.

Scandinavian Family

Avant garde, nontraditional coloring is exceptionally success- ful in this family version of traditional Fair Isle pattern work. A cardinal rule of Fair Isle is broken though—for 13 rows in the adult pullover, there is a transition between patterns, and three colors of yarn are used. The child's pullover is a smaller, diamond-based motif. Patterns for the mittens and hat are also included.

Design: **Kristin Nicholas**
Knitting rating: **Very challenging**

Sizes
Small(Medium,Large)
Finished measurements at chest:
44(48,52)" (112,122,132 cm)

Materials
Boston (100% wool; 50 grams = approx. 85 yards) OR Paisley (50% wool, 50% rayon; 50 grams = approx. 90 yards): 11(12,13) hanks of color A; 2(2,2) hanks of color B; 3(3,3) hanks of color C; 8(8,9) hanks of color D
Equivalent yarn: 990(1080,1170) yards/904(988,1070) meters of worsted weight in color A, 180(180,180) yards/165(165,165) meters of color B, 270(270,270) yards/247(247,247) meters of color C, and 720(720,810) yards/659(659,741) meters of color D
Knitting needles in sizes 6 and 8 U.S. (4 and 5 mm)
16" (40.5 cm) circular needles in sizes 6 and 8 U.S. (4 and 5 mm)
Note: Models are wearing the follow- ing yarns and color combinations (from left to right):
Woman in Paisley: A—#1753, B—#1750, C—#1738, D—#1784
Child in Boston: A—#1952, C—#1959, D—#1943

Woman in Boston: A—#1944, B—#1948, C—#1942, D—#1943
Child in Boston: A—#1913, C—#1953, D—#1928
Man in Boston: A—#1952, B—#1928, C—#1943, D—#1959

Gauge
Fair Isle technique on larger needles: 21 sts and 24 rows = 4" (10 cm)
Because of colorwork charts, it is extremely important to get the correct row gauge, or the smock will not be the proper length.
Take time to save time—check your gauge.

Pattern Stitches
Stockinette Stitch
Row 1: (RS) K all sts.
Row 2: P all sts.
In round for neckline: K all sts.

Fair Isle Pattern
Work in St st.
When spacing between colors is more than 5 sts, weave the contrasting color in by twisting yarn behind work.

Adult's Smock
Back
Hemmed edge: With smaller needles and color A, c.o. 110(120,132) sts.
Work in St st for 2¾" (7 cm) ending with WSR.
In last row, inc 7 sts evenly across to give 117(127,139) sts.
Purl 1 row (turning edge).
Begin Patt A: Using Fair Isle technique beg with stitch 8(7,1) using colors indi- cated on chart.
When you have completed 18 rows of A, begin Patt B where shown for size, beg with stitch 23(18,28) and using larger needles.
Work to row 32, then work 2 complete repeats of B—84(99,102) rows.
Then begin working transition rows in 3 colors as indicated for 13 rows, weav- ing yarns not used behind work to avoid long floats.

Work Patt C using colors A and C, ending where indicated.

B.O. all sts.

FRONT

Work as for back.

Shape neckline when piece meas 24 (25½,27)" (61,64.5,68.5 cm) excluding hem.

Work 44(47,52) sts, join second ball of yarn (base color) and b.o. center 29(33, 35) sts, work to end.

Cont working shoulder in patt and b.o. 1 st every other row at neck edge 4 times to give 40(43,48) sts at shoulders.

Work until piece meas same as back.

SLEEVES

Using smaller needles and color A, c.o. 44(44,52) sts.

Work in St st for 2¾" (7 cm).

In last WS row, inc 4 sts evenly across to give 48(48,56) sts.

Purl 1 row.

Work Patt A as done on body.

In 17th row of patt, inc 5(7,1) sts evenly across to give 53(55,57) sts.

Begin Patt B using colors indicated on chart, beg with stitch 7(6,5) and using larger needles.

Work as est inc 1 st each end every 4th row 21(23,25) times to give 95(101, 107) sts.

When sleeve meas 18(19,20)" (45.5, 48.5,51 cm) excluding hem, b.o. all sts.

FINISHING

Sew shoulder seams.

Using smaller circular needle and color A, p.u. 88(88,96) sts evenly around neckline.

P 1 rnd.

Work Patt A for 18 rounds.

P 1 rnd.

Dec 6 sts evenly around and work in St st for 18 rnds.

Sew neckband loosely to inside of neckline so it will fit over head.

Meas down 9(9½,10)" (23,24,25.5 cm) from shoulder seams in front and back and mark points.

Sew sleeves bet these points.

Sew underarm and sleeve seams.

Turn up bottom hem and sew down.

Optional: You may want to encase a 2½" (6.5 cm) piece of elastic in the hem so it doesn't flare after continued wear.

Turn up sleeve hems and sew down.

CHILD'S SMOCK

SIZES

2(4,6,8,10)

Finished measurements: 24(27½,30, 33½,36½)" (61,70,76,85, 92.5 cm)

MATERIALS

4(4,4,5,5) hanks of colors A and D and 1 hank of color C

BACK

Using smaller needles and color C, c.o. 60(68,76,84,92) sts.

Work in St st for 8 rows.

In last WS row, inc 4 sts evenly across to give 64(72,80,88,96) sts.

Purl 1 row (turning row) in color C.

Begin Patt D using colors C and D.

Work for 8 rows.

Change to larger needles and beg Patt E: Using colors A and D, beg on stitch 1(29,25,23,1).

Work until piece meas 14(16,18,20, 21)" (35.5,40.5,45.5,51,53.5 cm).

B.o.

FRONT

Work as for back.

When piece meas 12½(14½,16½,18½, 19½)" (31.5,37,42,47,49.5 cm), shape neck.

Work 21(24,27,30,34) sts, join second ball of base color yarn and b.o. center 22(24,26,28,28) sts in patt.

Work to end.

Working each side sep, at every other neck edge b.o. 1 st 3 times to give 18(21,24,27,31) sts at shoulders.

SLEEVES

With smaller needles and color C, c.o. 32(32,40,40,48) sts.

Work in St st for 8 rows ending with WSR.

Purl 1 row in C (turning row).

Beg Patt D over 8 st repeat.

Work for 8 rows.

In last row in color C, inc 6(4,4,4,4) sts evenly across to give 38(36,44,44,52) sts.

Change to larger needles.

Beg Patt E on stitch 30(31,27,27,23).

At the same time while working patt, inc 1 st each end every 3rd row 17(19, 9,10,0) times, then every 4th row 0(0,8,10,19) times to give 72(74,78,84, 90) sts.

When piece meas 10(11,12,13,14)" (25.5,28,30.5,33,35.5 cm), b.o. all sts.

FINISHING

Sew shoulder seams.

With larger circular needle, p.u.

64(72,72,72,80) sts around neck edge using color B.

Purl 1 round in B.

Then work Patt D for 8 rounds.

Change to smaller circular needle and purl 1 round.

Work in St st in color B for 8 rounds.

Turn neckband to inside.

Sew down loosely without binding off.

Meas down 7(7,7½,8,8½)" (18,18,19, 20.5,21.5 cm) from each shoulder seam in front and back.

Sew sleeve bet points.

Sew sleeve and side seams.

Turn up hem at bottom and sew.

Turn up sleeve hems and sew down.

MITTENS

SIZES

Child's medium(Woman's medium, Man's large)

MATERIALS

1(2,2) hanks each colors A and B and 1 hank color D

Double-pointed needles (dpn) in sizes 6 and 8 U.S. (4 and 5 mm)

Note: These mittens are worked in rnd on dpn.

INSTRUCTIONS

Using smaller dpn and color B, c.o. 30(38,44) sts.

Divide sts onto 3 needles and join in round.

Work in St st for 1½" (4 cm).

In last round, inc 4 sts evenly around to give 34(42,48) sts.

Purl 1 round.

Change to larger needles and work Patt F using colors indicated.

Then beg stripe patt using colors D and A.

Work in round until piece meas 4(5½, 6)" (10,14,15 cm).

Work thumb as foll: K1 st; break yarn and, using a contrast yarn, work 5(6,7) sts; finish round in patt stitch.

Next round, knit around working contrast yarn into mitten. This will become thumb opening later.

For left mitten: Work 12(14,16) sts across mitten, work 5(6,7) sts with

scrap yarn, work around in patt.

When piece meas 7½(10,11)" (19,25.5, 28 cm) or desired length, shape tip.

Place marker at halfway points of mitten—bet 1st and last sts and bet 17th and 18th(21st and 22nd,24th and 25th) sts.

First dec round: * Sl 1st marker, sl 1 st, k1 st, pass sl st over k st; knit to within 2 sts of next marker, k2tog *. Rep from * to finish round.

Cont dec this way (4 sts each round) until 6(10,12) sts rem.

Weave ends.

For thumb opening: Remove contrast scrap.

P.u. 12(14,16) sts around opening and work in stripe patt.

When thumb meas 2½(3,3½)" (6.5,7.5, 9 cm) or desired length, dec 4 sts evenly around by k2tog.

Weave ends tog.

Using 4 strands of each color yarn, make a braid long enough to go around the cuff, knot both ends and sew on.

Make a small tassel and sew on over joining point.

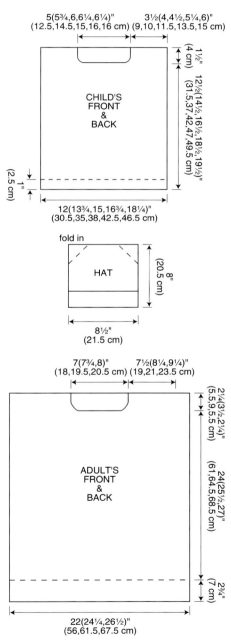

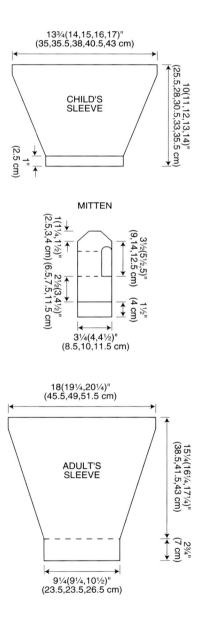

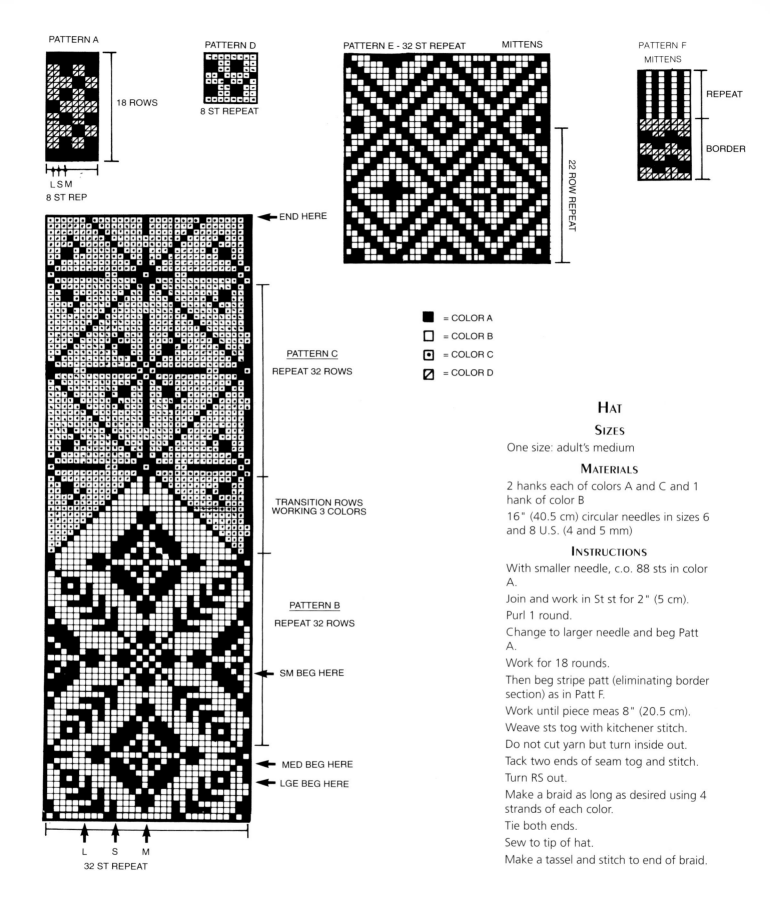

PATTERN A

18 ROWS

L S M
8 ST REP

PATTERN D

8 ST REPEAT

PATTERN E - 32 ST REPEAT

MITTENS

22 ROW REPEAT

PATTERN F
MITTENS

REPEAT

BORDER

← END HERE

PATTERN C
REPEAT 32 ROWS

TRANSITION ROWS
WORKING 3 COLORS

PATTERN B
REPEAT 32 ROWS

← SM BEG HERE

← MED BEG HERE
← LGE BEG HERE

L   S   M
32 ST REPEAT

■ = COLOR A

□ = COLOR B

▣ = COLOR C

◩ = COLOR D

Hat

Sizes

One size: adult's medium

Materials

2 hanks each of colors A and C and 1 hank of color B

16" (40.5 cm) circular needles in sizes 6 and 8 U.S. (4 and 5 mm)

Instructions

With smaller needle, c.o. 88 sts in color A.

Join and work in St st for 2" (5 cm).

Purl 1 round.

Change to larger needle and beg Patt A.

Work for 18 rounds.

Then beg stripe patt (eliminating border section) as in Patt F.

Work until piece meas 8" (20.5 cm).

Weave sts tog with kitchener stitch.

Do not cut yarn but turn inside out.

Tack two ends of seam tog and stitch.

Turn RS out.

Make a braid as long as desired using 4 strands of each color.

Tie both ends.

Sew to tip of hat.

Make a tassel and stitch to end of braid.

SIZES

Small(Medium,Large,Extra Large)
Finished measurements: 40(44,48,52)" (101.5,112,122,132 cm)

MATERIALS

Tapestry (75% wool, 25% mohair; 50 grams = approx. 95 yards)

For cardigan: 4(4,4,5) hanks of color A—#2284 Sacred Saffron; 7(7,7,8) hanks each of colors B—#2280 Ibex and C—#2213 Yak Black; 2(2,3,3) hanks of of color D—#2252 Merchant's Eggplant

For pullover: 4(4,4,5) hanks of color A—#2252 Merchant's Eggplant; 7(7,7, 8) hanks each of colors B—#2251 Tibetan Gold and C—#2246 Loomed Teal; 2(2,3,3) hanks of color D—#2238 Scrolled Olive

Equivalent yarn (for cardigan or pullover): 380(380,380,475) yards/348(348,435, 435) meters of worsted-weight wool in color A, 665(665,665, 760) yards/608 (608,608,695) meters each of colors B and C, and 190(190, 285,285) yards/ 174(174,261,261) meters of color D

Knitting needles in sizes 5 and 8 U.S. (3.75 and 5 mm)

For cardigan: 36" (91.5 cm) circular needle in size 5 U.S. (3.75 mm)

1" (2.5 cm) Pueblo buttons, style #B104 Navaho (7)

For pullover: 16" (40.5 cm) circular needle in size 5 U.S. (3.75 mm)

GAUGE

Stockinette stitch on larger needles: 21 sts and 21 rows = 4" (10 cm)

Take time to save time—check your gauge.

PATTERN STITCHES

CORRUGATED RIBBING AND GARTER STITCH

See chart on page 86.

STOCKINETTE STITCH

Row 1: (RS) K all sts.

Row 2: P all sts.

FAIR ISLE TECHNIQUE

Work as specified in colors as shown on chart.

Yarn not being worked should be carried loosely but with even tension throughout entire body.

If pattern float is more than 5 sts long, color not being used should be twisted behind work.

Note: Body is knit in one piece from bottom of back up to neck, then down front(s).

CORNWALL COVERLET

Antique American blue and white coverlets inspired the charts for both of these dramatic graphic designs. The individual blocks of two-color Fair Isle stranded knitting are separated by reverse stockinette stitch ridges in contrasting colors. Corrugated ribbing completes this challenging duo.

Design: **Kristin Nicholas**
Knitting rating: **Very challenging**

BACK (CARDIGAN AND PULLOVER)

With smaller needles and color A, c.o. 94(102,110,122) sts.

Work 1st 3 rows garter band as shown on corrugated rib chart.

Joining colors B and C, work in corrugated rib for 2" (5 cm).

Work last 3 rows of garter band in color A, inc 12(14,16,14) sts evenly across in 1st row of garter band to give 106(116, 126,136) sts.

Change to larger needles and work plaid patt beg on row 1(35,30,25).

Work for 120(126,131,136) rows.

Mark each end for shoulders.

Work 37(39,42,45) sts, sl center 32(38, 42,46) sts to holder, join 2nd ball of yarn and work to end.

CARDIGAN FRONT

Work as est in plaid patt, inc 1 st at each neck edge every 3rd row 11(7,0,0) times, then every 2nd row 0(6,16,19) times to give 48(52,58,64) sts.

Work fronts sep until each meas same as back.

Dec 6(6,8,10) sts in last row of patt to give 42(46,50,54) sts.

Change to smaller needles and beg garter band and corrugated ribs to correspond with back.

B.o. all sts loosely.

PULLOVER FRONT

Work same as for back.

Shape neck: After shoulder point, work each side sep for 2" (5 cm).

Then inc 1 st at neck edge every other row 4 times.

Then c.o. center 24(30,34,38) sts for center front and work as for back.

Work bottom rib to correspond with back.

SLEEVES (CARDIGAN AND PULLOVER)

Meas down 9½(9½,10,10½)" (24,24, 25.5,26.5 cm) from shoulder on front and back, and mark underarm point.

You should be at same point in a plaid patt on both front and back, centering garter band at center of piece.

P.u. 100(100,106,110) sts for sleeve, with 17 sts bet each plaid line and 2 sts at each 3-row plaid line.

Est patt, matching plaids to body.

At the same time, dec 1 st each end every 3rd row 28(19,19,24) times, then every 4th row 0(7,8,5) times to give 44(48,52,52) sts.

Change to smaller needles and k 1 RSR or p 1 WSR in color A, dec 2 sts evenly across to give 42(46,50,50) sts.

Work garter band and corrugated ribbing same as for body.

B.o. all sts loosely.

CARDIGAN FINISHING

Sew underarm and sleeve seams.

Mark buttonhole (BH) placement for 7 buttons.

Work 7 BH's on left side for man's sweater, on right side for woman's sweater.

Using longer circular needle and color A, with RS facing, p.u. 99(105,111,110) sts from bottom edge to beg of V-neck shaping, 33(33,32,38) sts to shoulder, 30(38,40,46) sts at back neck, 33(33, 32,38) sts to next V-neck shaping, and 99(105,111,110) sts to bottom edge.

Work band as on body for 1½" (4 cm).

Work BH's where marked on body of sweater as foll:

Work to marker, * b.o. 2 sts, work to next marker *, rep bet *'s.

Next row, c.o. 2 sts over b.o. sts.

Work for 1½" (4 cm).

B.o. all sts loosely.

Sew on buttons.

PULLOVER FINISHING

Sew underarm and side seams.

Using shorter circular needle, p.u. 92(100,112,120) sts evenly around neckline and work in garter ridge and corrugated ribbing for 2" (5 cm).

CORRUGATED RIBBING:
MULTIPLE OF 4 PLUS 2

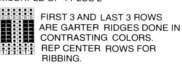

FIRST 3 AND LAST 3 ROWS ARE GARTER RIDGES DONE IN CONTRASTING COLORS. REP CENTER ROWS FOR RIBBING.

★ = PURL ON RS IN COLOR A, KNIT ON WS IN COLOR A
☆ = KNIT ON RS IN COLOR A, PURL ON WS IN COLOR A
■ = KNIT ON RS IN COLOR C, PURL ON WS IN COLOR C
□ = KNIT ON RS IN COLOR B, PURL ON WS IN COLOR B
◉ = PURL ON RS IN COLOR B, KNIT ON WS IN COLOR B
• = PURL ON RS IN COLOR D, KNIT ON WS IN COLOR D

WOMAN'S COVERLET PATTERN

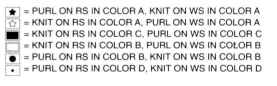

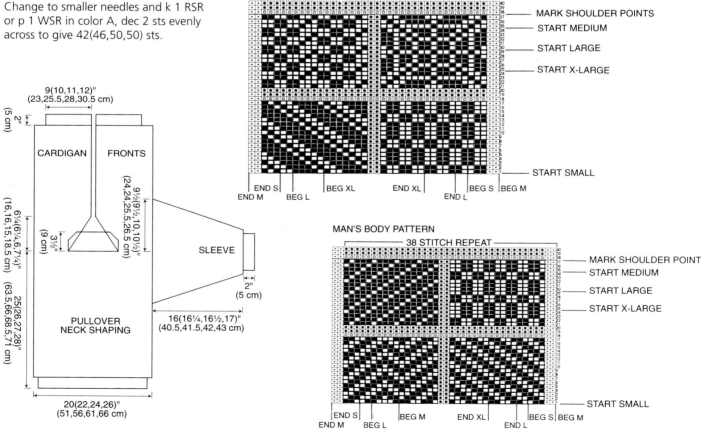

MAN'S BODY PATTERN

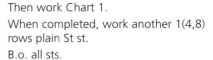

Before the Fall

The Garden of Eden "before the fall"—complete with Adam, Eve, and a menagerie of beasts—is depicted on this intarsia knit pullover worked in pure alpaca and camel hair yarns. It's edged in a German herringbone stitch at the cuffs, neckline, and border, and the entire alphabet is included in the charts so that you can personalize your sweater however you like. This sweater is very entertaining to knit!

Design: **Julie Hoff**
Knitting rating: **Very challenging**

Sizes

Small(Medium,Large)
Finished measurements: 44½(46½,49)" (113,118,124.5 cm)
Finished length: 24¾(25¼,26)" (63,64,66 cm)

Materials

Inca Alpaca (100% alpaca; 50 grams = approx. 115 yards): 10(11,11) hanks of main color A—#1127; 1 hank each of colors B—#1143, C—#1160, D—#1184, E—#1152, F—#1158, G—#1157, J—#1113, and L—#1140; approx. 1 yard/1 meter of color K—light peach or pink

Caravan 2 Ply (65% lambswool, 35% camel down; 50 grams = approx. 130 yds): 1 hank each of colors H—#6216 and I—#6203

Equivalent yarn: 1150(1265,1265) yards/1052(1157,1157) meters of light worsted-weight alpaca or camel hair in A, 115 yards/106 meters each of contrasting colors B, C, D, E, F, G, H, I, J, and L, and 1 yard/1 meter of contrasting color K

Knitting needles in size 6 U.S. (4 mm)
Note: Entire sweater is worked with size 6 needles.

Gauge

Stockinette stitch on larger needles: 22 sts and 27 rows = 4" (10 cm)
Take time to save time—check your gauge.

Pattern Stitches

German Herringbone Pattern

Make One (m1): Make a stitch by lifting the running thread bet sts and knitting into the back of this thread.

Row 1: K1(1,4), p0(1,1), m1, k1(3,3), * p2, p3tog, p2, k3, m1, p1, m1, k3 *, rep bet *'s 8 times; last rep: P2, p3tog, p2, k1(3,3), m1, p0(1,1), k1(1,4).

Row 2: P3(1,4), k0(1,1), p0(4,4), * k5, p4, k1, p4 *, rep bet *'s 8 times; last rep: K5, p0(4,4), k0(1,1), p3(1,4).

Row 3: K1(1,4), p0(1,1), m1, k2(4,4), * p1, p3tog, p1, k4, m1, p1, m1, k4 *, rep bet *'s 8 times; last rep: p1, p3tog, p1, k2(4,4), m1, p0(1,1), k1(1,4).

Row 4: P4(1,4), k0(1,1), p0(5,5), * k3, p5, k1, p5 *, rep bet *'s 8 times; last rep: k3, p0(5,5), k0(1,1), p4(1,4).

Row 5: K1(1,4), p0(1,1), m1, k3(5,5), * p3tog, k5, m1, p1, m1, k5 *, rep bet *'s 8 times; last rep: p3tog, k3(5,5), m1, p0(1,1), k1(1,4).

Row 6: P5(1,4) * k1, p6 *, rep bet *'s, end p5(1,4).

Back

C.o. 123(129,135) sts and work in German herringbone patt.

Then work Chart 1.
When completed, work another 1(4,8) rows plain St st.
B.o. all sts.

Front

Work as for back until 4(7,11) rows above the elephant have been worked.

Shape neck: Work across 55(58,61) sts, b.o. next 13 sts, work to end of row.

Working each side sep in est patt, b.o. at neck edge 4 sts once, 3 sts once, 2 sts twice, and 1 st 3 times.

When chart and additional 1(4,8) rows have been worked, b.o. rem 41(44,47) sts for each shoulder.

Note for sleeves: Using the alphabet and numbers provided, change the year as desired and fill in your initials in the space outlined on Chart 2.

Try using your initials on one sleeve and the initials of the person for whom you are knitting the sweater on the other sleeve (if applicable).

Sleeves

C.o. 59 sts and work in German herringbone patt, following directions for size medium.

Then work Chart 2 (inserting your initials in blank box at lower right) and, **at the same time,** inc 1 st each side every 4th row 10 times and every 6th row 10 times to give 99 sts.

Work to end of chart or to desired length.

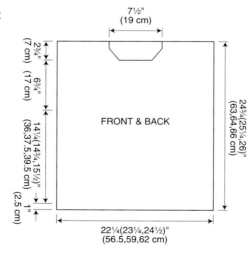

7½"
(19 cm)

2¾"
(7 cm)

6¾"
(17 cm)

14¼(14¾,15½)"
(36,37.5,39.5 cm)

1"
(2.5 cm)

FRONT & BACK

24¾(25¼,26)"
(63,64,66 cm)

22¼(23¼,24½)"
(56.5,59,62 cm)

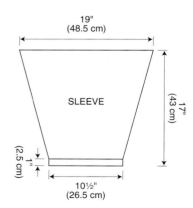

19"
(48.5 cm)

17"
(43 cm)

SLEEVE

1"
(2.5 cm)

10½"
(26.5 cm)

CHART 1

Collar

C.o. 115 sts.

Work in German herringbone patt, following instructions for size medium.

Rep 6 rows of patt 4 times, b.o. all sts.

Finishing

Work in all loose ends.

Block as foll: Lay pieces face down and pin flat.

Place dampened cloth over pieces and steam with iron.

Allow to dry completely before proceeding.

Sew shoulder seams.

Set in sleeves.

Sew underarm and side seams.

Turn sweater inside out and gently steam seams.

Sew collar to neck, leaving an opening in front to form a polo-style collar.

☐ = A   C = G

Z = B   · = H

☒ = C   V = I

◎ = D   ▲ = J

● = E   ◣ = K

✳ = F   L = L

CHART 2

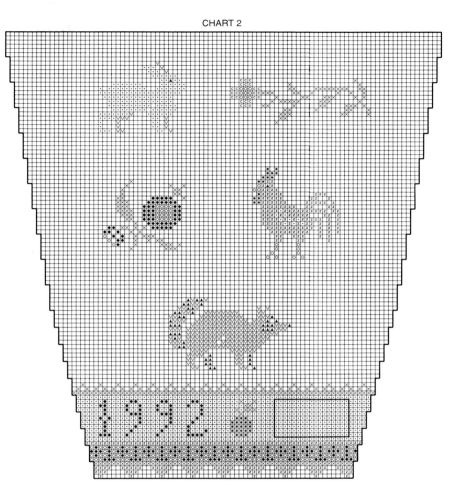

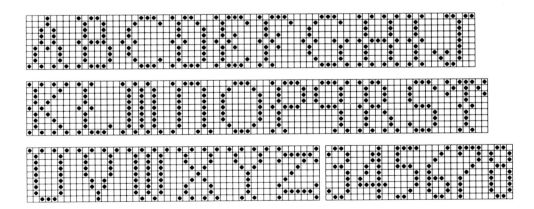

91

SANTORINI & MYKONOS

Antique Greek and Byzantine mosaics inspired both of these colorful pullovers. Each sweater is edged in multicolored borders, which make only a small section of the design a challenge. Repetitive, easy-to-knit textured stitches compose the main fabric of each sweater.

Design: MICHELE ROSE
Knitting rating: EXPERIENCED

SIZES

Small(Medium,Large)
Finished measurements: 42(44,46)" (106.5,112,117 cm)

MATERIALS

Pullover with Greek mosaic border:
Paisley (50% wool, 50% rayon; 50 grams = approx. 95 yards): 12(13,13) skeins of color A—#1710 Marine Blue; 3 skeins of color B—#1743 Spice

Equivalent yarn: 1140(1235,1235) yards/1042(1129,1129) meters of worsted-weight wool in color A and 285(285,285) yards/261(261,261) meters of color B

Pullover with diamond pattern:
11(12,12) skeins color of A—#1743 Spice; 2 skeins each of colors B—#1750 Mountain Moss and C—#1752 Eggplant; 1 skein each of colors D—#1784 Saffron and E—#1718 Harvest Squash

Equivalent yarn: 1045(1140,1140) yards/956(1042,1042) meters of worsted-weight wool in color A, 190(190,190) yards/174(174,174) meters each of B and C, and 95(95,95) yards/87(87,87) meters each of D and E

Knitting needles in sizes 6 and 8 U.S. (4 and 5 mm)

16" (40.5 cm) circular needle in size 6 U.S. (4 mm)

Cable needle (cn) for Greek mosaic pullover

GREEK MOSAIC PULLOVER

PATTERN STITCHES

STOCKINETTE STITCH
Row 1: (RS) Knit all sts.
Row 2: Purl all sts.

CABLED RIB
See chart.

GREEK KEY PATTERN
See chart.

BYZANTINE PATTERN
See chart.

PURL DOT PATTERN
See chart.

GAUGE

Byzantine pattern on larger needles: 20 sts and 22 rows = 4" (10 cm)
Take time to save time—check your gauge.

BACK

With smaller needles and color A, c.o. 105(109,113) sts.

Starting with st 5(3,1), beg cabled rib patt over 12 rows.

Next RS row, change to larger needles and work 2 rows in St st.

Next RS row, starting with st 4(2,15), beg Greek key patt and cont over next 13 rows.

Using color A, starting with st 9(7,5), beg Byzantine patt.

Work over next 32 rows.

Next WS row using color A, starting with st 1(5,3), beg purl dot patt.

Work even until piece meas 10½(11, 11½)" (26.5,28,29 cm) from beg.

Mark armholes.

Cont even in patt until armhole meas 9½(10,10½)" (24,25.5,26.5 cm).

Next RS row, **beg shoulder and neck shaping:** B.o. 11(12,13) sts at beg of next 4 rows, 13 sts at beg of next 2 rows.

At the same time, b.o. center 25 sts for neck, join 2nd ball of yarn, and working both sides at once, b.o. from each neck edge 3 sts once and 2 sts once.

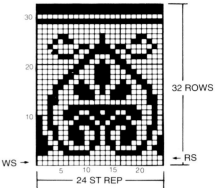

BYZANTINE PATTERN

30

20

10

32 ROWS

WS →

← RS

5   10   15   20

24 ST REP

COLOR KEY FOR BYZANTINE & GREEK KEY PATTERNS

☐ COLOR 1, K ON RS, P ON WS
■ COLOR 2. K ON RS, P ON WS

GREEK KEY PATTERN

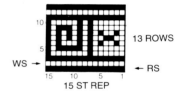

10

5

13 ROWS

WS →

← RS

15   10   5   1

15 ST REP

PURL DOT PATTERN

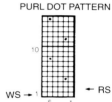

10

WS → 1

← RS

5   1

CABLED RIB

10

WS → 1

← RS

5   1

STITCH KEY FOR PURL DOT & CABLED RIB PATTERNS

☐ = K ON RS, P ON WS

I = P ON RS, K ON WS

 = LEFT TWIST—SL TO CN, HOLD AT FRONT, K1, K2 FROM CN

Front

Work as for back until piece meas 19(20,21)" (48.5,51,53.5 cm) from beg.

Next RS row beg **neck shaping:** Work across 43(45,47) sts in purl dot patt, join 2nd ball of yarn and b.o. center 19 sts, work to end.

Working both sides sep in est patt, b.o. from each neck edge 4 sts once, 2 sts once, 1 st every other row 2 times.

At the same time, when same length as back to shoulder, work **shoulder shaping** same as for back.

Sleeves

With smaller needles and color A, c.o. 35(39,43) sts.

Starting with st 5(3,1), beg cabled rib patt.

Work over 12 rows.

Next RS row, change to larger needles.

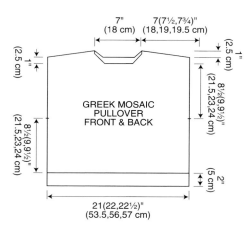

7" (18 cm) 7(7½,7¾)" (18,19,19.5 cm)

1" (2.5 cm)

1" (2.5 cm)

8½(9,9½)" (21.5,23,24 cm)

GREEK MOSAIC PULLOVER FRONT & BACK

8½(9,9½)" (21.5,23,24 cm)

2" (5 cm)

21(22,22½)" (53.5,56,57 cm)

19½(20¼,21)" (49.5,51.5,53.5 cm)

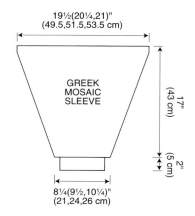

GREEK MOSAIC SLEEVE

17" (43 cm)

2" (5 cm)

8¼(9½,10¼)" (21,24,26 cm)

With color A, work 2 rows St st, inc 8 sts evenly across to give 43(47,51) sts.

Next RS row starting with st 6(4,2), beg Greek key patt.

Work Greek key over next 13 rows.

Next WS row using color A, starting with st 3(1,5), beg purl dot patt.

Work even in purl dot patt.

At the same time, inc 1 st each edge every other row 5 times, alternately every 3rd and every 4th rows 11 times to give 97(101,105) sts.

When piece meas 19" (48.5 cm), b.o. all sts.

Finishing

Sew shoulder seams.

Using circular needle and color A, p.u. 90 sts around neck edge.

Work Byzantine patt for 13 rows (starting with st 14).

Next row using color A, k 1 row, p 1 row, k 16 rows.

B.o. 90 sts.

Turn collar to inside along p row fold line, stitch down along neck seam.

Attach sleeves.

Sew side and sleeve seams.

Diamond-Bordered Pullover

Pattern Stitches

2 x 2 Rib

Row 1: K2, p2 to end.

Row 2: Work sts as they appear.

Large Moss Diamond Pattern

See chart.

Cable Box Pattern

See chart.

Small Moss Diamond Pattern

See chart.

Gauge

Cable box pattern on larger needles: 18 sts and 25 rows = 4" (10 cm)

Take time to save time—check your gauge.

Back

With smaller needles and color B, c.o. 92(96,100) sts.

Work 4 rows 2 x 2 rib, inc 3 sts evenly across last row to give 95(99,103) sts.

Next RS row starting with st 7(3,5) and larger needles, beg large moss diamond patt and work over next 18 rows.

Next RS row with color A, k 1 row.

Next WS row starting with st 10(8,6), beg cable box patt and cont until piece meas 8(8½,9)" (20.5,21.5,23 cm) from beg.

Mark armholes and continue until armhole meas 10(10½,11)" (25.5,26.5,28 cm).

Beg shoulder and neck shaping: B.o. 10(11,12) sts at beg of next 4 rows, 12 sts at beg of next 2 rows.

At the same time, b.o. center 19 sts for neck, join 2nd ball of yarn, and working each side sep, b.o. from each neck edge 4 sts once and 2 sts once.

FRONT

Work as for back until piece meas 16½(17½,18½)" (42,44.5,47 cm) from beg.

Next RS row, **beg neck shaping:** Work 42(44,46) sts, join 2nd ball of yarn and b.o. center 11 sts, work to end.

Working each side sep in est patt, b.o. at each neck edge 4 sts once, 2 sts once, 1 st twice, 1 st every other row twice.

At the same time, when same length as back to shoulder, **shape shoulders** as for back.

SLEEVES

With smaller needles and color B, c.o. 31(35,39) sts.

Work 4 rows in 2 x 2 rib.

Next RS row starting with st 3(1,11) and larger needles, beg large moss diamond patt and work over next 18 rows.

Next RS row with color A, k 1 row.

Next WS row starting with st 4(2,10), beg cable box patt.

At the same time, work inc into patt as foll: Inc 1 st each edge every other row 3 times, alt every other and every 4th row 4 times, every 4th row 19 times.

Work even until piece meas 19" (48.5 cm) from beg.

B.o. 91(95,99) sts.

FINISHING

Sew shoulder seams.

Using circular needle and color A, p.u. 96 sts around neck edge.

Starting with st 8, work small moss diamond patt for 13 rows.

Work 2 x 2 rib over next 4 rows in color B.

B.o. all sts.

Sew in sleeves.

Sew side and underarm seams.

LARGE MOSS DIAMOND PATTERN

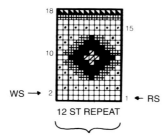

WS → 2   1 ← RS

12 ST REPEAT

SMALL MOSS DIAMOND PATTERN

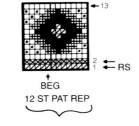

← 13

2 ← RS
1

↑ BEG

12 ST PAT REP

CABLE BOX PATTERN

WS → 1   2 ← RS

10 ST PAT REP

STITCH KEY

☐ = K ON RS, P ON WS

⊟ = P ON RS, K ON WS

▨ = RIGHT TWIST—K 2ND ST, K 1ST ST, SLIP BOTH STS FROM NEEDLE

COLOR KEY

■ = COLOR B, K ON RS, P ON WS

☐ = COLOR C, K ON RS, P ON WS

⊞ = COLOR D, K ON RS, P ON WS

◪ = COLOR E, K ON RS, P ON WS

◙ = COLOR C, P ON RS, K ON WS

◤ = COLOR E, P ON RS, K ON WS

⊠ = COLOR D, P ON RS, K ON WS

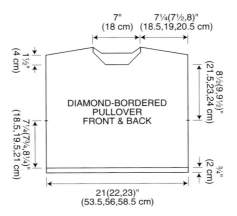

7" (18 cm)   7¼(7½,8)" (18.5,19,20.5 cm)

1½" (4 cm)

8½(9,9½)" (21.5,23,24 cm)

7¼(7¾,8¼)" (18.5,19.5,21 cm)

DIAMOND-BORDERED PULLOVER FRONT & BACK

¾" (2 cm)

21(22,23)" (53.5,56,58.5 cm)

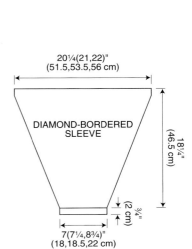

20¼(21,22)" (51.5,53.5,56 cm)

DIAMOND-BORDERED SLEEVE

18¼" (46.5 cm)

¾" (2 cm)

7(7¼,8¾)" (18,18.5,22 cm)

This oversized tunic with side slits has an abundance of textures, both in yarns and stitch work. The pleasing sequence of stripes includes a variety of easy-to-knit stitches such as seed stitch, reverse stockinette stitch, garter stitch, and basketweave. The choice of luxury yarns and fibers makes this a very special pullover.

Design: **Michele Rose**
Knitting rating: **Intermediate**

SIZES

Small(Medium,Large)
Finished measurements: 44(48,52)"
(112,122,132 cm)

MATERIALS

Nature's Palette worsted wool (80% wool, 20% recycled mohair; 100 grams = approx. 190 yards): 2 hanks of color A—#5544; 1 hank of color B—#5542

Diva (29% mohair, 61% cotton, 5% wool, 5% nylon; 50 grams = approx. 60 yards): 3 hanks of color C—#2103; 2 hanks each of colors D—#2128 and E—#2116

Mouton (21% kid mohair, 73% wool, 6% nylon; 50 grams = approx. 51 yards): 1 hank of color F—#4613

Onyx Wool Tweed (40% wool, 40% cotton, 20% polyester; 100 grams = approx. 242 yards): 1 hank of color G—#5570

Equivalent yarn:

Worsted-weight wool: 380 yards/347 meters of color A; 190 yards/174 meters of color B

Bulky mohair: 180 yards/165 meters of color C; 120 yards/110 meters each of colors D and E

Bulky looped mohair: 51 yards/47 meters of color F

Textured novelty worsted-weight wool: 242 yards/221 meters of color G

Knitting needles in size 10 U.S. (6 mm)

16" (40.5 cm) circular needle in size 9 U.S. (5.5 mm)

GAUGE

Stockinette stitch on larger needles: 13 sts and 18 rows = 4" (10 cm)

Take time to save time—check your gauge.

PATTERN STITCHES

(All patt over even number of sts.)

STOCKINETTE STITCH

Row 1: (RS) K all sts.
Row 2: P all sts.

SEED STITCH

Row 1: (RS) * K1, p1, rep from *.
Row 2: * P1, k1, rep from *.

GARTER STITCH

All rows: K all sts.
In the round:
Rnd 1: K all sts.
Rnd 2: P all sts.

REVERSE STOCKINETTE STITCH

Row 1: (RS) P all sts.
Row 2: K all sts.

BASKETWEAVE STITCH

Row 1: (WS) P2, * p next st, wrapping yarn twice around needle, rep from * to last 2 sts, p2.

Row 2: K2, * sl next 4 sts, dropping extra wraps to form 4 long sts, sl same 4 sts to left-hand (LH) needle, insert right-hand (RH) needle purlwise into 3rd and 4th sts and lift these sts tog over first 2 sts, placing them nearest the point of LH needle to be knitted first, then k all 4 sts, rep from *, end k2.

Row 3: P4, rep from * of row 1 to last 4 sts, p4.

Row 4: K4, * sl 4 sts, dropping extra wraps, insert LH needle into 1st and 2nd sts and pass them over 3rd and 4th sts and onto LH needle, sl rem 2 sts back to LH needle, then k all 4 sts, rep from *, end k4.

Repeat rows 1-4.

STRIPED PATTERN

This pattern is a combination of the sts above and is worked repeatedly over entire sweater. Odd rows are WS.

Rows 1 and 2: Color A in seed st.
Row 3: Color B in purl.
Row 4: Color B in knit.
Rows 5-8: Color C in basketweave st.
Rows 9-10: Color A in purl.
Rows 11-12: Color G in purl.
Row 13: Color B in knit.
Row 14: Color B in seed st.
Rows 15-16: Color F in St st.
Rows 17-18: Color C in St st.
Rows 19-20: Color A in garter st.
Rows 21-24: Color D in basketweave st.
Rows 25-26: Color A in garter st.
Rows 27-28: Color E in basketweave st.
Rows 29-32: Color G in rev St st.
Rows 33-35: Color B in seed st.
Row 36: Color C in seed st.
Rows 37-38: Color C in St st.
Rows 39-40: Color A in St st.
Row 41: Color F in St st.
Row 42: Color B in rev St st.
Rows 43-46: Color G in St st.
Rows 47-50: Color A in garter st.
Rows 51-52: Color E in basketweave st.
Rows 53-54: Color B in seed st.
Repeat rows 1-54.

BACK

With color A, c.o. 72(76,84) sts.

Beg working stripe patt.

Work until piece meas 6" (15 cm).

C.o. 2 sts at end of next 2 rows to give 76(80,88) sts.

Cont in patt, working additional 4 sts into est patt until piece meas 28" (71 cm) from beg.

Shape shoulder and neck: B.o. 9(9,11) sts at beg of next 4 rows, b.o. 8(10,10) sts at beg of next 2 rows.

At the same time, b.o. center 14 sts and, working both sides at once, b.o. 3 sts once, 2 sts once from each neck edge.

FRONT

Work same as for back until piece meas

25½" (64.5 cm) from beg, ending on WSR.

Neck shaping: Cont in patt, b.o. center 10 sts and, working both sides at once, b.o. from each neck edge 3 sts once, 2 sts once, 1 st twice.

Cont in est patt until piece meas same as back to shoulder.

Work shoulder shaping as given for back.

SLEEVES

With color A, c.o. 26(32,32) sts.

Beg working stripe patt.

Work sleeve shaping into patt as foll: Inc 1 st each edge every 4th row 18(17,17) times to give 62(66,66) sts.

Work even in patt until piece meas 17(18,18½)" (43,45.5,47 cm) or desired length.

B.o. all sts.

FINISHING

Work side slit trim as foll: On one 6" (15 cm) section at bottom side, with color A, p.u. 20 sts.

Work 2 rows garter st.

B.o. 20 sts.

Rep for other 3 bottom side sections.

Lightly steam all pieces.

Sew shoulder seams.

With circular needle and color A, p.u. 72 sts.

Work 4 rows garter st.

B.o. all sts.

Meas down 9½(10,10)" (24,25.5,25.5 cm) from shoulder seam in front and back.

Sew in sleeves bet markers.

Sew side and sleeve seams, ending side seam 6" (15 cm) up from bottom where garter st trim beg.

Lightly block garment to even out various sts.

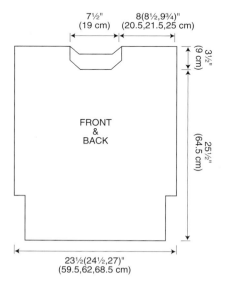

7½"
(19 cm)

8(8½,9¾)"
(20.5,21.5,25 cm)

3½"
(9 cm)

FRONT
&
BACK

25½"
(64.5 cm)

23½(24½,27)"
(59.5,62,68.5 cm)

19(20,20)"
(48.5,51,51 cm)

SLEEVE

17(18,18½)"
(43,45.5,47 cm)

8(8,9)"
(20.5,20.5,23 cm)

Cardigans

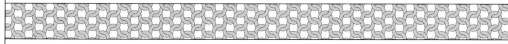

WATCH HILL BUTTONDOWN

Cardigans are versatile garments that quickly become wardrobe favorites. This one is great for men or women and is very easy to knit. A simple moss rib stitch makes up the body of the sweater, and the border is done in a knit and purl diamond pattern that is framed by a row of garter stitch for added interest.

Design: CATHY PAYSON
Knitting rating: INTERMEDIATE

SIZES

Small(Medium,Large)
Finished measurements: 40(44,48)" (101.5,112,122 cm)

MATERIALS

Paisley (50% wool, 50% rayon; 50 grams = approx. 95 yards): 14(15,16) skeins

Equivalent yarn: 1330(1425,1520) yards/1216(1303,1390) of worsted-weight wool

Knitting needles in sizes 4 and 6 U.S. (3.5 and 4 mm)

36" (91.5 cm) circular needle in size 4 U.S. (3.5 mm)

1" (2.5 cm) buttons (6)

GAUGE

Moss diamond pattern on larger needles: 20 sts and 28 rows = 4" (10 cm)
Take time to save time—check your gauge.

PATTERN STITCHES

2 x 2 RIB

(over multiple of 2 sts)
Row 1: K2, p2 across row.
Row 2: Work sts as they appear.

MOSS DIAMOND PATTERN

(over multiple of 18 sts)
See chart.

MOSS RIB

(over multiple of 4 sts)
Row 1: * P1, k3 *, rep bet *'s across row, end p1.
Row 2: K2, * p1, k3 *, rep bet *'s across row, end p1, k2.

BACK

With smaller needles, c.o. 120(130,140) sts.
Work 2 x 2 rib for 3" (7.5 cm).
Change to larger needles and work rows 1-4 of diamond patt, dec 1 st at end of row to give 119(129,139) sts.
Set up row 5 as foll:
Small(Med): K6(2), work 6(7) reps of 18 st patt, k5(1).
Large: Beg at st 3, complete patt, work 7 rep of 18 st patt, ending last rep on st 15.
Complete diamond patt as set to row 32.
P next 2 rows, inc 7 sts evenly across 2nd row to give 126(136,146) sts.
Work moss rib until piece meas 23(24, 25½)" (58.5,61,64.5 cm).
B.o. all sts.

LEFT FRONT

With smaller needles, c.o. 60(66,70) sts.
Work 2 x 2 rib for 3" (7.5 cm).
Change to larger needles and work rows 1-4 of diamond patt, inc 0(1,0) st at end of last row to give 60(67,70) sts.
Set up row 5 as foll:
Small: K6, work 3 reps of 18 st patt.

Med: Beg at st 3, work to end of patt, work 3 reps but end last rep on st 15.

Large: Beg at st 3, work to end of patt, work 3 reps of patt.

Complete 32 row patt as set.

P next 2 rows, inc 3(3,7) sts evenly across last row to give 63(70,77) sts.

Work moss rib until piece meas 9(10,11)" (23,25.5,28 cm).

Shape front: Dec 1 st at neck edge: Small(Med): every 4th row 25(28) times; Large: alt every 3rd then 4th row 15 times (30 dec) to give 38(42,47) sts.

When front meas same as back to shoulders, b.o. all sts.

RIGHT FRONT

Work same as for left front but reverse shapings.

SLEEVES

With smaller needles, c.o. 42(48,52) sts.

Work 2 x 2 rib for 3" (7.5 cm), inc 0(1,0) sts across last row to give 42(49, 52) sts.

Beg working moss rib, inc 1 st in patt on each end every other row 24(23,24) times to give 90(95,100) sts.

When piece meas 16(17,18)" (40.5,43, 45.5 cm), b.o. all sts.

FINISHING

Sew shoulder seams.

With circular needle, p.u. 350(354,358) sts along right front, back neck, and left front.

Work 2 x 2 rib for 3 rows.

In next row, make 6 buttonholes on left side (for man's sweater), evenly spaced bet bottom and beg of V-neck shaping.

Make buttonholes by yo, k2tog.

Work 2 x 2 rib for 3 more rows and b.o. all sts.

Meas down 8½(9,9½)" (21.5,23,24 cm) in front and back.

Sew sleeve bet points.

Sew side and underarm seams.

Sew on buttons.

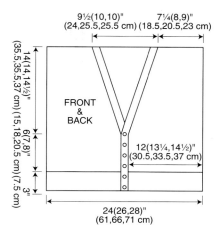

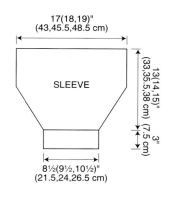

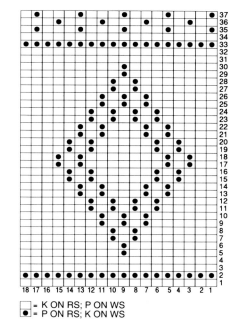

= K ON RS; P ON WS
= P ON RS; K ON WS

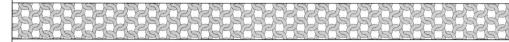

TARTAN TRELLIS

Art nouveau graphic designs by E. A. Seguy inspired this dramatic cardigan, which is worked in a mercerized cotton yarn. The square-cut sleeves, deep rib, and scooped neck give this sweater a nontraditional look. Bobbles and fringed ties add interest to an intarsia design.

Design: **Sally Lee**
Knitting rating: **Very challenging**

Sizes

Small(Medium,Large)
Finished measurements: 36(40,44)" (91.5,101.5,112 cm), including 3" (7.5 cm) front band

Materials

Newport Light (100% cotton; 50 grams = approx. 93 yards): 5 hanks of colors A—#3351, E—#3322, and H—#3310; 4 hanks of colors B—#3347 and C—#3320; 2 hanks of color D—#3372; 6 hanks of color F (MC)—#3381; 3 hanks of color G—#3316

Equivalent yarn: 465 yards/426 meters of worsted-weight mercerized cotton in colors A, E, and H; 372 yards/340 meters of colors B and C; 186 yards/170 meters of color D; 558 yards/510 meters of color F; 279 yards/255 meters of color G

Knitting needles in sizes 4 and 6 U.S. (3.5 and 4 mm)

1⅛" (2.9 cm) buttons (4)

Gauge

Stockinette stitch on larger needles: 20 sts and 28 rows = 4" (10 cm)

Take time to save time—check your gauge.

Pattern Stitches

Stockinette Stitch

Row 1: (RS) K all sts.
Row 2: P all sts.

3 x 3 Ribbing

Row 1: (RS) K3, p3 across.
Row 2: Work sts as they appear.
Repeat rows 1-2.

Moss Stitch

Row 1: * K1, p1 *, rep bet *'s.
Row 2: * P1, k1 *, rep bet *'s.
Repeat rows 1-2.

Make Bobble (MB)

Using color A worked double, (k1, yo, k1, yo, k1) in 1 st, making 5 sts from 1, turn and k5, turn and p5, turn and (k1, sl1, k2tog, psso, k1), turn and p3tog, completing bobble.

Make Mini-Bobble (MMB)

K into front and back of same stitch 3 times; then pass 1st 5 of these sts over last made st and off needle.

Note: MB on body is worked in doubled color A. MMB on body is worked in single color G. MB on sleeve is worked in single color B.

Pocket Backs

Make 2.
With larger needles and MC, c.o. 24 sts.
Work in St st for 10" (25.5 cm).
Place sts on holder.

Body

Body is made in one piece.
With smaller needles and MC, c.o. 189(207,231) sts.
Work in 3 x 3 ribbing for 6½(7,7½)" (16.5,18,19 cm).
In last row (RS, pocket row) work 9 sts, place next 24 sts on holder, work 24 sts of pocket back, work across dec 3(1,5) sts, until 33 sts rem; then place next 24 sts on holder, work 24 sts of pocket back, work last 9 sts, for a total of 186(206,226) sts.
Next row: Change to larger needles and work across in St st, foll graph for color and st changes.
Work as est until graph is completed.
B.o. all sts.

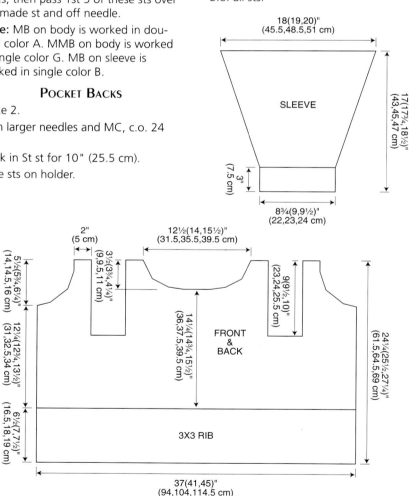

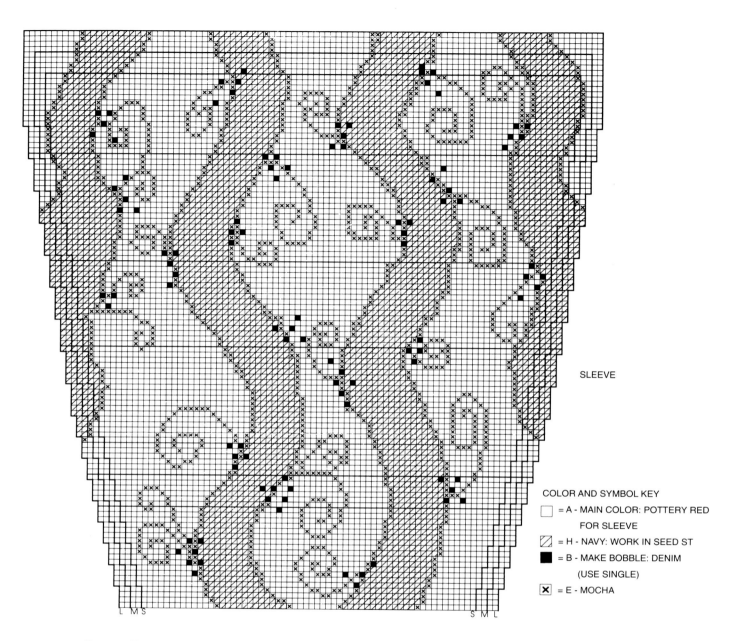

SLEEVE

COLOR AND SYMBOL KEY

☐ = A - MAIN COLOR: POTTERY RED
    FOR SLEEVE

▨ = H - NAVY: WORK IN SEED ST

■ = B - MAKE BOBBLE: DENIM
    (USE SINGLE)

☒ = E - MOCHA

L M S   S M L

POCKET TOPS

With smaller needles and MC, p.u. the 24 sts from holders and work in 3 x 3 rib for 1" (2.5 cm).

B.o. all sts.

SLEEVES

With smaller needles and MC, c.o. 60(64,68) sts.

Work in 2 x 2 ribbing for 3" (7.5 cm).

Change to larger needles and work in St st, foll graph for inc, color, and st changes.

Work as est until graph is completed.

B.o. all sts.

FINISHING

Sew shoulder seams.

Set in sleeves.

Sew sleeve seams.

With smaller needles and MC, p.u. 78(94,110) sts around neck edges and work in 2 x 2 ribbing for 3" (7.5 cm).

B.o. all sts.

With smaller needles, MC and RS facing, beg at bottom right side, p.u. 96(100,104) sts along front band.

Work 2 x 2 rib for 8 rows.

Row 9: Beg at top, work 8(6,8) sts, k2tog, yo, * work 16(18,18) sts, k2tog, yo *, rep bet *'s 3 times, work to end in 2 x 2 rib.

Work 2 x 2 rib patt for 7 more rows.

B.o. all sts.

Work left band same as right band, omitting buttonholes.

Fold pockets up and attach on the inside, 1" (2.5 cm) below ending of rib.

Sew side seams together.

Sew buttons on right band.

Stitch pocket top down carefully.

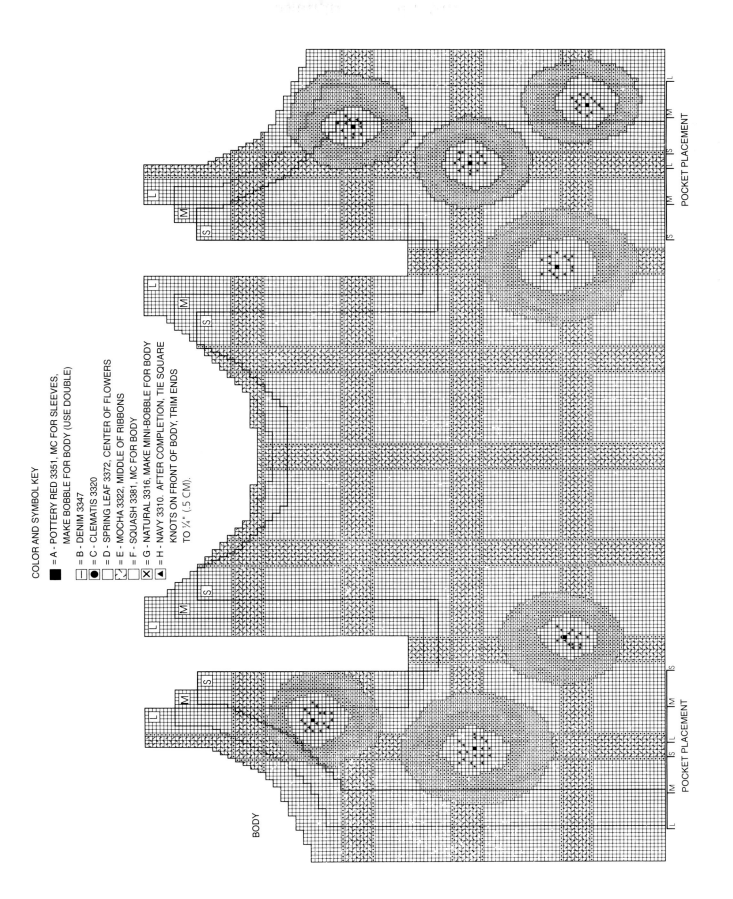

COLOR AND SYMBOL KEY

■ = A - POTTERY RED 3351, MC FOR SLEEVES,
    MAKE BOBBLE FOR BODY (USE DOUBLE)

▯ = B - DENIM 3347

● = C - CLEMATIS 3320

▱ = D - SPRING LEAF 3372, CENTER OF FLOWERS

◪ = E - MOCHA 3322, MIDDLE OF RIBBONS

▨ = F - SQUASH 3381, MC FOR BODY

✕ = G - NATURAL 3316, MAKE MINI-BOBBLE FOR BODY

◣ = H - NAVY 3310. AFTER COMPLETION, TIE SQUARE
    KNOTS ON FRONT OF BODY, TRIM ENDS
    TO ¼" (.5 CM).

BODY

POCKET PLACEMENT

POCKET PLACEMENT

Little Miss Riding Hood & Friend

Two strands of mohair are used in these quick-knitting warm, hooded coats for women and children. Simple garter stitch is used throughout, with contrasting colors used for the edgings. The child's coat flares at the base, which makes it the perfect choice to wear over a smocked dress all winter long.

Design: **Julie Hoff**
Knitting rating: **Intermediate**

Sizes

Adult's Small(Medium,Large) <Child's 4-5(6-7,8-9)>
Finished measurements: 46(50,54)" (117,127,137 cm), <28(32,36)" (71,81.5,91.5 cm)>

Materials

La Gran (74% mohair, 13% wool, 13% nylon; 1½ oz. = approx. 90 yards): 30(30,31) <14(15,16)> balls of main color (MC)—#504 <#585>; 2 <2(2,3)> balls of color B—#513 <#595>; <1> ball of color C—#557

Equivalent yarn: 2700(2700,2790) yards/2468(2468,2551) meters <1260(1350,1440) yards/1152(1234, 1317) meters> of bulky brushed mohair in main color, 180 yards/165 meters <180(180,270) yards/165(165,247)> of color B, and <90 yards/83 meters> of color C

Knitting needles in size 11 U.S. (8 mm)
Crochet hook in size 10 U.S. (6 mm)
1½" (4 cm) painted buttons for child's coat (5)
1¼" (3 cm) Pueblo buttons for adult's coat (5 #B105 and 4 #B104)

Gauge

Garter stitch, using two strands of yarn held together: 12 sts and 20 rows = 4" (10 cm)
Take time to save time—check your gauge.

Pattern Stitches

Garter Stitch
K every row.

Stockinette Stitch
Row 1: (RS) K all sts.
Row 2: P all sts.

Child's Coat

Back
With two strands of MC held tog, c.o. 68(78,88) sts.
Work in garter stitch (first row is WSR) for 2½" (6.5 cm).
Next row (RS): k1, k2tog, work to last 3 sts, k2tog, k1.
Rep dec on RS every 3(2½,2½)" (7.5,6.5,6.5 cm) 3(4,5) times more to give 60(68,76) sts.
Work straight until piece meas 13(14½, 16)" (33,37,40.5 cm).
On RS row; k3(4,5) sts, * k2tog, k1.
Rep from * 17(19,21) times, end k3(4,5) to give 42(48,54) sts.
Cont as est until piece meas 20(22,24)" (51,56,61 cm).
B.o. all sts.

Right Front
With two strands MC held tog, c.o. 35(40,45) sts.
Work in garter st, sl 1st st of each RS row with yarn in front (wyif) (button band edge) throughout all of coat front.
When piece meas 2½" (6.5 cm) on RS, knit until 3 sts rem, k2tog, k1.
Rep this row every 3(2½,2½)" (7.5,6.5, 6.5 cm) 3(4,5) times more to give 31(35,39) sts.
When piece meas 13(14½,16)" (33,37, 40.5 cm) on RS, work 3(4,5) sts, * k2tog, k1.
Repeat from * 8(9,10) times, end k1 to give 22(25,28) sts.

Work as est until piece meas 17½(19½, 21½)" (44.5,49.5,54.5 cm).
At beg of next RSR, b.o. 3 sts, then at beg of next neck edge 2 sts 0(1,2) times, then 1 st 3(2,1) times to give 16(18,20) sts.
When piece meas same as back, b.o. rem sts.

Left Front
Work as for right front, reversing all shaping and sl 1 st at beg of WS rows wyif.

Sleeves
With two strands of MC held tog, c.o. 29(31,33) sts.
Work in garter st, inc 1 st each edge when piece meas 7, 9 and 11 (7, 9 and 11; 7, 9½ and 12)" (18, 23, and 28; 18, 23, and 28; 18, 24, and 30.5 cm) to give 35(37,39) sts.
Work even until sleeve meas 12(12½, 13)" (30.5,31.5,33 cm).
B.o. all sts.

Hood
With 2 strands of MC held tog, c.o. 21(22,23) sts.
Sl first st of row wyif on right edge throughout hood.
Work in garter st, inc on left edge 1 st every 2½(2½,2¾)" (6.5,6.5,7 cm) 3 times to give 24(25,26) sts.
When piece meas 10(10½,11)" (25.5,26.5,28 cm), beg dec on left edge.
Dec 1 st every 2½(2½,2¾)" (6.5,6.5,7 cm) 3 times to give 21(22,23) sts.
Cont until piece meas 20(21,22)" (51,53.5,56 cm).
B.o. all sts.
See Finishing on page 108.

Adult's Coat

Back
With 2 strands MC held tog, c.o. 69(75,81) sts.
Work garter st until piece meas 17(18, 19)" (43,45.5,48.5 cm).

Shape armholes: B.o. 2 sts at beg next 4 rows, then 1 st at beg next 6 rows to give 55(61,67) sts.

Cont in garter st until piece meas 27(28,29)" (68.5,71,73.5 cm).

B.o. 6(7,8) sts at beg of next 6 rows, then b.o. rem 19 sts.

Continue in est patt until piece meas 28(29,30)" (71,73.5,76 cm).

B.o. all sts.

POCKET BACKS

Make 2.

With 2 strands MC held tog, c.o. 18 sts.

Work in St st for 7" (18 cm).

Place sts on holder.

LEFT FRONT

With 2 strands MC held tog, c.o. 38(41, 44) sts.

Work in garter st, sl 1st st of each WSR wyif (button band edge).

When piece meas 10" (25.5 cm) ending with a WSR, place pockets.

On next row work 10(12,13) sts, b.o. next 18 sts, work to end.

On next row work to bound off sts, k 18 sts from holder, work to end.

Cont as est until piece meas 17(18,19)" (43,45.5,48.5 cm).

Shape armhole: B.o. on armhole edge 2 sts twice and 1 st 3 times.

Cont until piece meas 2½" (6.5 cm) less than back.

Shape neck: B. o. 6 sts at neck edge once.

B.o. at neck edge 2 sts 3 times, 1 st once and, **at the same time,** when front meas same as back to shoulder, b.o. 6(7,8) sts on shoulder edge 3 times.

RIGHT FRONT

Work as for left front, reversing all shaping and position of pockets and sl 1st st wyif of each RSR.

At same time, work buttonholes on RS as follows: When piece meas ¾(1¼, 1¾)" (2,3,4.5 cm), b.o. the 3rd and 4th sts.

On next row, c.o. 2 sts over bound off sts.

Work buttonholes every 3" (7.5 cm) for a total of 9 buttonholes.

SLEEVES

With 2 strands of MC held tog, c.o. 32(34,36) sts.

Work in garter st for 5¾" (14.5 cm).

On RS inc 1 st each edge every 4th row 15(10,5) times and every 6th row 0(4,8) times to give 62 sts.

When piece meas 17¾(18¾,19¾)" (45, 47.5,50 cm), **shape top sleeve:** B.o. 2 sts at beg of next 4 rows, then 1 st at beg of next 6 rows.

B.o. rem 48 sts.

HOOD

With 2 strands of MC held tog, c.o. 29 sts.

Sl 1st st of row wyif on right edge throughout hood.

Work in garter st, inc on left edge 1 st every 2½" (6.5 cm) 5 times to give 34 sts.

When piece meas 15" (38 cm), beg dec on left edge 1 st every 2½" (6.5 cm) 5 times to give 29 sts.

Cont until piece meas 30" (76 cm).

B.o. all sts.

FINISHING

Gently block all pieces.

Sew shoulder seams.

Sew sleeves to body.

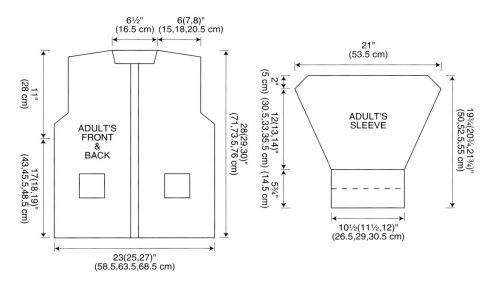

6½"
(16.5 cm)

6(7,8)"
(15,18,20.5 cm)

11"
(28 cm)

ADULT'S
FRONT
&
BACK

17(18,19)"
(43,45.5,48.5 cm)

28(29,30)"
(71,73.5,76 cm)

23(25,27)"
(58.5,63.5,68.5 cm)

21"
(53.5 cm)

ADULT'S
SLEEVE

2"
(5 cm)

12(13,14)"
(30.5,33,35.5 cm)

5¾"
(14.5 cm)

19¾(20¾,21¾)"
(50,52.5,55 cm)

10½(11½,12)"
(26.5,29,30.5 cm)

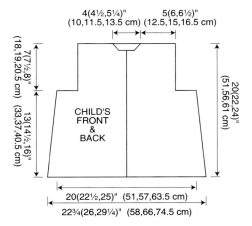

4(4½,5¼)"
(10,11.5,13.5 cm)

5(6,6½)"
(12.5,15,16.5 cm)

7(7½,8)"
(18,19,20.5 cm)

CHILD'S
FRONT
&
BACK

13(14½,16)"
(33,37,40.5 cm)

20(22,24)"
(51,56,61 cm)

20(22½,25)" (51,57,63.5 cm)

22¾(26,29¼)" (58,66,74.5 cm)

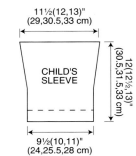

11½(12,13)"
(29,30.5,33 cm)

CHILD'S
SLEEVE

12(12½,13)"
(30.5,31.5,33 cm)

9½(10,11)"
(24,25.5,28 cm)

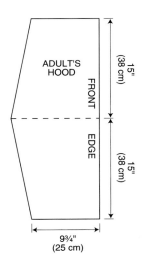

ADULT'S
HOOD

FRONT

EDGE

15"
(38 cm)

15"
(38 cm)

9¾"
(25 cm)

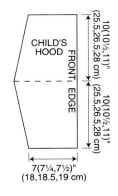

CHILD'S
HOOD

FRONT EDGE

10(10½,11)"
(25.5,26.5,28 cm)

10(10½,11)"
(25.5,26.5,28 cm)

7(7¼,7½)"
(18,18.5,19 cm)

Sew sleeve seams allowing 4½" (11.5 cm) <3" (7.5 cm)> for cuff.

(Make cuff by leaving seam on the outside of first 4½" <3"> of sleeve).

Sew side seams.

Fold hood in half and sew back seam.

Sew hood to neckline, matching center backs.

With crochet hook and 2 strands B, work double crochet into each st around entire edge of coat, beg at lower left back.

Work a single chain before and after each corner st.

Child's version: With B and C, make pompons and attach to hood with crocheted cord (using single strand of yarn).

With single strand of C, make 3 crochet cords for button loops of required length.

Sew evenly spaced in upper 7(7½,8)" (18,19,20.5 cm) of right front.

Sew on buttons opposite loops.

Adult's version: With 2 strands B and crochet hook, work double crochet into each st across pocket top.

Sew on buttons.

DOWN AT THE O.K. CORRAL

Bicolored intarsia diamond motifs frame the edges of this man's or woman's cardigan and are echoed in knit and purl textured stitches around the inner borders of the sweater. The cardigan opening is bound using a traditional hemmed technique, which gives a firm, durable cardigan edging. Double buttonholes are whipped together upon completion.

Design: **Kristin Nicholas**
Knitting rating: **Experienced**

SIZES

Small(Medium,Large,Extra Large)
Finished measurements: 40¼(43½,46¾, 50)" (102,110.5,118.5,127 cm)

MATERIALS

Montera (50% llama, 50% wool, 100 grams = approx. 127 yards): 9(10,10, 11) hanks of main color (MC) and 1 hank each of colors A and B
Equivalent yarn: 1143(1270,1270,1397) yards/1045(1161,1161,1277) meters of bulky wool in main color and 127 yards/ 117 meters each of colors A and B
Knitting needles in sizes 5 and 7 U.S. (3.75 and 4.5 mm)
29" (73.5 cm) circular needles in sizes 5 and 7 U.S. (3.75 and 4.5 mm)
⅝" (1.6 cm) buttons (7)

GAUGE

Stockinette stitch on larger needles: 17 sts and 24 rows = 4" (10 cm)
Take time to save time—check your gauge.

PATTERN STITCHES

2 x 2 Rib
(over multiple of 4 + 2)
Row 1: (RS) * K2, p2 *, rep bet *'s, end k2.

Row 2: * P2, k2 *, rep bet *'s, end p2.

FRONT AND BACK

Note: Front and back are knit together in one piece and then split for armholes.
With smaller circular needle and color A, c.o. 162(174,190,202) sts.
Work in 2 x 2 rib for 1" (2.5 cm), ending with a WSR.
K 1 row in color A, inc 9(11,9,11) sts evenly across to give 171(185,199,213) sts.
Change to larger needles and beg chart using MC.
Start at left side of chart on WSR.
Work in St st and beg patt on row 4 on RS.
Work sts 1-20, work 14 st repeat 9(10, 11,12) times; then work last 25 sts of chart.
Work diamonds in intarsia not in Fair Isle technique, as yarn requirements are for intarsia.
Work diamonds in both intarsia and knit/purl sts going up center front.
When piece meas 15(15½,16½,17)" (38,39.5,42,43 cm), split body for armholes.
Work 42(45,49,53) sts and sl to holder; work center 87(95,101,107) sts; sl rem 42(45,49,53) sts to holder.
Back: Dec for armholes: B.o. 1 st at beg of next 8 rows to give 79(87,93,99) sts.
Work straight until piece meas 24(25, 26,27)" (61,63.5,66,68.5 cm) incl rib.
B.o. all sts.

RIGHT FRONT

Place sts on needles so that RSR will be first row.
Work 1 RSR.
Then b.o. 1 st at armhole edge every other WSR 4 times to give 38(41,45,49) sts.
When piece meas 18(19,20,21)" (45.5, 48.5,51,53.5 cm), **shape V-neck:**
For decrease on RSR: K5, ssk (Sl the 1st and 2nd sts one at a time as if to k; then insert point of left-hand needle into fronts of these 2 sts and k them tog).

K to end of row.
Stop working diamond motif when next motif is complete.
Dec 1 st every 2nd row 0(0,4,6) times, then 3 sts every 4th row 8(9,7,6) times to give 30(32,34,37) sts.
When piece meas same as back, b.o. all sts.

LEFT FRONT

Work same as for right front, reversing shaping.
For V-neck shaping, work dec on RS as foll: K across until 7 sts from end, k2tog, k5.

SLEEVES

With color A and smaller needles, c.o. 38(38,40,44) sts.
Work in 2 x 2 rib for 1" (2.5 cm), ending with a WSR.
K 1 row in color A, inc 2(4,4,2) sts evenly across to give 40(42,44,46) sts.
Change to larger needles and work in St st in MC, centering sleeve patt chart around bottom of wrist.

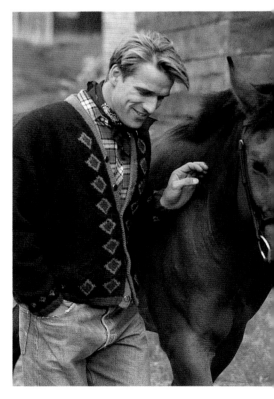

BODY INTARSIA PATTERN

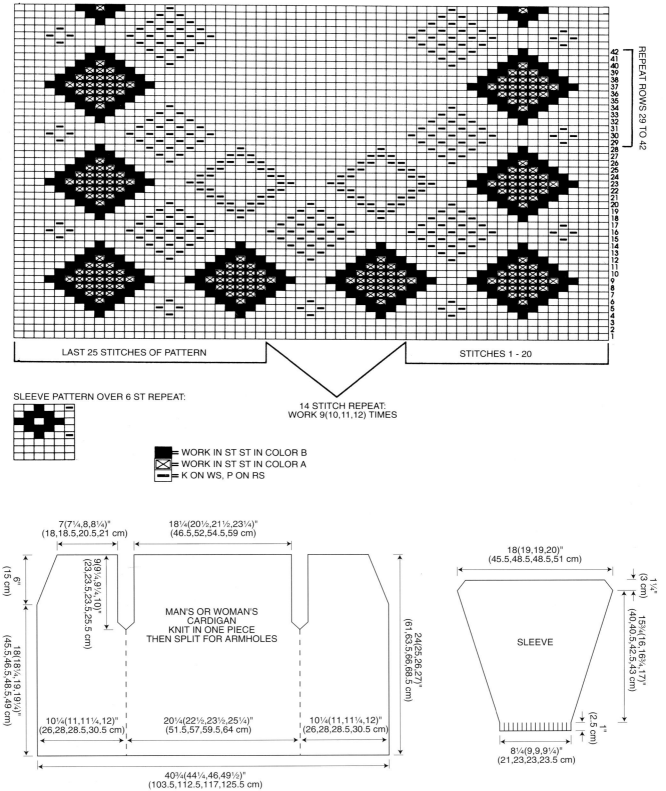

LAST 25 STITCHES OF PATTERN

STITCHES 1 - 20

14 STITCH REPEAT:
WORK 9(10,11,12) TIMES

SLEEVE PATTERN OVER 6 ST REPEAT:

■ = WORK IN ST ST IN COLOR B
⊠ = WORK IN ST ST IN COLOR A
▬ = K ON WS, P ON RS

7(7¼,8,8¼)"
(18,18.5,20.5,21 cm)

18¼(20½,21½,23¼)"
(46.5,52,54.5,59 cm)

6"
(15 cm)

9(9¼,9¼,10)"
(23,23.5,23.5,25.5 cm)

MAN'S OR WOMAN'S
CARDIGAN
KNIT IN ONE PIECE
THEN SPLIT FOR ARMHOLES

18(18¼,19,19¼)"
(45.5,46.5,48.5,49 cm)

24(25,26,27)"
(61,63.5,66,68.5 cm)

10¼(11,11¼,12)"
(26,28,28.5,30.5 cm)

20¼(22½,23½,25¼)"
(51.5,57,59.5,64 cm)

10¼(11,11¼,12)"
(26,28,28.5,30.5 cm)

40¾(44¼,46,49½)"
(103.5,112.5,117,125.5 cm)

18(19,19,20)"
(45.5,48.5,48.5,51 cm)

1¼"
(3 cm)

15¾(16,16¾,17)"
(40,40.5,42.5,43 cm)

SLEEVE

1"
(2.5 cm)

8¼(9,9,9¼)"
(21,23,23,23.5 cm)

At the same time, inc 1 st each end every 5th row 20(21,21,22) times to give 80(84,86,90) sts.

When piece meas 18(18½,19,19½)" (45.5,47,48.5,49.5 cm) incl rib, **shape sleeve cap.**

B.o. 1 st every row 8 times to give 72 (76,78,82) sts.

B.o. all sts.

FINISHING

Sew shoulder and underarm seams.

Sew sleeve into armhole.

Mark buttonhole placement for 7 buttons on sweater front.

Mark 7 buttonholes on left side for man's sweater, on right side for woman's sweater.

With color C and RS facing, p.u. 84(88, 93,97) sts from bottom edge to beg of V-neck shaping, 15(15,17,17) sts to shoulder, 24(24,26,26) sts at back of neck, 15(15,17,17) sts to next V-neck shaping, and 84(88,93,97) sts to bottom edge.

Work band as foll: In St st, work 1 row.

Work buttonholes where marked on body of sweater as foll: When a marker is reached, b.o. 2 sts, work in St st to next marker, work another buttonhole.

Next row, c.o. 2 sts over bound off sts.

Next row, complete buttonholes by inc 2 above b.o. sts.

Work 3 rows in St st.

P 1 row (RS).

Work 3 rows in St st.

Work buttonholes to correspond with other buttonholes on next row.

Finish buttonholes on next row.

Work 1 row in St st.

B.o. all sts.

Fold band in half and sew down.

Whip stitch around buttonholes, sewing the two layers together.

Sew on buttons.

SIZES

Small(Medium,Large)
Finished measurements: 40(42,44)"
(101.5,106.5,112 cm)

MATERIALS

La Gran (74% mohair, 13% wool, 13% nylon; 1½ oz. = 90 yards): 3 balls of color A—#513 Black; 4 balls each of colors B—#542 Vienna Waltz, C—#584 Warmed Saffron, D—#548 Slate, and E—#582 Peach Blossom

Equivalent yarn: 270 yards/247 meters of bulky brushed mohair in color A and 360 yards/330 meters each of colors B, C, D, and E

Knitting needles in sizes 6 and 9 U.S. (4 and 5.5 mm)

Long circular needle in size 6 U.S. (4 mm)

Stitch holders (4)

GAUGE

Chart pattern on larger needles: 4 sts and 5 rows = 1" (2.5 cm)

Take time to save time—check your gauge.

PATTERN STITCHES

1 x 1 RIB

(over odd number)
Row 1: * K1, p1 *, rep bet *'s, end k1.

Row 2 and all following rows: Work sts as they appear.

STOCKINETTE STITCH

Row 1: (RS) K all sts.
Row 2: P all sts.

POCKET BACKS

Make 2.
With larger needles and color D, c.o. 20 sts and work in St st for 25 rows.
Place sts on holder.

BODY

Make in one piece.
With color A and smaller needles, c.o. 161(169,177) sts.

Work 1 x 1 rib in striped sequence as foll: A D C B E A D B A C E D for 3" (7.5 cm), changing colors every row.

Change to larger needles and work in St st, following the chart for color changes.

In 1st row, place markers for side seams as foll: Work 40(42,44) sts, place marker, work 81(85,89) sts, place marker, work 40(42,44) sts.

Work according to chart for 30(32,34) rows; then place pockets.

Work 19(20,21) sts, place next 20 sts on holder, work until 39(40,41) sts rem,

place next 20 sts on holder, work to end.

On the next row, insert pocket backs as foll: sl the 20 sts from pocket back in place of sweater sts now on holder; then knit them.

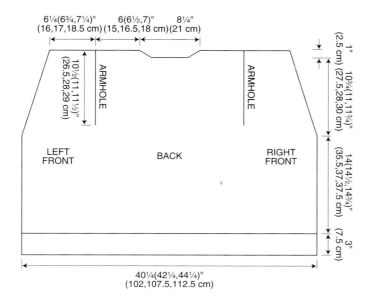

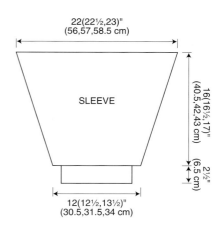

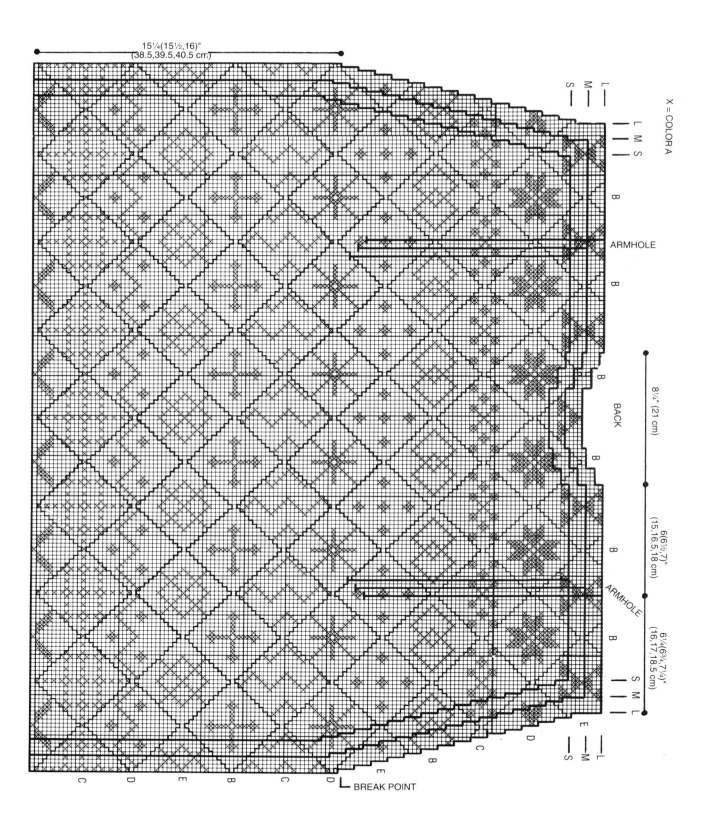

X = COLOR A

15¼(15½,16)"
(38.5,39.5,40.5 cm.)

L
M
S

L M S

B

ARMHOLE

B

8¼" (21 cm)

B

BACK

B

6(6½,7)"
(15,16.5,18 cm)

B

ARMHOLE

B

6¼(6¾,7¼)"
(16,17,18.5 cm)

S M L

L
M
S

C

D

E

B

C

D

E

B

C

D

E

BREAK POINT

Cont until 70(72,74) rows have been worked.

Begin front neck shaping by dec 1 st at each front edge on next and every following 4th row 15 times.

At the same time, when row 76(78, 80) has been worked, divide piece for armholes on next row as foll: Work across 38(40,42) sts; change to 2nd ball of yarn and work across 81(85,89) sts for back; change to third ball of yarn and work across rem 38(40,42) sts.

When row 123(127,131) has been worked, shape back neck on next row as foll: B.o. center 15 sts.

At each neck edge, b.o. 5 sts once, 4 sts once.

When chart has been completed, b.o. all sts.

SLEEVES

With color A and smaller needles, c.o. 33(35,37) sts.

Work 1 x 1 rib in striped sequence for 2½" (6.5 cm), inc 15(15,17) sts evenly spaced across last row to give 48(50,54) sts.

Change to larger needles and work rev St st in striped sequence as for rib, inc 1 st each end every other row 0(0,4) times, then every 4th row 20 times (all sizes) to give 88(90,92) sts.

When sleeve meas 18½(19,19½)" (47,48.5,49.5 cm), b.o. all sts.

FINISHING

Sew shoulder and sleeve seams.

Set in sleeves.

With RS facing, using circular needle and color A, p.u. 81(83,85) sts from bottom to V-neck shaping, 63(65,67) sts along front neck edge, 28 sts from back of neck, 63(65,67) sts along left front neck, and 81(83,85) sts along left front to bottom of sweater, giving a total of 316(324,332) sts.

Work 1 x 1 rib in stripe patt for 4 rows, changing colors as for previous ribs.

Buttonhole row: On RS, work 5 sts, b.o. 2 sts, * work 17 sts, b.o. 2 sts *; rep bet *'s 4 more times to give 5 buttonholes, ending at beg of V-neck shaping.

On the next row, make 2 sts where they were b.o. in the previous row to form buttonholes.

Cont 1 x 1 rib until 8 rows have been completed.

B.o. all sts.

Sew on 5 buttons.

Pocket tops: Sl sts from holder onto smaller needle.

Work 1 row each in rib with colors as foll: D C E A.

B.o. in rib.

Sew down ends.

Shoulder pads: With larger needles and color E, c.o. 24 sts and work in St st for 6" (15 cm).

B.o.

Fold into triangle and pad with piece of foam.

Sew edges.

Tack in place.

POMO SPICE

Textile designers all over the world derive inspiration from the American southwest. In this cardigan, a number of designs indicative of the region—cactus, chile peppers, and floral motifs—are rendered in brilliant, sun-filled colors. Buttons crocheted in a swirl design provide a clever finish to the edges. In technique this cardigan is a traditional Fair Isle pattern, but the bright palette gives it a festive, contemporary flair.

Design: **Michele Rose**
Knitting rating: **Very challenging**

SIZES

Small(Medium,Large)
Finished measurements: 44(46,48)" (112,117,122 cm)

MATERIALS

Regatta (100% cotton; 50 grams = approx. 123 yards): 3 hanks of color A—#3013; 1 hank of color B—#3001; 2 hanks of color C—#3030

Newport Light (100% mercerized cotton; 50 grams = approx. 93 yards): 6 skeins of color D—#3350; 3 skeins of color E—#3317; 2 skeins each of colors F—#3346 and G—#3308; 5 skeins of color H—#3358

Metro (100% rayon; 50 grams = approx. 110 yards), 1 hank of color I—#4002

Equivalent yarn: 369 yards/338 meters of sport-weight mercerized cotton in color A, 123 yards/113 meters of color B, 246 yards/225 meters of color C, 558 yards/510 meters of color D, 279 yards/255 meters of color E, 186 yards/170 meters of color F, 186 yards/170 meters of color G, 465 yards/425 meters of color H, 110 yards/101 meters of sport-weight space-dyed rayon in color I

Knitting needles in sizes 4 and 6 U.S. (3.5 and 4 mm)
#1 (2.5 mm) steel crochet hook
Black and white crocheted buttons (5); directions at end of pattern

GAUGE

Stockinette stitch on larger needles: 24 sts and 34 rows = 4" (10 cm)
Take time to save time—check your gauge.

PATTERN STITCHES

STOCKINETTE STITCH

Row 1: (RS) K all sts.
Row 2: P all sts.

REVERSE STOCKINETTE STITCH

Row 1: (RS) P all sts.
Row 2: K all sts.

2 x 2 RIBBING

Row 1: K2, p2.
Row 2: Work sts as they appear.

Note: Matching row gauge is very important! Matching stitch gauge is very, very important!

BACK

With smaller needles and color A, c.o. 130(138,142) sts.

Work in 2 x 2 ribbing for 2 rows.

Next RS row, change to 2-color ribbing as foll: K2 in color B, p2 in color A.

Cont for 4 rows.

Next RS row, work 2 x 2 ribbing in color B for 2 rows, inc 3(1,3) sts on last row to give 133(139,145) sts.

Next RS row, change to larger needles and beg working Fair Isle patt, beg and end as indicated.

Work in patt until piece meas 20" (51 cm) from beg.

Next RS row, beg shoulder and neck shaping: B.o. 16(17,18) sts at beg of next 6 rows.

At same time, b.o. center 27 sts and, working each side sep, b.o. from each neck edge 3 sts once, then 2 sts once. B.o. all sts.

RIGHT FRONT

With smaller needles and color A, c.o. 62(66,70) sts.

Work ribbing as for back, inc 1(0,dec 1) in last row.

Next RS row, change to larger needles and beg Fair Isle patt beg and ending as indicated on chart.

Work in patt until piece meas 17¾" (45 cm) from beg.

In next RS row, beg neck shaping as foll: At beg of next 8 RS rows, b.o. 4 sts once, 3 sts once, 2 sts twice, and 1 st 4 times.

Work until piece meas same as back to shoulder.

Shape shoulder: B.o. 16(17,18) sts at beg of next 3 WS rows.

LEFT FRONT

Work as for right front, rev shaping.

SLEEVES

With smaller needles and color A, c.o. 46(46,50) sts.

Work in 2 x 2 rib as for back, inc 1(3,1) sts in last row to give 47(49,51) sts.

Next RS row, change to larger needles and work according to chart, beg and end as indicated.

At the same time, work sleeve shaping into patt as foll: inc 1 st each end on 1st row, then every 4th row 35(37, 39) times to give 117(123,129) sts.

Work even until piece meas 18½(19, 19½)" (47,48.5,49.5 cm) from beg.

B.o. all sts.

FINISHING

Lightly block all pieces.

Sew shoulder seams.

Work right placket as foll: With RS facing, smaller needles and color B, p.u. 106 sts along right front edge.

Work 2 x 2 rib for 2 rows, then 2-color 2 x 2 rib for 2 rows.

Next RS row (row 5), work 4 sts, b.o. 4 sts, (work 22 sts, b.o. 4 sts) 3 times, work 20 sts.

Next row, work as est and c.o. 4 sts over b.o. sts on previous row.

In color A, work 2 x 2 rib for 2 more rows.

B.o. 106 sts with color A.

Work left placket same way, but omit buttonholes.

With smaller needles and color B, p.u. 90 sts around neck.

Work 6 rows 2 x 2 rib same as for plackets.

Next RS row (row 7), work 2 sts, b.o. 4 sts, work to end.

Next row, work as est and c.o. 4 sts over b.o. sts on previous row.

Work 2 x 2 rib in color A for 2 more rows.

B.o. all sts.

Meas and mark 9½(10,10½)" (24,25.5, 26.5 cm) down from shoulder seam on front and back.

Set in sleeves bet markers.

Sew side and sleeve seams.

Work in and tie off all loose ends.

Buttons

Make 5

Rnd 1: With crochet hook and color A, chain 6, join to form rnd.

Rnd 2: With color B, work 2 single crochet (sc) in each sc around.

Rnd 3: With color A, * work 2 sc in next sc, work 1 sc *, rep bet *'s (18 sc).

Rnd 4: With color B, * work 2 sc in next sc, work 2 sc *, rep bet *'s (24 sc).

Rnd 5: With color A, work 24 sc.

Rnd 6: With color B, * skip 1 sc, work 3 sc *, rep bet *'s (18 sc).

Rnd 7: With color A, * skip 1 sc, work 2 sc *, rep bet *'s (12 sc).

Rnd 8: With color B, * skip 1 sc, work 1 sc *, rep bet *'s (6 sc).

Cut yarn.

Flatten piece so rnd 5 is at outer edge and rnds 1 and 8 are at center; pull loose ends from rnd 1 through to center back and tie off with loose ends from rnd 8 to form button shank.

Sew on buttons.

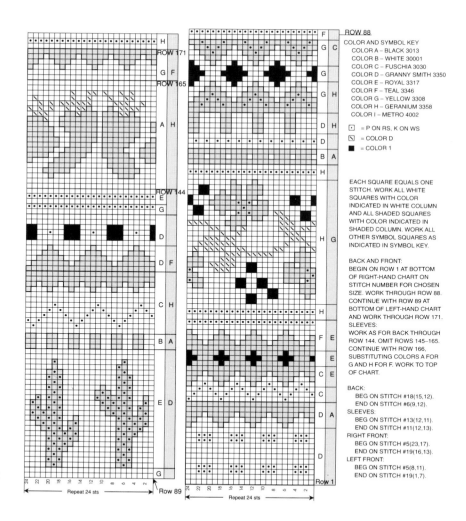

ROW 88

COLOR AND SYMBOL KEY
COLOR A – BLACK 3013
COLOR B – WHITE 30001
COLOR C – FUSCHIA 3030
COLOR D – GRANNY SMITH 3350
COLOR E – ROYAL 3317
COLOR F – TEAL 3346
COLOR G – YELLOW 3308
COLOR H – GERANIUM 3358
COLOR I – METRO 4002

□ = P ON RS, K ON WS

◩ = COLOR D

■ = COLOR 1

EACH SQUARE EQUALS ONE STITCH. WORK ALL WHITE SQUARES WITH COLOR INDICATED IN WHITE COLUMN AND ALL SHADED SQUARES WITH COLOR INDICATED IN SHADED COLUMN. WORK ALL OTHER SYMBOL SQUARES AS INDICATED IN SYMBOL KEY.

BACK AND FRONT:
BEGIN ON ROW 1 AT BOTTOM OF RIGHT-HAND CHART ON STITCH NUMBER FOR CHOSEN SIZE. WORK THROUGH ROW 88. CONTINUE WITH ROW 89 AT BOTTOM OF LEFT-HAND CHART AND WORK THROUGH ROW 171.
SLEEVES:
WORK AS FOR BACK THROUGH ROW 144. OMIT ROWS 145–165. CONTINUE WITH ROW 166, SUBSTITUTING COLORS A FOR G AND H FOR F. WORK TO TOP OF CHART.

BACK:
BEG ON STITCH #18(15,12).
END ON STITCH #6(9,12).
SLEEVES:
BEG ON STITCH #13(12,11).
END ON STITCH #11(12,13).
RIGHT FRONT:
BEG ON STITCH #5(23,17).
END ON STITCH #19(16,13).
LEFT FRONT:
BEG ON STITCH #5(8,11).
END ON STITCH #19(1,7).

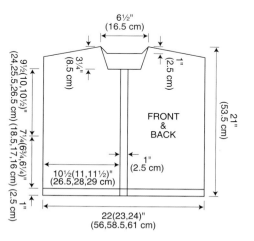

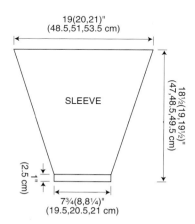

SIZES

Small(Medium,Large)

Finished measurements: 44(48,52)" (112,122,132 cm)

MATERIALS

Montera (50% llama, 50% wool; 100 grams = approx. 127 yards): 11(11,12) hanks

Equivalent yarn: 1397(1397,1524) yards/1277(1277,1394) meters of bulky-weight yarn

36" (91.5 cm) circular knitting needle in size 9 U.S. (5.5 mm)

Straight knitting needles in sizes 8 and 9 U.S. (5 and 5.5 mm)

Cable needle (cn)

Stitch markers (small scraps of yarn in a contrasting color)

Holders or scrap yarn for pockets

1" (2.5 cm) Akoya shell buttons (5)

GAUGE

Garter stitch on larger needles: 16 sts and 30 rows = 4" (10 cm)

Box stitch: 17 sts and 26 rows = 4" (10 cm)

Cable = 2⅝" (6.7 cm)

Take time to save time—check your gauge.

PATTERN STITCHES

ABBREVIATIONS

SSK: Sl the 1st and 2nd sts one at a time as if to knit; then insert point of left-hand needle into fronts of these 2 sts and knit them tog from this position.

BOX STITCH

See chart on page 122.

BLITHEWOLD CARDIGAN

With its interesting combination of stitches, this cardigan looks quite complex but is actually easy to work. The main section of the design features a 12-row cable that twists only once, for simple, repetitive knitting. The lower border is done in a fun-to-knit box stitch, and the sleeves, side panels, and bands are worked in basic garter stitch.

Design: **Kristin Nicholas**
Knitting rating: **Experienced**

CABLE

(over 16 sts)

Rows 1, 3, 5, and 7: (WS) P4, k3, p2, k3, p4.

Rows 2, 4, and 6: K4, p3, k2, p3, k4.

Row 8: Sl 4 sts to cn and hold in front of work, k4, k4 from cn, sl 4 sts to cn and hold in back, k4, k4 from cn.

Row 9: P16.

Row 11: As row 1.

Rows 10 and 12: As row 2.

GARTER STITCH (GS)

Back and forth: K all rows.

In the round:

Rnd 1. K all sts.

Rnd 2. P all sts.

Note: Cardigan is knit in one piece. Front and back are split at underarm, then worked separately.

POCKETS

Make 2.

Using size 9 straight needles, c.o. 18 sts.

Work in St st for 5" (12.5 cm).

Sl sts to holder.

BODY

With circular needle, c.o. 196(210,224) sts.

Work in box stitch for 2 complete reps (48 rows).

K 2 rows.

Pocket row: Knitting all sts, work 8 sts, sl next 18 sts to holder, and replace with 18 pocket sts.

Work until 26 sts rem on needles, slip next 18 sts to holder and replace with 2nd pocket, work rem 8 sts.

K 2 more rows, inc 28(30,30) sts evenly across last row to give 224(240,254) sts.

Est cable/garter st patt: Work 3 sts in GS, pm, work cable over 16 sts, pm, work 2 in GS, pm, work cable over 16 sts, pm, work 18(23,26) in GS, pm for side seam, work 22(25,29) in GS, pm, * work cable over 16 sts, pm, work 2 in GS, pm, rep from * twice, work cable over 16 sts, pm, work 22(25,29) in GS, pm, work 18(23,26) in GS, pm, work cable over 16 sts, pm, work 2 in GS, pm, work cable over 16 sts, pm, work 3 in GS.

Work in est patt until piece meas 17 (17½,18)" (43,44.5,45.5 cm).

Split for armholes, working back and two fronts in est pattern.

Work back until piece meas 26(27,28)" (66,68.5,71 cm) or desired length.

B.o. all sts.

RIGHT FRONT

Work as est until piece meas 19(20, 21)" (48.5,51,53.5 cm).

Shape V-neckline: On RS, work across 1st 37 sts of patt (this should be directly after 2nd cable), k2tog, work to end of row.

Cont to dec 1 st every 2nd row 0(0,2) times, then every 4th row 10(13,12) times to give 44(46,49) sts at front.

When piece meas same as back, b.o. all sts.

Note: Front cables will not match back cables at shoulder seams.

LEFT FRONT

Work same as right front, working SSK before cable begins on RSR.

SLEEVES

With smaller needles, c.o. 32(32,34) sts. Work in GS for 8 rows, inc 4 sts evenly across last row to give 36(36,38) sts.

Change to larger needles and inc 1 st each end every 6th row 18(20,21) times to give 72(76,80) sts while cont in GS.

When piece meas 16(16½,17)" (40.5, 42,43 cm) or desired length excluding 1st 8 rows GS, b.o. all sts.

FINISHING

Sew shoulder seams.

Sew sleeve seams.

Sew in sleeve bet opening.

Pockets: P.u. 18 sts at holder.

Work 7 rows of GS and b.o. all sts.

Sew pocket lining to inside of garment and sew pocket band at corners.

Using circular needle at lower edge of sweater, p.u. 1st, 2nd, 3rd sts; skip 4th st, and rep across bottom of sweater; p.u. every 2nd and 3rd st to shoulder seam, every 2nd and 3rd st at back of neck, and every 2nd and 3rd st to bottom of sweater.

Now work GS in round on circular needles.

Mark 2 corner bottom sts.

Inc 1 st at either side of marker every other rnd to miter corner.

Work 2 rnds in GS.

Mark 5 buttonholes evenly spaced at right front.

Next rnd: B.o. 2 sts at marker.

Next rnd: C.o. 2 sts over b.o. sts.

Cont working in GS for entire button band.

When 10 rnds have been completed, b.o. all sts.

Sew on buttons.

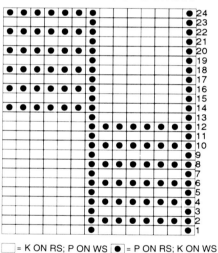

BOX STITCH – OVER 14 STS AND 24 ROWS

☐ = K ON RS; P ON WS ● = P ON RS; K ON WS

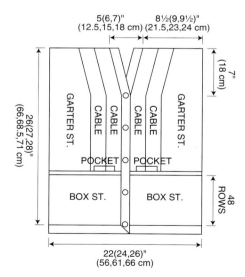

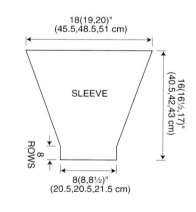

HARLEQUIN CARDIGAN

A Pucci-inspired colorway à la the 1960s makes these diamond-shaped motifs pop! The colored motifs are echoed in a textured seed stitch that is superimposed at odd intervals over the entire sweater. Bicolored seed stitch bands give a nice finishing touch.

Design: MICHELE ROSE
Knitting rating: VERY CHALLENGING

SIZES

Small(Medium,Large)
Finished measurements: 42(44,46)" (106.5,112,117 cm)

MATERIALS

Paisley (50% wool, 50% rayon; 50 grams = approx. 95 yards): 6(6,7) hanks of color A—#1732 Raspberry; 4(5,5) hanks each of colors B—1711 Rococo Gold, C—1796 Sacred Saffron, D—1708 Persian Purple, and E—#1709 Harlequin Pink
Equivalent yarn: 570(570,665) yards/ 521(521,608) meters of worsted-weight wool in color A and 380(475,475) yards/ 348(435,435) meters of colors B, C, D, and E
Knitting needles in sizes 5 and 7 U.S. (3.75 and 4.5 cm) or size to give gauge
¾" (2 cm) buttons (4)

GAUGE

Argyle seed stitch on larger needles: 20 sts and 28 rows = 4" (10 cm)
Take time to save time—check your gauge.

PATTERN STITCHES

TWO-COLOR SEED STITCH RIB

See chart on page 126.

ARGYLE SEED STITCH

See chart on page 126.

Note: Patterns should be worked using intarsia method with separate bobbins of yarn for each color section.

BACK

With smaller needles and color A, c.o. 107(111,115) sts.
K 1 row.
Next RSR, beg 2-color seed stitch rib.
Work in rib for 8 more rows.
Next RSR, change to larger needles and beg working argyle chart as indicated.
Work in argyle pattern until piece meas 11½(11,10½)" (29,28,26.5 cm) from beg.
Mark beg of armholes.
Cont in patt until piece meas 21" (53.5 cm).

Beg shoulder and neck shaping:
Cont in patt, b.o. 12(13,14) sts at beg of next 4 rows, 13 sts beg of next 2 rows.
At same time, b.o. center 17 sts and, working both sides at same time, b.o. from each neck edge 5 sts once, 3 sts once.

RIGHT FRONT

Using smaller needles and color A, c.o. 50(52,54) sts.
K 1 row.
Next RSR, beg 2-color seed stitch rib.
Work in rib for 8 more rows.
Next RSR, change to larger needles and beg working argyle chart as indicated.
Work in patt until piece meas 7" (18 cm) from start.
Next RSR, **beg neck shaping:** B.o. 1 st at neck edge this and every 8th row 13 times.
When piece meas 11½(11,10½)" (29, 28,26.5 cm) from start, mark beg of armholes.
Cont in patt.
When piece meas 21" (53.5 cm), work shoulder shaping same as for back.

LEFT FRONT

Work same as right front, reversing patt placement and shaping.

SLEEVES

Using smaller needles and color A, c.o. 37(41,45) sts.
K 1 row.
Next RSR, beg 2-color seed stitch rib.
Work rib for 8 more rows.
Next RSR, change to larger needles and beg working argyle chart as indicated.
Working in patt, shape sleeve by inc 1 st each end this and every 4th row 30 times.
When piece meas 19(19½,20)" (48.5, 49.5,51 cm) from beg incl rib, b.o. 97 (101,105) sts.

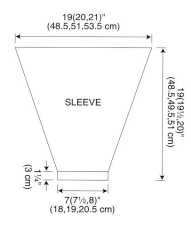

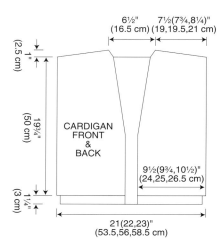

CARDIGAN FRONT & BACK

6½" (16.5 cm) 7½(7¾,8¼)" (19,19.5,21 cm)
1" (2.5 cm)
19¾" (50 cm)
1¼" (3 cm)
9½(9¾,10½)" (24,25,26.5 cm)
21(22,23)" (53.5,56,58.5 cm)

SLEEVE

19(20,21)" (48.5,51,53.5 cm)
19(19½,20)" (48.5,49.5,51 cm)
1¼" (3 cm)
7(7½,8)" (18,19,20.5 cm)

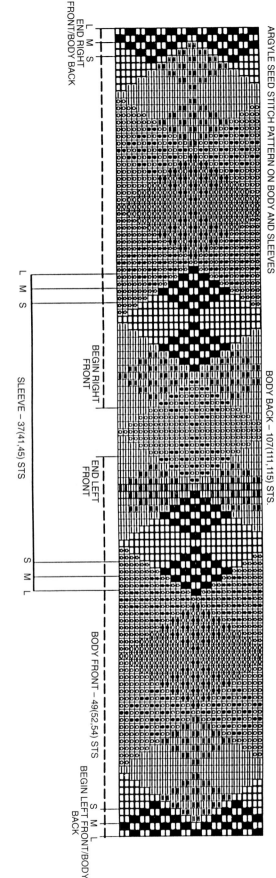

ARGYLE SEED STITCH PATTERN ON BODY AND SLEEVES

END RIGHT
FRONT/BODY BACK

L
M
S

BEGIN RIGHT
FRONT

END LEFT
FRONT

BODY BACK – 107(111,115) STS.

SLEEVE – 37(41,45) STS

L
M
S

S
M
L

BODY FRONT – 49(52,54) STS

S
M
L
BEGIN LEFT FRONT/BODY
BACK

Legend:

★ ✧ ◆ ◇ ● ▮ ‖ | ■ □

KNIT ON RS/PURL ON WS IN COLOR C (SACRED SAFFRON 1796)
PURL ON RS/KNIT ON WS IN COLOR C (SACRED SAFFRON 1796)
KNIT ON RS/PURL ON WS IN COLOR A (RASPBERRY 1732)
PURL ON RS/KNIT ON WS IN COLOR A (RASPBERRY 1732)
KNIT ON RS/PURL ON WS IN COLOR D (PERSIAN PURPLE 1708)
PURL ON RS/PURL ON WS IN COLOR D (PERSIAN PURPLE 1708)
KNIT ON RS/PURL ON WS IN COLOR B (ROCOCO GOLD 1711)
PURL ON RS/KNIT ON WS IN COLOR B (ROCOCO GOLD 1711)
KNIT ON RS/PURL ON WS IN COLOR E (HARLEQUIN PINK 1709)
PURL ON RS/KNIT ON WS IN COLOR E (HARLEQUIN PINK 1709)

TWO-COLOR SEED STITCH RIB OVER MULTIPLE OF 2 STS

CARDIGAN EDGE IN SEED STITCH RIB:

BIND OFF ROW ON WS IN KNIT ST — WSR
KNIT IN COLOR A ON RS — RSR
WSR – BUTTONHOLE FINISHING ROW
RSR
RSR – BUTTONHOLE ROW
WSR
RSR
WSR
WSR IN COLOR 2
PICK UP ROW IN COLOR B

FINISHING

Block all pieces.

Sew shoulder seams.

Using smaller needles and **color B**, p.u. 311 sts evenly around neck and fronts.

P 1 row.

Next RSR, beg 2-color seed stitch rib.

Work for 2 rows.

Next RSR, work in patt for 3 sts, b.o. 4 sts, (work in patt for 19 sts, b.o. 4 sts) 3 times, cont in patt.

Next row, work patt, c.o. 4 sts at points where they were b.o. on previous row.

Work 4 rows in patt.

B.o. all sts **in color A.**

Sew sleeves between points marked on body.

Sew side and sleeve seams.

Tie off and work in all loose ends on inside.

Sew on buttons.

Block entire garment.

NOTES:
1) USE SEPARATE BOBBINS OF EACH COLOR. WRAP YARNS AROUND EACH OTHER AT POINTS WHERE COLOR CHANGES TO PREVENT HOLES.
2) NECK SHAPING: WORK NECK DEC 2 STS IN FROM EDGE. ON RIGHT FRONT: K2, SL1, K1, PSSO. ON LEFT FRONT: WORK X STS TO 4 STS BEFORE END OF WORK, K2TOG, K2.
3) CONT WORKING IN PATTERNS DURING NECK AND SLEEVE SHAPING AS LONG AS IS REASONABLE.

ROSA RUGOSA BLOUSE

By choosing the proper weight and quality of yarn, you can easily transform a knit cardigan into a blouse. This short-sleeved cardigan has a very flattering V-shaped neckline that is accented with a pointed collar. The delicate rose motif and lacy borders make this a perfect sweater for dressy occasions.

Design: **Michele Rose**
Knitting rating: **Intermediate**

SIZES

Small(Medium,Large)
Finished measurements: 40(42,44)" (101.5,106.5,112 cm)

MATERIALS

Newport Light (100% mercerized cotton; 50 grams = approx. 93 yards): 10 skeins of color A and 1 skein each of colors B, C, D, E, F, and G
Equivalent yarn: 930 yards/851 meters of worsted-weight cotton in color A and 93 yards/85 meters of colors B, C, D, E, F, and G
Knitting needles in size 6 U.S. (4 mm)
½" (1.5 cm) buttons (5)

GAUGE

Stockinette stitch: 21 sts and 26 rows = 4" (10 cm)
Take time to save time—check your gauge.
Notes: On charts C and D, use sep bobbins for each color change, making sure to twist yarns where colors change to prevent holes.
On front panels, seed st buttonhole and button bands are knit in with fronts.

PATTERN STITCHES

SEED STITCH
(multiple of 2 + 1)
Row 1: * K1, p1 *, k1.

Row 2: * K1, p1 *, k1.

POINTELLE CHEVRON
(multiple of 8 + 1)
Row 1: (RS) * K1, yo, sl1, k1, psso, k3, k2tog, yo *, rep bet *'s to last st, k1.
Rows 2, 4, and 6: P all sts.
Row 3: * K2, yo, sl1, k1, psso, k1, k2tog, yo, k1 *, rep bet *'s to last st, k1.
Row 5: * K3, yo, sl1, k2tog, psso, yo, k2 *, rep bet *'s to last st, k1.

BACK

With color A, c.o. 103(107,111) sts.
Work 6 rows in seed st.
Next RS row, k3(1,3) sts, work 12(13, 13) rep of pointelle chevron over 97 (105,105) sts, k3(1,3) sts.
Cont over next 5 rows, keeping first and last 3(1,3) sts in St st.
Next RS, beg working in St st.
Cont until piece meas 10½" (26.5 cm) from beg.

Mark for armholes.
Cont in St st until piece meas 19½(20, 20½)" (49.5,51,52 cm) from beg.
Shape shoulder by b.o. 13 sts at beg of next 2 rows, then 12(13,14) sts at beg of next 4 rows.
At the same time, b.o. center 21 sts and, working each side sep, b.o. at each neck edge, 3 sts once and 1 st once.
B.o. rem sts.

RIGHT FRONT

With color A, c.o. 54(56,58) sts.
Work 6 rows in seed st, working first buttonhole in row 3 as foll: Seed st 2, yo, sl1, k1, psso, seed st to end of row.
Note: Work rem 4 buttonholes in rows 21, 39, 57, and 75.
Next RS row: Seed st 5 for buttonhole band, work pointelle over next 49 sts, k 0(2,4) sts.
Cont as est over next 5 rows to complete pointelle.

Next row (row 13): Seed st 5, k5, work row 1 of chart C over next 36 sts, k8 (10,12) sts.

Cont as est over next 35 rows to complete chart C.

Next RS row (row 49): Seed st 5, k to end.

Cont in St st with seed st buttonhole band until front meas 10½" (26.5 cm) from beg.

Mark for armhole.

Cont until row 76 has been completed.

Next row, **shape neck:** K5, k2tog, k to end.

Cont to dec 1 st at neck edge, 5 sts in from neck edge as foll: every other and every 4th row, alt 6 times, then every 4th row 5 times.

At the same time, when front meas same length as back to shoulder, shape shoulder as for back.

LEFT FRONT

Work as for right front, but rev shaping and omit buttonholes.

SLEEVES

With color A, c.o. 53(57,61) sts.

Work 6 rows in seed st.

Next row (RS): K2(0,2), work row 1 of pointelle 6(7,7) times over 49(55,55) sts, k2(0,2), cont in pointelle over next 5 rows, work rem of sleeve in St st.

At the same time, work inc as foll: Beg on row 1 of pointelle, inc 1 st each edge of first and every other row 20 times to give 93(97,101) sts. When piece meas 8½" (21.5 cm) from beg, b.o. all sts.

COLLAR

With color A, c.o. 147 sts.

Work 2 rows seed st, beg with p1.

Row 3: Seed st 3, sl1, k1, psso, seed st 137, k2tog, seed st 3.

Row 4 and all WS rows: Seed st 3, p until last 3 sts, seed st 3.

Row 5: Seed st 3, sl1, k1, psso, k3, work row 1 pointelle 16 times, k3, k2tog, seed st 3.

Cont in patt as est, dec 1 st each edge (3 sts in from edge) until pointelle is complete.

Row 11 and all foll RS rows: Seed st 3, sl1, k1, psso, k to last 5 sts, k2tog, seed st 3.

Work until row 24 is complete.
B.o. all sts.

FINISHING

Block all pieces.

Sew shoulder seams.

Attach collar.

Set in sleeves.

Sew side and sleeve seams.

Sew on buttons.

FLORAL INTARSIA
36 ST MOTIF

CHART C – RIGHT FRONT

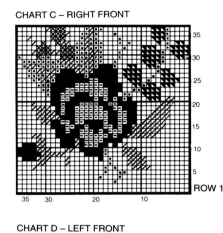

ROW 1

CHART D – LEFT FRONT

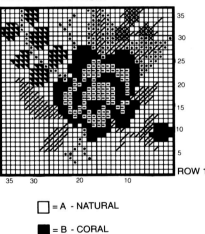

ROW 1

☐ = A - NATURAL

■ = B - CORAL

⊟ = C - PEACH

⊡ = D - TOURMALINE

◥ = E - SQUASH

◿ = F - PYRITE

⊠ = G - AMBER

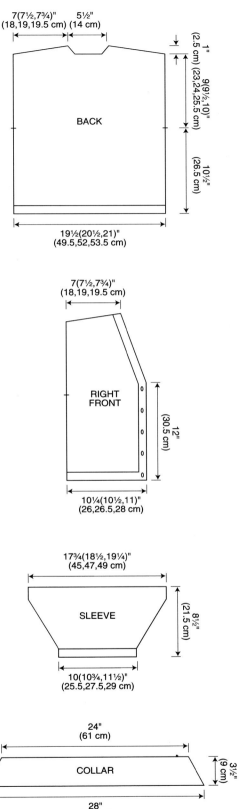

7(7½,7¾)" 5½"
(18,19,19.5 cm) (14 cm)

1" (2.5 cm)
9(9½,10)" (23,24,25.5 cm)
10½" (26.5 cm)

BACK

19½(20½,21)"
(49.5,52,53.5 cm)

7(7½,7¾)"
(18,19,19.5 cm)

RIGHT FRONT

12" (30.5 cm)

10¼(10½,11)"
(26,26.5,28 cm)

17¾(18½,19¼)"
(45,47,49 cm)

SLEEVE

8½" (21.5 cm)

10(10¾,11½)"
(25.5,27.5,29 cm)

24"
(61 cm)

COLLAR

3½" (9 cm)

28"
(71 cm)

PEGGY & NORIKO

Garter stitch combined with slipping and passing slip stitches over previous stitches creates a zigzag border. The shape of the border is echoed with a knit and purl chevron design on a stockinette stitch ground, making a summer sweater for women that is as easy to knit as it is comfortable to wear. A matching cardigan is given in children's sizes.

Design: Kristin Nicholas
Knitting rating: Intermediate

ADULT'S PULLOVER

SIZES

Small(Medium,Large)
Finished measurements: 39½(45,49)" (100.5,114.5,124.5 cm)

MATERIALS

Willough (65% cotton, 35% silk; 50 grams = approx. 136 yards): 8(9,10) hanks
Equivalent yarn: 1088(1224,1360) yards/995(1119,1244) meters of worsted-weight cotton
Knitting needles in sizes 6 and 8 U.S. (4 and 5 mm)
36" (91.5 cm) circular needle in size 6 U.S. (4 mm)

GAUGE

Chevron stitch on **smaller** needles: 20 sts and 26 rows = 4" (10 cm)
Contrary to most patterns, this one uses smaller needles for the body and larger needles for the trim.
Take time to save time—check your gauge.

PATTERN STITCHES

SCALLOPED BORDER
(multiple of 12 plus 3)
C.o. and k 1 row.
Then repeat rows 1 and 2.

Row 1 (RS): K1, ssk, * k9, sl2, k1, p2sso; rep from *, end k9, k2tog, k1.
Row 2: K1, * p1, k4, (k1, yo, k1) in next st, k4; rep from *, end p1, k1.

SSK
Sl 1st and 2nd sts one at a time as if to knit; then insert point of left-hand needle into fronts of these 2 sts and knit them tog from this position.

GARTER STITCH
(in the round)
K 1 row.
P 1 row.

BACK

With **larger** needles, c.o. 99(111,123) sts.
K 1 row.
Work in scalloped edge for 12 rows, ending with row 2.
Change to **smaller** needles and work in chevron stitch.
Work until piece meas 11½(12,12½)" (29,30.5,31.5 cm).
Then **shape armholes:** B.o. 1 st at beg of next 14 rows to give 85(97,109) sts.
Work as est in patt.
When piece meas 18½(19½,20½)" (47,49.5,52 cm), **shape neck:** Work 25(30,35) sts, join second ball of yarn and b.o. center 35(37,39) sts, work to end.
Working each side sep, b.o. 1 st at neck edge every row 5 times to give 20(25, 30) sts at shoulder.
When piece meas 20(21,22)" (51,53.5, 56 cm), b.o. all sts.

FRONT

Work same as for back.
When piece meas 16(17,18)" (40.5,43, 45.5 cm), shape neck: Work 27(32,37) sts, join second ball of yarn and b.o. center 31(33,35) sts, work to end.
Working each side sep, b.o. 1 st every other row 7 times to give 20(25,30) sts at shoulder.
When piece meas same as back, b.o. all sts.

SLEEVES

With **larger** needles, c.o. 75 sts.

K 1 row.
Work scalloped edging for 10 rows, ending with Row 2.
Change to **smaller** needles and work chevron stitch, inc 1 st each end as foll:
For size small: Inc 1 st each end every 6th row 5 times.
For size medium: Inc 1 st each end every 4th row 5 times, then every 5th row 3 times.
For size large: Inc 1 st each end every 4th row 10 times.
You should have 85(91,95) sts.
When chevron st meas 5½(6,6½)" (14,15,16.5 cm), **shape armhole:** B.o. 1 st at beg of each row 12 times to give 73(79,83) sts.
B.o. all sts.

FINISHING

Sew shoulder seams.
With circular needle, p.u. 102(104,106) sts evenly around neck and work in garter stitch in round for 1¼" (3 cm).
Sew sleeves corresponding to armhole shaping on body.
Sew underarm and side seams.

CHILD'S CARDIGAN

SIZES

2(4,6,8,10)
Finished measurements: 23½(24½,25¾, 28,30)" (59.5,62,65.5,71,76 cm)

MATERIALS

Newport Light (100% mercerized cotton; 50 grams = approx. 93 yards): 5(6,6,7,7) skeins
Equivalent yarn: 465(558,558,651,651) yards/426(511,596,596) meters of worsted-weight cotton
29" (73.5 cm) circular needles in sizes 6 and 8 U.S. (4 and 5 mm)
Stitch holders (1 long, 1 short)
⅝" (1.6 cm) buttons 6(7,7,8,8)

GAUGE

Chevron stitch on **smaller** needles: 21 sts and 26 rows = 4" (10 cm)
Take time to save time—check your gauge.

PATTERN STITCHES

SCALLOPED BORDER

(multiple of 12 + 3)

The multiple will work out for all sizes **except** size 4.

For size 4: Eliminate the first 3 sts of the pattern and beg where marked below with a + on Row 1. On Row 2, eliminate the last 2 sts of pattern after the +.

For all sizes: C.o. and k 1 row.

Then repeat rows 1 and 2:

Row 1 (RS): K1, ssk, + * k9, sl2, k1, p2sso; rep from *, end k9, k2tog, k1.

Row 2: K1, * p1, k4, (k1, yo, k1) in next st, k4; rep from *, + end p1, k1.

FRONT AND BACK

Note: This cardigan is knit back and forth on circular needles until armholes. Then it is split and worked in separate pieces.

With **larger** needles, c.o. 123(129,135, 147,159) sts.

Work in scalloped border pattern for 8 rows, ending with row 2.

Change to **smaller** needles and beg chevron stitch, beg with st 1(4,1,1,1).

Work until piece meas 8(8½,9,9½,10)" (20.5,21.5,23,24,25.5 cm) incl trim.

Split for armholes as foll: On RS at right center front, work 31(32,33,37,40) sts, slip next 61(65,69,73,79) sts to long holder for back, slip rem 31(32,33,37, 40) sts to short holder for left front.

Work right front as foll: Work in chevron patt as est until piece meas 11(12,13,14,15)" (28,30.5,33,35.5,38 cm) and you are on RSR.

B.o. first 7(6,7,8,9) sts, work to end.

At each RS neck edge, b.o. 1 st 7(7,5,6, 7) times to give 17(19,21,23,24) sts at shoulder.

When piece meas 13½(14½,15½,16½, 17½)" (34,37,39.5,42,44.5 cm), b.o. all sts.

Work left front as for right, reversing shaping.

BACK

Work straight as est in patt until piece meas same as front to shoulders.

B.o. all sts.

SLEEVES

With larger needles, c.o. 39 sts.

Work in scallop trim for 8 rows, beg where indicated.

Change to smaller needles and beg chevron pattern.

At the same time, inc 1 st each end every 6th(6th,5th,5th,5th) row 6(8,11,13,15) times, for 51(55,61,65, 69) sts.

When piece meas 10(10½,11,12¼,13)" (25.5,26.5,28,31,33 cm), b.o. all sts.

FINISHING

Before any finishing, block body to correspond with diagram.

Using pins and lots of steam, manipulate the scallops up and down, pulling sts with pins to emphasize the shape.

Sew shoulder seams.

CHEVRON STITCH – 12 ST REPEAT

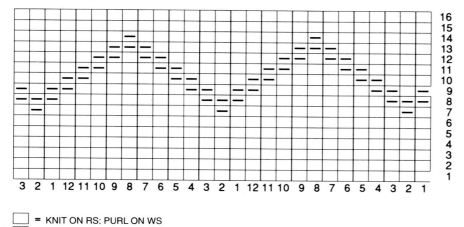

16
15
14
13
12
11
10
9
8
7
6
5
4
3
2
1

3 2 1 12 11 10 9 8 7 6 5 4 3 2 1 12 11 10 9 8 7 6 5 4 3 2 1

☐ = KNIT ON RS; PURL ON WS

⊟ = PURL ON RS; KNIT ON WS

Using larger circular needle, p.u. 46(51, 56,61,66) sts along right front edge, place marker, p.u. corner st, pm, p.u. 54(56,56,58,58) sts evenly around neck, pm, p.u. 46(51,56,61,66) sts down left front.

Work in garter st, inc 2 sts at marked st by (k1, yo, k1) into marked corner st every other row to make mitered edge.

In the 3rd row, make 6 buttonholes evenly spaced on right front (for girl's cardigan) by k2tog, yo.

When garter st meas 1¼" (3 cm), b.o. all sts.

Sew in sleeves.

Sew on buttons.

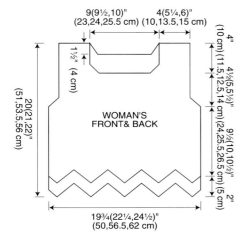

9(9½,10)" (23,24,25.5 cm)   4(5¼,6)" (10,13.5,15 cm)

1½" (4 cm)

4" (10 cm)

4½(5,5½)" (11.5,12.5,14 cm)

9½(10,10½)" (24,25.5,26.5 cm)

2" (5 cm)

20(21,22)" (51,53.5,56 cm)

WOMAN'S FRONT & BACK

19¾(22¼,24½)" (50,56.5,62 cm)

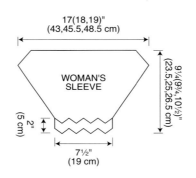

17(18,19)" (43,45.5,48.5 cm)

WOMAN'S SLEEVE

9¼(9¾,10½)" (23.5,25,26.5 cm)

2" (5 cm)

7½" (19 cm)

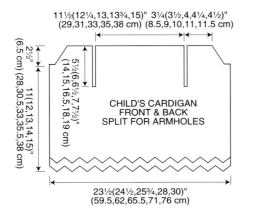

11½(12¼,13,13¾,15)" (29,31,33,35 cm)   3¼(3½,4,4¼,4½)" (8.5,9,10,11,11.5 cm)

2½" (6.5 cm)

5½(6,6½,7,7½)" (14,15,16.5,18,19 cm)

11(12,13,14,15)" (28,30.5,33,35.5,38 cm)

CHILD'S CARDIGAN FRONT & BACK SPLIT FOR ARMHOLES

23½(24½,25¾,28,30)" (59.5,62,65.5,71,76 cm)

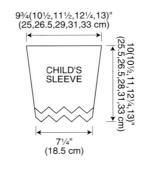

9¾(10½,11½,12¼,13)" (25,26.5,29,31,33 cm)

CHILD'S SLEEVE

10(10½,11,12¼,13)" (25.5,26.5,28,31,33 cm)

7¼" (18.5 cm)

SIZES

Small(Medium,Large)
Finished measurements: 37½(41,43½)"
(95.5,104,110.5 cm)

MATERIALS

Newport (100% mercerized cotton; 50
grams = approx. 70 yards): 12(13,14)
skeins

Equivalent yarn: 840(910,980) yards/
768(832,896) meters of bulky worsted-
weight cotton

Knitting needles in sizes 6 and 8 U.S. (4
and 5 mm) or size to give gauge

Cable needle (cn)

GAUGE

Brocade stitch on larger needles: 18 sts
= 4" (10 cm)

*Take time to save time—check your
gauge.*

PATTERN STITCHES

CABLED RIB

(over multiple of 9 + 5)

Row 1: (RS) * P1, k1-b (k into back of
st), p1, k1-b, p1, k4 *, rep bet *'s, end
p1, k1-b, p1, k-1b, p1.

Rows 2 and 4: * K1, p1, k1, p1, k1, p4
*, rep bet *'s, end k1, p1, k1, p1, k1.

Row 3: * P1, k1-b, p1, k1-b, p1, sl 2 sts
to cn and hold in front, k2, k2 from cn *,
rep bet *'s, end p1, k1-b, p1, k1-b, p1.

BROCADE STITCH

(over multiple of 14 sts)

Rows 1, 3, and 5: (WS) K3, * p8, k6,
rep from *, end p8, k3.

Rows 2 and 4: K all sts.

Row 6: K2, * p2, k6, p2, k4, rep from
*, end last repeat k2.

Row 7: P3, * k2, p4, k2, p6, rep from *,
end last repeat p3.

Row 8: K4, * p2, k2, p2, k8, rep from
*, end last repeat k4.

Row 9: P5, * k4, p10, rep from *, end
k4, p5.

Rows 10, 11, and 12: Repeat rows 8, 7,
and 6.

BACK

With smaller needles, c.o. 77(86,95) sts.

Work in cabled rib for 2½" (6.5 cm).

In last RS row of rib, inc 7(6,3) sts evenly across to give 84(92,98) sts.

Change to larger needles and beg
working in brocade stitch.

Work 0(4,0) sts in St st, work 6(6,7)
repeats of brocade st over 84(84,98)
sts., work 0(4,0) sts in St st.

Cont in patt as est until piece meas
11(11½,12)" (28,29,30.5 cm).

B.o. 4 sts at beg of next 2 rows, then 1
st at beg of next 12 rows to give 64(72,
78) sts.

When piece meas 17(18,19)" (43,45.5,
48.5 cm), shape back of neck.

Work 15(18,20) sts, join a second ball
of yarn and b.o. center 34(36,38) sts,
work to end.

Working both sides sep, b.o. 1 st at
each neck edge 4 times to give 11(14,
16) sts.

When piece meas 19(20,21)" (48.5,51,
53.5 cm), b.o. all sts.

FRONT

Work same as for back.

When piece meas 14(15,16)" (35.5,38,
40.5 cm), shape front neck.

Work 22(26,29) sts, join a second ball of
yarn and b.o. center 20 sts, work to end.

Working both sides sep, b.o. 1 st every
other row at neck edge 11(12,13) times
to give 11(14,16) sts.

When piece meas same as back at
shoulder, b.o. all sts.

SLEEVES

With smaller needles, c.o. 59 sts.

Work in cabled rib for 2½" (6.5 cm).

In last RS row of rib, inc 11 sts evenly
across to give 70 sts.

Change to larger needles and beg brocade patt: Work 5 repeats.

Then inc 1 st each end 1(3,6) times
every 4th row to give 72(76,82) sts,

Here is a short-sleeved summer
sweater that looks great on
many figure types. The design
on this scoop-neck pullover
resembles a trellis, but it is
actually a knit and purl brocade
pattern that is both easy and fun
to knit. A cabled rib variation
adds a contrasting texture at the
edges, and mercerized cotton
yarn gives a gentle sheen overall.

Design: **KRISTIN NICHOLAS**
Knitting rating: **INTERMEDIATE**

building out in patt st.

When piece meas 7½" (19 cm), b.o. 4 sts
at beg of next 2 rows, then 1 st at beg of
next 12 rows to give 52(56,62) sts.

B.o. all sts.

FINISHING

Sew one shoulder seam.

Using smaller needles, p.u. 122(131,
131) sts evenly around neckline.

Work in cable rib for 2½" (6.5 cm).

B.o. neatly.

Sew shoulder and neck seam.

Sew in sleeves.

Sew underarm and side seams.

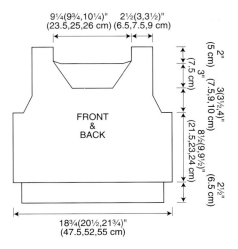

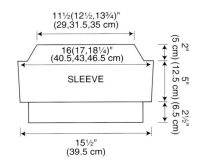

FIELDSTONE FINERY

The snowflake has been a favorite motif of knitters throughout the centuries. Here it's rendered in a combination of knit and purl stitches to make a summer-weight cotton pullover. The borders of the garment are worked in an easy chevron design, and the V-shaped neckline is finished with a collar fashioned in rib and seed stitch.

Design: Michele Rose
Knitting rating: Intermediate

SIZES

Small(Medium,Large)
Finished measurements: 42(44,46)"
(106.5,112,117 cm)

MATERIALS

Batik (100% cotton; 100 grams = approx. 176 yards): 6(6,7) skeins
Equivalent yarn: 1056(1056,1232) yards/966(966,1127) meters of worsted-weight cotton
Knitting needles in sizes 6 and 8 U.S. (4 and 5 mm)

GAUGE

Snowflake pattern on larger needles: 16 sts and 25 rows = 4" (10 cm)
Take time to save time—check your gauge.

PATTERN STITCHES

1 x 1 Rib
Row 1: (RS) K1, p1 across row.
Row 2: Work all sts as they appear.

Chevron Pattern
See chart on page 138.

Snowflake Pattern
See chart on page 138.

Seed Stitch
Row 1: * K1, p1 *, rep bet *'s, end k1.
Row 2: K the p sts and p the k sts.

BACK

With smaller needles, c.o. 85(89,93) sts.
Work 5 rows in 1 x 1 rib.
Next WS row, beg with st 17(15,13) and work 15 rows of chevron patt.
Next RS row: Change to larger needles and start snowflake patt at st 25(27, 29).
Work until piece meas 9(9½,10)" (23, 24,25.5 cm).
Mark for armholes.
Cont until armholes meas 10(10½,11)" (25.5,26.5,28 cm).
B.o. center 15 sts for neck and, working both sides sep, b.o. from each neck edge 3 sts once and 2 sts once.
At the same time, shape shoulders by b.o. 10 sts at beg of next 2 rows, then 10(11,12) sts at beg of next 4 rows.

FRONT

Work as for back until piece meas 12(13,14)" (30.5,33,35.5 cm).
Next row work patt st for 41(43,45) sts, k2tog at center, giving 42(44,46) sts on each needle.
Put rem 42(44,46) sts on holder.
Working each side sep, b.o. at neck edge 1 st at next and every other row 3 times, every 4th row 8 times.
Cont without further shaping until piece meas same as back to shoulder and shape as for back.
With RS facing, p.u. sts from holder and work as for left side, reversing shaping.

SLEEVES

With smaller needles, c.o. 33(37,41) sts.
Work 5 rows in 1 x 1 rib.
Next WS row, beg with st 11(9,7) and work chevron patt for 15 rows.
Next RS row, change to larger needles and start snowflake patt. (St 19 should fall on center st of sleeve.)
Inc 1 st each end every other row 3(4,5) times, every 4th row 15 times, every 6th row 6 times to give 83(87,91) sts.
When piece meas 19" (48.5 cm), b.o. all sts.

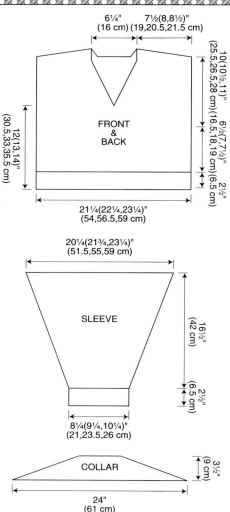

COLLAR

With smaller needles, c.o. 115 sts.
Work 1st 5 rows in 1 x 1 rib and rem of collar in seed st.
At the same time, on row 3 of rib, beg shaping as foll: B.o. 1 st at beg of next 2 rows, 2 sts at beg of next 4 rows, 4 sts at beg of next 4 rows, 6 sts at beg of next 4 rows, 10 sts at beg of next 4 rows.
B.o. rem 25 sts.

FINISHING

Block all pieces.
Sew shoulder seams.
Set in collar.
Sew in sleeves.
Sew side and sleeve seams.

CHEVRON PATTERN

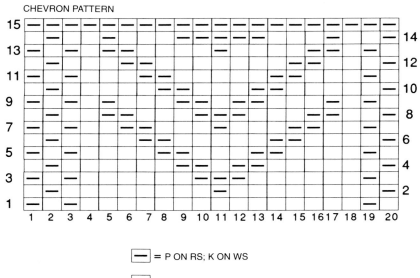

☐ = P ON RS; K ON WS

☐ = K ON RS; P ON WS

SNOWFLAKE PATTERN

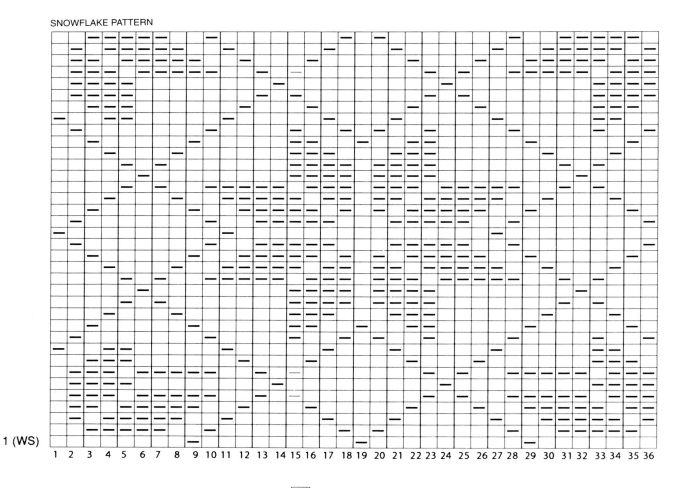

☐ = P ON RS; K ON WS

☐ = K ON RS; P ON WS

138

SIZES

Small(Medium,Large)

Finished measurements: 40(44,48)" (101.5,112,122 cm)

MATERIALS

Willough (65% cotton, 35% silk; 50 grams = approx. 135 yards): 11(12,13) hanks

Equivalent yarn: 1485(1620,1755) yards/1358(1481,1605) meters of light worsted-weight cotton

Knitting needles in sizes 5 and 6 U.S. (3.75 and 4 mm)

GAUGE

Stockinette stitch on larger needles: 20 sts and 28 rows = 4" (10 cm)

Take time to save time—check your gauge.

Note: The shell and eyelet border does not show in the photograph.

PATTERN STITCHES

ABBREVIATIONS

Sl2-k1-p2sso: Insert needle into fronts of 2nd and 1st sts on left-hand (LH) needle as if to k2tog; do not k these sts tog, but sl them, both at once, from this position. K the next st on LH needle; then insert LH needle point into both sl sts at once and draw them tog over the k st and off RH needle, just as in psso.

Sl2-p1-p2sso: This is a double dec from WS. Turn work over slightly, keep yarn in front, and insert needle from left into back loops of 2nd and 1st sts, in that order, as if to p2tog-b; do not p these sts tog, but sl them, both at once, from

POINT D'ESPRIT

Knits for summer wear should be lightweight and comfortable. To achieve this result, nothing is more effective than knitted lace. This design is a lace sampler incorporating a pointed lace border, a thin eyelet insert, and two different easy-to-knit lace panels. The proportions and placement of the lace make this a flattering design for many figure types.

Design: **Kristin Nicholas**
Knitting rating: **Experienced**

this position. P next st on LH needle; then insert LH needle point into both sl sts at once and draw them tog over the p st and off RH needle. The p2sso is just the same as when dec is worked from RS.

SSK: Sl the 1st and 2nd sts one at a time as if to knit; then insert point of LH needle into fronts of these 2 sts and k them tog from this position.

SHELL AND EYELET BORDER

(multiple of 14 + 5)

Rows 1 and 2: K all sts.

Row 3: (RS) K5, * yo, k3, sl2-k1-p2sso, k3, yo, k5 *, rep bet *'s.

Row 4: P6, * yo, p2, sl2-p1-p2sso, p2, yo, p7 *, rep bet *'s, end last rep p6.

Row 5: K7, * yo, k1, sl2-k1-p2sso, k1, yo, k9 *, rep bet *'s, end last rep k7.

Row 6: P8, * yo, sl2-p1-p2sso, yo, p11 *, rep bet *'s, end last rep p8.

Row 7: K8, * yo, sl2-k1-p2sso, yo, k11 *, rep bet *'s, end last rep k8.

Row 8: P all sts.

LACE GARTER INSET

(multiple of 2)

Rows 1-6: K all sts.

Rows 7 and 9: * Yo, k2tog *, rep bet *'s.

Row 8 and 10: * Yo, p2tog *, rep bet *'s.

Rows 11-16: K all sts.

EYELET DIAMONDS

(multiple of 10 + 1)

Row 1: K1, * yo, ssk, k5, k2tog, yo, k1 *, rep bet *'s.

Row 2 and all WS rows: P all sts.

Row 3: K1, * k1, yo, ssk, k3, k2tog, yo, k2 *, rep bet *'s.

Row 5: K1, * k2, yo, ssk, k1, k2tog, yo, k3 *, rep bet *'s.

Row 7: K1, * k3, yo, sl1, k2tog, psso, yo, k4 *, rep bet *'s.

Row 9: K1, * k2, k2tog, yo, k1, yo, ssk, k3 *, rep bet *'s.

Row 11: K1, * k1, k2tog, yo, k3, yo, ssk, k2 *, rep bet *'s.

Row 13: K1, * k2tog, yo, k5, yo, ssk, k1 *, rep bet *'s.

Row 15: K2tog, * yo, k7, yo, sl1, k2tog, psso *, rep bet *'s.

Repeat rows 1-16.

VINE LACE ZIGZAG

(multiple of 11 + 1)

Row 1: K1, * k2tog, k4, (yo, k1) twice, ssk, k1 *, rep bet *'s.

Row 2 and all WS rows: P all sts.

Row 3: K1, * k2tog, k3, yo, k1, yo, k2, ssk, k1 *, rep bet *'s.

Row 5: K1, * k2tog, k2, yo, k1, yo, k3, ssk, k1 *, rep bet *'s.

Row 7: K1, * k2tog, (k1, yo) twice, k4, ssk, k1 *, rep bet *'s.

Row 9: K1, * k2tog, yo, k1, yo, k5, ssk, k1 *, rep bet *'s.

Row 11: Repeat row 7.

Row 13: Repeat row 5.

Row 15: Repeat row 3.

Row 17: Repeat row 1.

Row 19: K1, * k2tog, k5, yo, k1, yo, ssk, k1 *, rep bet *'s.

Repeat rows 1-20.

Note: There is 1 edge st on each end of each piece. These sts are not included in determining gauge. These edge sts are used for seaming.

BACK

With smaller needles, c.o. 103(103,117) sts.

Work shell and eyelet border for 8 rows.

In last row of patt, dec 3(inc 7,inc 3) sts evenly across to give 100(110,120) sts.

Change to larger needles.

Work 1 edge st in St st, work lace garter inset to last st, work 1 st in St st for edge st.

In last row of rep, inc 1 st evenly across to give 101(111,121) sts.

Beg eyelet diamond patt: Work for 8" (20.5 cm), dec 1 st in last row to give 100(110,120) sts.

Work lace garter inset as before.

In last row, inc 0(1,2) sts to give 100 (111,122) sts.

Work vine lace zigzag patt for 12(13, 14)" (30.5,33,35.5 cm).

B.o. all sts.

FRONT

Work as for back until piece meas 22(23,24)" (56,58.5,61 cm) from beg.

Shape neck: Work 40(44,48) sts, join 2nd ball of yarn and b.o. center 22(25, 28) sts, work to end.

Working each side sep, b.o. 1 st at neck edge every other row 10 times to give 30(34,38) sts at shoulder.

When piece meas same as back at shoulders, b.o. all sts.

SLEEVES

With smaller needles, c.o. 47(61,61) sts.

Work shell and eyelet border for 8 rows, inc 3(1,1) sts in last row to give 50(62,62) sts.

Change to larger needles.

Work lace garter inset for 16 rows, keeping 1st and last st in St st for seaming as on body.

In last row of rep, inc 8(7,7) sts evenly across to give 58(69,69) sts.

Work vine lace zigzag patt, inc 1 st at each end every 2 rows 8(0,4) times, every 4 rows 8(13,12) times to give 90(95,101) sts.

When piece meas 17(18,19)" (43,45.5, 48.5 cm), b.o. all sts.

FINISHING

Sew one shoulder.

With smaller needles, p.u. 108(114, 120) sts evenly around neckline.

Work in garter stitch for 8 rows.

B.o. loosely.

Sew 2nd shoulder and neck edge.

Mark underarm points 9(9½,10)" (23, 24,25.5 cm) down from shoulder in front and back.

Sew sleeve bet points.

Sew underarm and side seams.

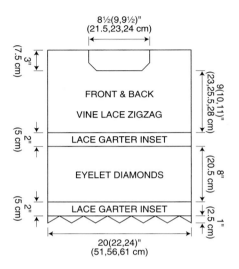

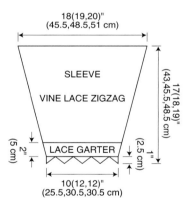

WOMAN'S PULLOVER

SIZES

Small(Medium,Large)
Finished measurements: 46(50,55)"
(117,127,139.5 cm)

MATERIALS

Newport (100% cotton; 50 grams =
approx. 70 yards): 25(26,27) skeins
Equivalent yarn: 1750(1820,1890)
yards/1600(1664,1728) meters of bulky
worsted-weight cotton
Knitting needles in sizes 6 and 8 U.S. (4
and 5 mm)

GAUGE

Pattern stitch on larger needles: 22 sts =
5" (12.5 cm) and 22 rows = 4" (10 cm)
*Take time to save time—check your
gauge.*

PATTERN STITCHES

BOBBLE

(K1, yo) twice in next st, k1-b (k1 into
back of st) of same st, turn, sl1, p4,
turn, (sl1, k4, turn, sl1, p4, turn) twice,
sl1, (k2tog) twice, turn, sl1, p2tog,
psso.

BACK

With larger needles, c.o. 101(111,121)
sts.
Beg with a k row, work 5 rows rev St st,
work 4 rows St st.
Rib row 1: (RS) K1, * k2, p3 *, rep bet
*'s.
Row 2: * K3, p2 *, rep bet *'s, end p1.
Rep these 2 rows for 2¼" (5.5 cm) from
beg of rib, end with row 1.
Work 4 rows St st, 4 rows rev St st.
P next row.
Work row 1 of chart from C(D,C) to A
once, A to B 4(5,5) times, B to E(F,E)
once.
Work in patt as est until piece meas
18(18,20)" (45.5,45.5,51 cm) from beg.
Shape raglan armholes: B.o. 5 sts at
beg of next 2 rows to give 91(101,111)
sts.
K2, sl2, k1, p2sso, work in patt to last 5
sts, k3tog, k2 to give 87(97,107) sts.

Keeping 3 sts at each edge in St st,
work 1 row even.
* [Dec 1 st each edge of next row, work
1 row even] 3(3,2) times, dec 2 sts each
edge of next row, work 1 row even *.
Rep bet *'s 4(5,7) more times for a total
of 5(6,8) times to give 37(37,43) sts.
[Dec 1 st each edge of next row, work 1
row even] 2(0,0) times to give 33(37,43)
sts.
B.o. all sts.

FRONT

Work to armholes as for back.
Shape raglan armholes: B.o. 5 sts at
beg of next 2 rows to give 91(101,111)
sts.
Keeping 3 sts at each edge in St st,
work 1 row even.
* [Dec 1 st each edge of next row, work
1 row even] 3(3,2) times, dec 2 sts each
edge of next row, work 1 row even *.
Rep bet *'s 3(4,5) more times for a total
of 4(5,6) times.
[Dec 1 st each edge of every other row]
3(0,3) times, and **at the same time,**
when 45(51,57) sts rem, **shape neck:**
Work in patt so that 8(9,9) sts are on
needle after dec, join 2nd strand of yarn,
b.o. center 29(33,39) sts, work to end.
Work 1 row even.
Cont raglan dec and dec 1 st at each
neck edge every row 3 times.
When raglan decs are complete, b.o.
rem 3 sts each side.

LEFT SLEEVE

C.o. 46(46,56) sts.
Work rib patt as for back for 15 rows,
work 4 rows St st, then 4 rows rev St st,
p next row (WS row).
At the same time, inc 1 st each edge
every 4th row 5 times to give 56(56,66)
sts.
Next row, k3, inc 1, work row 1 of
chart from G(G,H) to B once, from A to
I(I,J) once, inc 1, k last 3 sts to give
58(58,68) sts.
Work in patt as est with 3 sts each edge
in St st, inc 1 st each end every 4th row
4(7,2) times, then every 6th row 7(6,10)
times to give 80(84,92) sts.

BABIES & BOBBLES

In this woman's cotton pullover,
the overall pattern of diamond
shapes is done in eyelet and
moss stitch and is made extra
special with the addition of
three bobbles in each repeat.
The raglan shaping of the
sleeves adds to the strong diagonal emphasis, and the edges are
completed with an innovative
rib treatment. The baby's cardigan sweater is worked in a very
easy garter stitch variation,
where only one color at a time is
used to create a fabric that looks
more complicated than it is.

Woman's pullover:
STEPHANIE GILDERSLEEVE
Child's cardigan:
CATHY PAYSON

Woman's pullover: **VERY CHALLENGING**
Child's cardigan: **INTERMEDIATE**

Shape raglan cap: B.o. 5 sts beg of
next 2 rows.
* Dec 2 sts each edge of next row,
work 1 row even, (dec 1 st each edge
of next row, work 1 row even) 3(3,2)
times *, rep bet *'s 4(4,6) times.
(B.o. 2 sts each edge of next row, work
1 row even) 0(2,1) times.
Shape neck edge: Dec 2(1,2) sts at
beg of row, work to end.
B.o. 6(4,6) sts at beg of next row, work
to end.
Dec 1(2,2) sts at beg of next row, work
to end.
B.o. 5(4,5) sts at beg of next row, work
to end.
K 6(5,7) sts of next row; then b.o.
Work right sleeve same as left, but
reversing shaping.

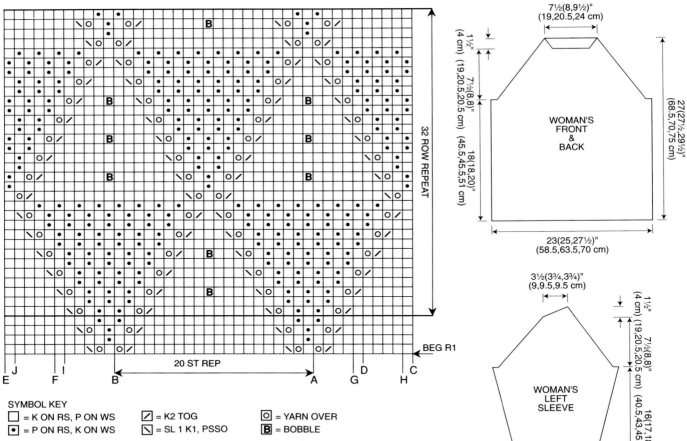

32 ROW REPEAT

20 ST REP

BEG R1

J   F I   B   A   G   H
E   F   B   A   D   C

SYMBOL KEY

☐ = K ON RS, P ON WS   ╱ = K2 TOG   ◻ = YARN OVER
⊡ = P ON RS, K ON WS   ◿ = SL 1 K1, PSSO   B = BOBBLE

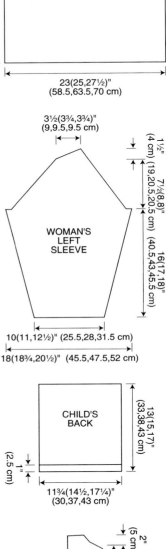

7½(8,9½)"
(19,20.5,24 cm)

1½"
(4 cm)

7½(8,8)" (19,20.5,20.5 cm)

18(18,20)"
(45.5,45.5,51 cm)

27(27½,29½)"
(68.5,70,75 cm)

WOMAN'S FRONT & BACK

23(25,27½)"
(58.5,63.5,70 cm)

3½(3¾,3¾)"
(9,9.5,9.5 cm)

1½"
(4 cm)

7½(8,8)" (19,20.5,20.5 cm)

16(17,18)"
(40.5,43,45.5 cm)

WOMAN'S LEFT SLEEVE

10(11,12½)" (25.5,28,31.5 cm)

18(18¾,20½)" (45.5,47.5,52 cm)

CHILD'S BACK

13(15,17)"
(33,38,43 cm)

1"
(2.5 cm)

11¾(14½,17¼)"
(30,37,43 cm)

FINISHING

Sew front and back raglan seams.

With larger needles, p.u. 120 sts evenly spaced along front, back, and sleeve edges.

Work 2 rows St st, 4 rows rev St st.

Change to smaller needles and work 4 rows in St st.

Work rib for 1¼" (3 cm).

Work 4 rows St st, 4 rows rev St st.

B.o. in purl.

Sew raglan and neck seam.

Sew side and sleeve seams.

CHILD'S CARDIGAN

SIZES

2-4(6-8,10-12)

Finished measurements: 23½(29,34½)"
(59.5,73.5,87.5 cm)

MATERIALS

Newport: 3(4,5) skeins of color A—
#2355 and 2(3,4) skeins of colors B—

#2322 and C—#2304

Equivalent yarn: 210(280,350) yards/192(256,320) meters of bulky worsted-weight cotton in color A; 140(210,280) yards/128(192,256) meters of color B; 140(210,280) yards/128(192,256) meters of color C

Knitting needles in sizes 6 and 8 U.S. (4 and 5 mm)

16" (40.5 cm) circular needle in size 6 U.S. (4 mm)

¾" (2 cm) buttons (8)

11(13,15)"
(28,33,38 cm)

CHILD'S SLEEVE

11(13,15)"
(28,33,38 cm)

1"
(2.5 cm)

6(7,8)"
(15,18,20.5 cm)

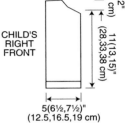

2"
(5 cm)

CHILD'S RIGHT FRONT

11(13,15)"
(28,33,38 cm)

5(6½,7½)"
(12.5,16.5,19 cm)

GAUGE

Garter stitch on larger needles: 16 sts and 28 rows = 4" (10 cm)

Take time to save time—check your gauge.

PATTERN STITCHES

GARTER STITCH

K every row.

REVERSIBLE STRIPED PATTERN

(multiple of 11 + 3)

Row 1: (RS) With color A, * K3, p8 *, rep bet *'s, end k3.

Row 2: Same as row 1.

Row 3: With color B, same as row 1.

Row 4: Same as row 3.

Row 5: With color C, same as row 1.

Row 6: Same as row 5.

Note: In photograph, this sweater is shown backwards on child.

BACK

With smaller needles and color A, c.o. 47(58,69) sts.

Work garter st for 1" (2.5 cm).

Change to larger needles and work striped patt until piece meas 13(15,17)" (33,38,43 cm) from beg.

B.o. all sts.

LEFT FRONT

With smaller needles and color A, c.o. 19(26,30) sts.

Work garter st for 1" (2.5 cm).

Change to larger needles and work striped patt as foll:

Row 1: (RS) With color A, p8, k3, p8, k0(3,3), p0(4,8).

Row 2: With color A, p0(4,8), k0(3,3), p8, k3, p8.

Row 3: With color B, same as row 1.

Row 4: With color B, same as row 2.

Row 5: With color C, same as row 1.

Row 6: With color C, same as row 2.

Work in stripe patt until piece meas 11(13,15)" (28,33,38 cm).

Shape neck: At every other neck edge, b.o. 2 sts twice, then 1 st 3 times.

When piece meas same as back at shoulder, b.o. all sts.

RIGHT FRONT

Work garter rib as for left front.

Change to larger needles and beg working striped patt as foll:

Row 1: (RS) With color A, P0(4,8), k0(3,3), p8, k3, p8.

Row 2: With color A, p8, k3, p8, k0(3,3), p0(4,8).

Row 3: With color B, same as row 1.

Row 4: With color B, same as row 2.

Row 5: With color C, same as row 1.

Row 6: With color C, same as row 2.

Work as for left front, but reverse shaping.

SLEEVES

With smaller needles and color A, c.o. 24(28,32) sts.

Work garter st for 1" (2.5 cm).

Change to larger needles and work as foll:

Rows 1 and 2: (RS) With color A, knit.

Rows 3 and 4: With color B, knit.

Rows 5 and 6: With color C, knit.

At the same time, shape sleeves by inc 1 st at each end every 6 rows 5(6,7) times in est garter patt, then every 8 rows 5(6,7) times to give 44(52,60) sts.

When piece meas 11(13,15)" (28,33,38 cm), b.o. all sts.

FINISHING

Sew shoulder seams.

With RS facing, smaller needles, and color A, p.u. 40(44,48) sts around neckline and work garter st for 1" (2.5 cm).

B.o. all sts.

With RS facing, smaller needles, and color A, p.u. 48(56,64) sts along left front edge and work garter rib for 2" (5 cm).

B.o. all sts.

Work right front as for left front, but at 1" (2.5 cm), make 8 buttonholes evenly spaced by yo, k2tog.

Sew underarm and side seams.

Sew on buttons.

FESTIVAL OF COLOR

This closely fitted, cropped top is worked in an easy slip stitch, using many colors of lustrous mercerized cotton yarn. The effect is reminiscent of afghans made with multicolored scraps. Black and white Fair Isle checks and diagonal lines are interspersed in just the right places among the rich, earthy tones of the chevron bands to add liveliness to a sporty summer pullover.

Design: **Sally Lee**
Knitting rating: **Experienced**

SIZES

Small(Medium,Large,Extra Large)
Finished measurements: 37(41,45,49)" (94,104,114.5,124.5 cm)

MATERIALS

Newport Light (100% pima cotton; 50 grams = approx. 93 yards): 2(2,3,3) skeins of colors A—#3347 Denim, B—#3313 Black, C—#3301 Bleach, D—#3350 Chartreuse, and H—#3384 Delphinium; 3(3,4,4) skeins of color E—#3351 Pottery Red; 1(1,2,2) skeins of colors F—#3372 Spring Leaf and G—#3332 Fuschia

Equivalent yarn: 186(279,279,279) yards/171(255,255,255) meters of worsted-weight cotton in colors A, B, C, D, and H; 279(279,372,372) yards/255 (255,340,340) meters of color E; 93(93,186,186) yards/85(85,170,170) meters of colors F and G

Knitting needles in size 4 and 6 U.S. (3.5 and 4 mm)

GAUGE

Afghan stitch on larger needles: 24 sts and 24 rows = 4" (10 cm)
Take time to save time—check your gauge.

PATTERN STITCHES

ABBREVIATIONS

SSK: Sl the 1st and 2nd sts one at a time as if to knit; then insert point of LH needle into fronts of these 2 sts and k them tog from this position.

AFGHAN GARTER STITCH (AGS)

(over multiple of 12 + 3)
Row 1: (RS) K1, ssk, * k9, sl2, k1, p2sso; rep from *, end k9, k2tog, k1.
Row 2: K1, * p1, k4, (k1, yo, k1) in next st, k4; rep from *, end p1, k1.

AFGHAN STOCKINETTE STITCH (AST)

(over multiple of 12 + 3)
Row 1: (RS) K1, ssk, * k9, sl2, k1, p2sso; rep from *, end k9, k2tog, k1.
Row 2: P1 * P5, (p1, yo, p1) in next stitch, p4; rep from *, end last repeat p2.

BACK

With smaller needles and color A, c.o. 111(123,135,147) sts.

Work 6 rows of afghan garter stitch (AGS).

Work 6 rows of afghan stockinette stitch (AST).

Change to larger needles and work 6 rows in patt #1 using colors B and C.

Work 8 rows of AST in color D.

Work 8 rows of AST in E.

Work 18 rows of pattern #2 in B and C, changing to smaller needles.

Work 6(8,10,10) rows of AGS in A, changing to larger needles.

Work 6(8,10,10) rows of AST in F.

Mark armhole point at 10(10½,11,11)" (25.5,26.5,28,28 cm) from beg.

Work 10 rows of pattern #3 in B and C.

Work 10 rows of AST in G.

Work 12 rows of AST in H.

Work 6 rows of AST in D.

Work 4 rows of AGS in A.

Work 17(20,23,23) rows of St st in E.

Cont working in color E, shaping shoulders and back neck at same time.

For shoulders, b.o. 10(12,13,15) sts at beg of next 6 rows.

At the same time, b.o. center 19(19,25,25) sts, then b.o. at each side of neck edge sep, 7 sts twice, then 2 sts once.

FRONT

Make same as back until you have worked 6(9,12,12) rows of last section of St st.

Place center 17(17,23,23) sts on holder.

Working each side sep, b.o. 4 sts at neck edge every other row 4 times, then 1 st once.

At the same time, when piece meas same as back to shoulder shaping, work same as for back.

SLEEVES

With smaller needles, c.o. 51(53,55,55) sts.

Work 6 rows of color A in AGS and 6 rows in AST.

Change to larger needles and cont working color sequence as follows **while increasing** along sides of sleeve:

Work 6 rows of pattern #1 in B and C.

Work 8 rows of AST in E.

Work 8 rows of AST in H.

Work 8 rows of AST in G.

Work 8 rows of AGS in D.

Work 8 rows of AST in F.

Work 18 rows of pattern #2 in B and C in St st.

Work 6(8,8,8) rows of AGS in E.

Work 8 rows of AST in H.

Work 12(15,18,18) rows of AST in A.

Inc 1 st each end every 3rd row 29(24, 20,20) times.

Note: Work in pattern only if you have enough sts to complete a repeat. Stitch markers will help you recognize the point in the pattern being worked.

Then **for size small:** Inc 1 st each end every row 3 times.

For sizes medium, large, and extra large: Inc 1 st each end every 2nd row 10(16,16) times.

B.o. all sts.

FINISHING

Sew shoulder seams.

With smaller needles, p.u. 150 sts evenly around neck.

Work in 1 x 1 corrugated rib for ⅝" (1.6 cm) using colors A and B.

B.o. in C in knit stitch.

Sew sleeves.

Sew side seams.

Set in sleeves.

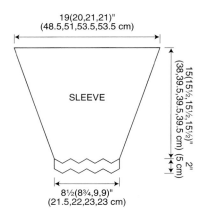

19(20,21,21)"
(48.5,51,53.5,53.5 cm)

SLEEVE

15(15½,15½,15½)"
(38,39.5,39.5,39.5 cm)

2"
(5 cm)

8½(8¾,9,9)"
(21.5,22,23,23 cm)

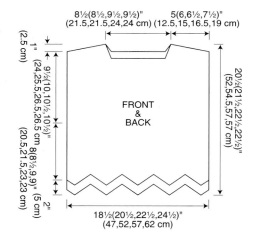

8½(8½,9½,9½)"
(21.5,21.5,24,24 cm)

5(6,6½,7½)"
(12.5,15,16.5,19 cm)

9½(10,10½,10½)"
(24,25.5,26.5,26.5 cm)

1"
(2.5 cm)

FRONT
&
BACK

20½(21½,22½,22½)"
(52,54,57,57 cm)

8(8½,9,9½)"
(20.5,21.5,23,23 cm)

2"
(5 cm)

18½(20½,22½,24½)"
(47,52,57,62 cm)

COLOR PATTERN #1
OVER MULTIPLE OF 10 STS

● = COLOR B
I = COLOR C

COLOR PATTERN #2
OVER MULTIPLE OF 6 STS

COLOR PATTERN #3
OVER MULTIPLE OF 6 STS

CORRUGATED RIB IN ROUND:
OVER MULTIPLE OF 2 STS

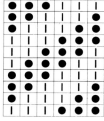

● = IN COLOR B, P ON RS
I = IN COLOR A, K ON RS

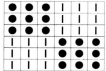

148

Tips for Knitters

THE BASICS

FIGURING YARN AMOUNTS

To calculate how much yarn to purchase, determine the number of yards in your chosen skein of yarn by referring to the ball band. Take that number and divide it into the total number of yards needed for the sweater. This figure is the number of balls required for the project.

Most knitters feel more at ease in having extra yarn, especially if the project will not be completed within a month. Manufacturers' supplies of dye lots change very rapidly, and frequently there will be no yarn available in a particular dye lot within a short period of time. Dye lots do change from batch to batch, and if you want to eliminate abrupt color variations within a sweater, purchase enough yarn to complete the project.

There are a couple of approaches to take if you do make an error and run out of yarn. When you're down to the last ball of the original dye lot, work a row of each ball—one from the new dye lot and one from the old—for a transition period of about 2" (5 cm) before completely switching to the new dye lot. Alternatively, if you work ribs and collars in a different dye lot, the difference in color often won't be noticeable because the texture of the stitch has also changed.

ON GAUGE

It is of vital importance for you to test your chosen yarn by doing a stitch gauge with the recommended needle size and yarn in the stitch specified. No matter how many times it is specified in directions to knit a gauge, even the best knitters eliminate this short, very worthwhile step. Do a swatch not only to check your gauge but also to serve as a practice piece for the stitch you will be working in the pattern.

The swatch must be at least 4" wide and 4" long (10 x 10 cm), not including selvage stitches. Measure over a 4" portion of the swatch and determine how many stitches and rows per inch are in the swatch. If there are more stitches than are specified in the gauge section of the pattern, increase the needle size you are using; if there are fewer stitches, decrease the needle size. Work swatches until you get the proper gauge. It is very important to complete this step successfully in order to produce a sweater that fits properly.

DETERMINING WHAT SIZE TO KNIT

The importance of choosing the right size to knit can't be overemphasized. No matter how beautiful it is, a sweater that doesn't fit well isn't enjoyable to wear.

To determine which size to make, a basic rule of thumb is to measure a comparable sweater that fits properly and comfortably. A comparable sweater is one that is made with a similar thickness of yarn and stitch design. Measure

the chest or bust of the sweater and work the instructions for the new sweater in the closest size. Don't make the mistake that many knitters do by knitting to fit their actual bust size; if you do, you'll have a very small sweater that is figure hugging and most likely unwearable.

When choosing the size sweater to knit, the following points should be noted:

Weight and loft of the yarn: The bulkier the yarn, the more ease is needed in order for the garment to hang properly. If you're using a very lightweight yarn, the amount of ease can be much less.

Stitches used: Heavily cable-patterned sweaters look better if they're loosely fitted. The stitches add more thickness and bulk to the garment, and if the sweater is too tight, the stitches will distort and look very unflattering.

Use of the sweater: Casual sweaters tend to look better and be more comfortable if they're loose and baggy. For dressy occasions, a tighter fit may be desired.

Several sizes are given for each design shown. The smallest size is given first, with increasingly larger sizes given in parentheses ( ). If you're going to work a size medium, and the sizes given are small, (medium, large, and extra large), always work the first set of numbers just inside the parentheses.

HOW TO READ A CHART

Colorwork charts represent the right side of the fabric. Where you begin the work and the direction you follow to read the chart depend on which side of the work you are knitting. When working the right side of the fabric, read the chart from right to left; when working on the wrong side of the fabric, the chart is read from left to right.

Most patterns are annotated to show the beginning and ending points for each size. Make sure you always begin and end on the same stitches on each side when you're on a particular side of the fabric. When the shaping for armholes and sleeves begins, the starting and ending points will change. It's an excellent idea to keep a notepad with your project to jot down the starting and ending points for each row if necessary. Most knitters will become familiar with a pattern and, after a few rows, will know where they should be.

Some of the charts given in this book are actually stitch charts for knit/purl combination fabrics or for cables. The above description also applies when working a stitch chart. Many knitters are afraid of working cabled and knit/purl stitches from charts, but it's actually much easier to knit from charts once that fear is conquered. The charts give a visual idea of what the stitch will look like, and they can be grasped much more quickly than several lines of written instructions.

On the right side of the fabric, work the symbols given, beginning and ending where indicated. On the wrong side

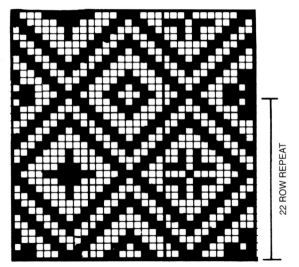

22 ROW REPEAT

SAMPLE COLORWORK CHART

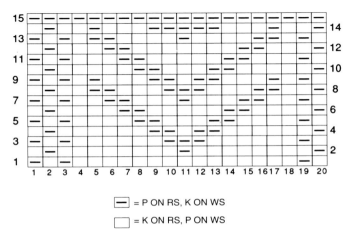

⊟ = P ON RS, K ON WS

□ = K ON RS, P ON WS

EXAMPLE OF A SIMPLE STITCH CHART

of the piece, work the opposite of the symbol given. For instance, if a knit stitch is shown, work a purl stitch on the wrong side.

Most cable and knit/purl charts that contain fancy techniques, such as cable crossings and yarn-over lace work, give a key to the exact technique you are to perform. The majority of the stitches in this book have difficult, manipulative stitches only on the right side. If a complicated stitch is done on the wrong side, the instructions are given in the key.

Don't be afraid of working cabled stitches from charts; after the first time, it becomes very easy.

STEAMING YOUR GARMENT

A garment is never completely finished until it has been properly steamed or washed. Many knitters don't realize that a proper steaming or washing will actually improve the finished look of their project. All of the garments shown in this book were steamed before being photographed so that they would hang and drape neatly.

Before seaming the pieces together, they should be properly blocked. If the gauge is slightly off, extra width can be obtained by stretching the pieces under tension; it's very difficult to shrink a garment.

While pinning the garment to a well-padded surface, stretch each finished piece until its measurements agree with the dimensions given in the schematic drawing for that design. Make sure the surface is covered with two to three layers of old towels in case the yarn runs or bleeds. For natural fibers, use a steam iron full of water on a high steam setting. Then slowly steam the entire piece, holding the iron 2" to 3" (5 to 7.5 cm) away from the garment. Don't touch the garment with the iron, as it will flatten the stitchwork and produce a fabric that appears machine made.

Wool or mohair can't take as much heat as cotton can, so refer to the iron's settings. There is danger that the garment may burn if the heat is too high for the fiber.

Let the pieces dry completely before seaming them together as instructed. If it takes too long for the fabric to dry, it may be necessary to lift the pieces off the blocking surface when partially dry so that they don't mildew.

LAUNDERING

You should always follow the instructions given on the yarn label when cleaning a hand-knit garment. The manufacturer has tested the yarn to conform to the washing standards given on the label.

Some colors have a tendency to bleed when being washed, and this can pose a problem, especially in multicolored garments. Colors including bright teals, reds, bright greens, and blacks tend to give the worst bleeding problems.

Use your gauge swatch to test the launderability of the yarn chosen, and always wash your swatch before washing your garment. If the colors bleed into each other, or if the swatch leaves a colored residue when it is laid on a white towel, you should change the washing procedure to dry cleaning. A solid-colored garment, if it has a tendency to run, may also be washed separately and dried on several old towels to absorb the dye. Most yarns that have excess dye residue will stop bleeding after the first few washings.

KNITTING TECHNIQUES

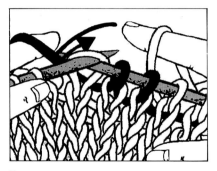

KNITTING WITH RIGHT HAND, STRANDING WITH LEFT

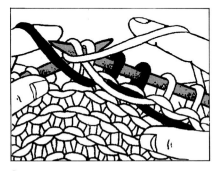

PURLING WITH RIGHT HAND, STRANDING WITH LEFT

KNITTING WITH LEFT HAND, STRANDING WITH RIGHT

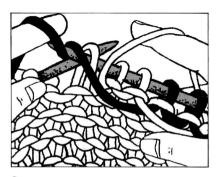

PURLING WITH LEFT HAND, STRANDING WITH RIGHT

FAIR ISLE KNITTING

Fair Isle is a well-established form of knitting that uses two colors in a single row of knitting. Traditional Fair Isle designs are often geometric ones, such as diamonds, snowflakes, and small overall dot patterns. In this technique, the color not being knitted is stranded behind the work and is later picked up. The resulting fabrics tend to be thick, since the carried yarn adds extra bulk.

The basic method for Fair Isle knitting is simple. Following a chart, knit the indicated color for the specified number of stitches; then drop it and pick up the next color according to the design. Although either right- or left-handed knitting can be used in Fair Isle, it's highly recommended that you learn both methods of knitting if you intend to do a fair amount of this type of work. Speed is easily reached by holding one color of yarn in the right hand and the second color in the left.

The biggest mistake made by beginners in this technique is to carry the unused yarn too tightly behind the work. This results in a puckered fabric that's uncomfortable and most likely too small. To avoid puckered fabric, stretch out the stitches on the right-hand needle just before you make each color change; then knit with the new color. This will result in a float of yarn that lies evenly across the back of the fabric. This is extremely important, especially in Fair Isle yoked sweaters, where the tension of the colorwork will affect the fit of the sweater. (Many beginner knitters have yoked sweaters in their closets that won't fit over anyone's shoulders.)

If you are an inexperienced knitter who's attempting Fair Isle for the first time, make sure to use a pure wool yarn for your first project. Wool has a very forgiving quality. When a Fair Isle piece is completed, it often looks lumpy and uneven. A very thorough steaming will flatten out the fabric. Some Fair Isle knitters become so adept at their work that it is difficult to tell if the fabric was done by machine or by hand.

You may notice that as you work a garment, the tension (or gauge) changes from day to day, depending on your mood. With Fair Isle knitting this is especially true and can be very noticeable. Using a concentrated amount of effort, try to keep an even tension from day to day. The easiest way to accomplish this is to relax and loosen up your thinking; this helps make each day's knitting very loose and consistent throughout the entire garment.

To weave or not to weave the yarn not in use when working Fair Isle is a bone of contention among knitters. Weaving the unused yarn is done by laying it in between the yarn being knit and the back side of the fabric, thereby catching the strand and keeping it neatly enclosed. Weaving should be done loosely so that the resulting fabric doesn't pucker.

Some knitters like to weave every other stitch, which produces a garment that is very neat on the wrong side; however, such garments are also stiffer and don't drape as nicely as those where the weaving is done less often.

An alternative method for catching the yarn not in use is to twist it with the knitting yarn behind the work. Whichever method is chosen, make sure to catch the unused yarn whenever it floats for more than five or six stitches. Long floats tend to result in a weaker fabric and cause easy snags and pulls.

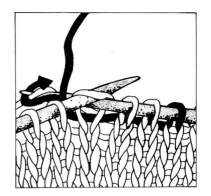

WEAVING YARNS WHEN CHANGING COLORS ON KNIT ROWS

INTARSIA KNITTING

Intarsia knitting is characterized by large sections of different colors on a piece of fabric. Instead of stranding the unused yarn behind the knitted piece, as in Fair Isle knitting, it is held on separate bobbins. The two colors of yarn are then twisted where they join to create a multicolored piece. This technique is very similar to the tapestry technique in weaving. Because each section has only a single thickness of yarn, intarsia knitting does not have the bulk of Fair Isle knitting.

To knit intarsia, wind bobbins with yarns of the different colors. (Commercial bobbins are available for this purpose.) Following the chart given, work the desired number of stitches in the first color. Join the second color of yarn by twisting the new color around the stitch just knit and continue with the new color. Continue twisting the yarns around each other every row to form a joint at each color change.

An alternative to using commercial bobbins is to make a "butterfly" of yarn for each color in your work. This is a yarn winding technique used by tapestry weavers. Leaving a tail of yarn between your ring and middle fingers, wrap the yarn in a figure eight until you have the needed amount. Remove the butterfly from your fingers and wrap the end still connected to the ball of yarn tightly around the center of the butterfly. End it off by tucking a loop of

USING BOBBINS FOR INTARSIA KNITTING

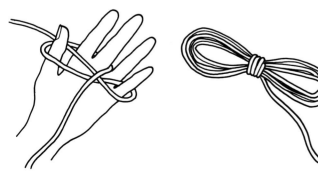

MAKING A BUTTERFLY

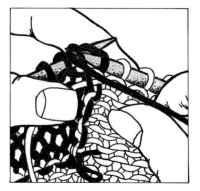

INTARSIA KNITTING WITH LONG STRANDS

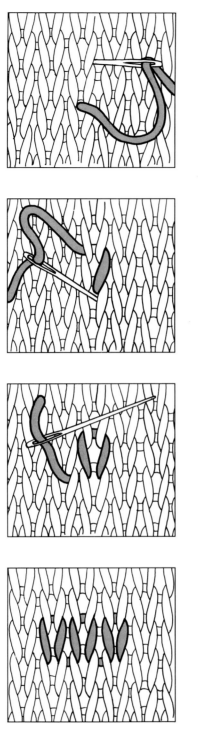

SEQUENCE FOR MAKING DUPLICATE STITCH

yarn under the just-wound section to form a knot. Begin knitting with the unknotted tail from between your fingers.

In recent years, it has become fashionable to use long strands of yarn instead of bobbins. This technique, popularized by Kaffe Fassett, author of *Glorious Color*, allows the knitter to become painterly with the yarn so that many colors can be added to a piece of intarsia knitting. Also, long strands can be untangled more easily, since there is little weight to them and no implement to add to the tangle.

DUPLICATE STITCH

Duplicate stitch is an embroidery technique sometimes called Swiss darning. It's used to add extra colors to a knitted fabric after the knitting is completed. A plain piece of stockinette-stitch knitting can be embroidered in duplicate stitch to form an insignia, a flower, or a small design to add interest to the fabric. A piece of two-color Fair Isle knitting can be duplicate stitched at certain sections that need more color for design enhancement.

Duplicate stitch actually retraces the knitted stitch to cover the original with a new color. If the stitching isn't worked neatly or with the appropriate size yarn, the original color will sometimes show through. Duplicate stitch makes the fabric thicker, and care must be taken to make the wrong side of the work neat. It's better to fasten off the colors being added rather than to stretch the yarn over large expanses of the back of the fabric.

To work duplicate stitch, use a large, blunt needle. A sharp needle will catch and pull the yarn. Using a manageable length of yarn will help you to avoid tangles and knots; too long a length will be unruly.

On the wrong side, take a small stitch through one of the plies of yarn to secure the end. Then come up through the center of the base of the stitch you wish to cover. Moving up along the stitch, thread the needle under the two strands of the base of the stitch above; then pull the yarn through. To complete the stitch, insert the needle next to the starting point at the base of the stitch. Pull the yarn to the wrong side and neaten the stitch.

Work duplicate stitch horizontally or diagonally. If you work it vertically along an entire row of stitches, the duplicate stitch will sink into the middle of the stitch and disappear.

TECHNICAL REFERENCES

This book is a collection of designs for knitters of all skill levels, and each pattern is rated according to its level of difficulty. Should you need further instructional guidance on techniques, consult any of the following basic knitting books for excellent diagrams and instruction:

Don, Sarah. *The Art of Shetland Lace.* London: Bell and Hyman, 1986.

Fassett, Kaffe. *Glorious Knits*. New York: Clarson Potter, 1985.

Goldberg, Rhoda Ochser. *The New Knitting Dictionary, 1000 Stitches and Patterns*. New York: Crown, 1984.

The Harmony Guide to Knitting Stitches, vols. 1, 2, and 3. London: Lyric, 1990.

The Harmony Guide to Aran Knitting. London: Lyric, 1991.

The Harmony Guide to Knitting Techniques. London: Lyric, 1990.

Mon Tricot. *1800 Patterns*. Paris, 1989

Mountford, Debra. *The Harmony Guide to Knitting Techniques and Stitches*. New York: Harmony, 1992.

Newton, Deborah. *Designing Knitwear*. Newtown, CT: Taunton, 1992.

Norbury, James. *Traditional Knitting Patterns*. New York: Dover, 1979.

Stanley, Montse. *The Reader's Digest Guide to Knitting*. Pleasantville, NY: Reader's Digest, 1993.

Starmore, Alice. *Alice Starmore's Book of Fair Isle Knitting*. Newtown, CT: Taunton, 1988.

Thomas, Mary. *Mary Thomas's Book of Knitting Patterns*. New York: Dover, 1972.

_____. *Mary Thomas's Book of Knitting*. New York: Dover, 1973.

Thompson, Gladys. *Patterns for Guernseys, Jerseys, and Arans*. New York: Dover, 1979.

Van der Klift-Tellegen, Henriette. *Knitting from the Netherlands*. Asheville, NC: Lark, 1983.

Vogue knitting editors. *Vogue Knitting Book*. New York: Pantheon, 1989.

Walker, Barbara G. *Charted Knitting Designs: A Third Treasury of Knitting Patterns*. New York: Charles Scribner's Sons, 1972.

_____. *A Second Treasury of Knitting Patterns*. New York: Charles Scribner's Sons, 1970.

_____. *A Treasury of Knitting Patterns*. New York: Charles Scribner's Sons, 1968.

Zimmermann, Elizabeth. *Knitting Without Tears*. New York: Charles Scribner's Sons, 1971.

and these knitting magazines:

Vogue Knitting Magazine, published by Butterick Co., 161 Avenue of the Americas, New York, NY 10013.

Knitters Magazine, Golden Fleece Publications, P.O. Box 1525, 824 West 10th St., Sioux Falls, SD 57101.

Wool Gathering, Schoolhouse Press, 6899 Cary Bluff, Pittsville, WI 54466.

ABBREVIATIONS

beg	beginning
b.o.	bind off
c.o.	cast on
cont	continue
dec	decrease
dpn	double-pointed needle(s)
est	established
foll	follows
inc	increase
k	knit
LH	left hand
m	make
MC	main color
meas	measures
p	purl
patt	pattern
pm	place marker
psso	pass slipped stitch over
p2sso	pass 2 slipped stitches over
p.u.	pick up
rem	remaining
rep	repeat
rev	reverse
RH	right hand
rnd	round
RS(R)	right side (row)
sep	separately
sl	slip
ssk	slip, slip, knit
st(s)	stitch(es)
St st	stockinette stitch
tog	together
WS(R)	wrong side (row)
wyif	with yarn in front
yo	yarn over

Choosing an Equivalent Yarn

The yarn featured in the photographs for each pattern is described in the materials section of the instructions. Also given are the generic type of yarn and the yards/meters needed to complete the project. This yardage and yarn type should be used only as a guide. Each yarn available in the marketplace has different characteristics and will knit differently. The thickness, loft, twist, and texture of the yarn all affect the gauge you will obtain when knitting.

All of the patterns in this book were designed for Classic Elite Yarns. As time passes, new yarns are developed and some older ones are discontinued. Below is a substitution guide to use when purchasing yarn for the sweater you wish to knit. NLA signifies that the yarn is no longer available.

FEATURED YARN SHOWN	SUGGESTED WEIGHT	AVAILABILITY/APPROPRIATE SUBSTITUTE
Applause	Bulky	Available
Batik	Worsted	NLA/Pure & Simple Worsted
Boston	Worsted	NLA/Tapestry
Cambridge	Worsted	NLA/Tapestry
Caravan	Worsted	NLA/Tapestry
Evergreen Cashmere/Wool	Worsted	Available
Evergreen Cotton/Wool	Worsted	Available
Inca Alpaca	Light Worsted	Available
La Gran Brushed Mohair	Bulky	Available
Metro	Light Worsted	Available
Montera	Bulky	Available
Newport Light Mercerized Cotton	Worsted	NLA/Pure & Simple Worsted
Newport Mercerized Cotton	Bulky/Worsted	NLA/Rockland
Paisley Light	Light Worsted	NLA/Tapestry 2 Ply
Paisley Wool/Rayon	Bulky/Worsted	NLA/Tapestry
Regatta	Light Worsted	Available
Sharon	Bulky	Available
Tapestry	Worsted	Available
Willough	Light Worsted	Available

If you already have some yarn on hand, the following chart will help you determine its weight. Look at the ball band and obtain the stitch gauge. The number of stitches will coordinate with the numbers below. Then choose a pattern appropriate for that yarn type.

YARN TYPE	APPROXIMATE No. STS/4" (10 CM)
Bulky	13 to 15
Bulky/Worsted	16 to 18
Worsted	19 to 20
Light Worsted	20 to 22
Sport Weight	22 to 24

WHO IS CLASSIC ELITE YARNS?

Classic Elite Yarns had its origin in the late 1940s, when Ernest Chew, the company's founder, became a partner in Warley Worsted Mills, an old-line textile mill in Lowell, Massachusetts.

The city of Lowell has been a major center for textile production since the beginning of the American Industrial Revolution. In the late 1800s, Frances Cabot Lowell and several business associates developed a canal system fed with water from the Merrimack River, paving the way for several mill complexes to be built throughout the city. In the basements of the mills, massive turbines fed power through leather pulley systems to the looms and spinning frames on the top floors.

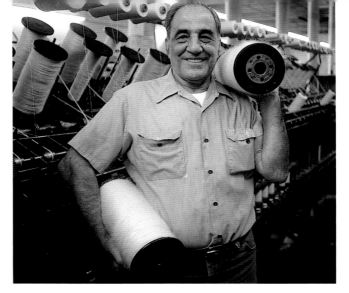

ALTHOUGH THE MACHINERY IS NO LONGER POWERED DIRECTLY BY THE RIVER BELOW, THE ORIGINAL MILL IN LOWELL IS STILL USED TO SPIN MOHAIR YARN. PHOTO: JOHN GOODMAN

TURBINE-DRIVEN LEATHER BELTS POWERED THE WEAVING LOOMS OF THE 1920S. PHOTO: PHILIP CHAPUT, COURTESY OF LOWELL NATIONAL HISTORICAL PARK

Mr. Chew's direction transformed Warley into a specialty mill, the only one of its day to produce fine brushed and looped mohair yarn. Mohair, a product of Angora goats, is a long, slick fiber that is difficult to process. To handle the fibers, Mr. Chew modified nineteenth-century equipment and designed custom machinery. His designs were never patented, however; Mr. Chew preferred instead to keep the secrets of his inventions in house.

Today, as in previous decades, Mr. Chew's machinery transforms the mohair fibers from a thick, ropelike mass into looped novelty yarn. Some of the looped yarn is packaged and sold under the trade name Sharon, but the majority receives additional processing, where it is brushed to produce a fuzzy, elegant, quick-knitting yarn known as La Gran.

In 1979, Classic Elite Yarns was created as a marketing division of Warley to cater mainly to hand weavers and designers. As hand knitting became popular in the early 1980s, Elite expanded its product line beyond mohairs to include

additional natural fibers produced under its direction by other mills worldwide. Prepackaged kits, new specialty yarns, and an annual collection of knitting designs were added. Soon Classic Elite became the parent company of the mill, and its new products and designs began to make the pages of international fashion magazines.

Today Classic Elite Yarns is owned by Patricia Chew and managed primarily by women. Maintaining its traditions, it's still located in the historic mill on the banks of the Merrimack, although the spinning frames are no longer powered by the water below. Its annual design collections have become increasingly popular among hand knitters everywhere, and its product line has grown to include yarns made of cotton, silk, llama, alpaca, wool, rayon, cashmere, and mohair fibers, all stocked in a large variety of classic and fashion-forward colors.

TODAY MOST MOHAIR FIBER COMES FROM TEXAS, WHERE THE MAJORITY OF THE WORLD'S ANGORA GOATS ARE RAISED. PHOTO: COURTESY OF THE MOHAIR COUNCIL OF AMERICA

CONTRIBUTING DESIGNERS

NORAH GAUGHAN

Best known for her innovative stitch designs, Norah Gaughan has been named one of *Vogue Knitting's* Master Knitters of the '90s. Her design talents surfaced early; she learned to knit when she was 14 years old and had her first knitwear design published just four years later. Currently Norah creates designs for several hand-knitting companies and the New York garment industry.

STEPHANIE GILDERSLEEVE

Stephanie Gildersleeve began her career as a textile artist by crocheting cotton bikini tops during the mid-1970s. Later she taught herself to knit and sharpened her design skills while working as a pattern editor for *McCall's Needlework and Crafts*. Now she works out of her home in California, where she creates designs for several yarn companies and knitwear magazines.

JULIE HOFF

While studying in Austria, Julie Hoff learned to design and knit simultaneously. Instead of using a pattern, she learned to knit a gauge swatch, determine the finished width of the garment, cast on, and go! For several years she designed a line of machine-knit sweaters that were sold in exclusive boutiques and larger stores. Currently she enjoys designing for yarn companies from her home in Wheeling, West Virginia.

SALLY LEE

Sally Lee grew up among talented needleworkers who taught her how to knit and encouraged her natural abilities. Although she's had no formal design training, she is one of the most talented colorists working in the United States today. At present she is the co-owner of the Flatiron Workshop in New York City, where she produces exceptional garments for better boutiques and large stores.

SUSAN MILLS

A self-taught knitter, Susan Mills took up weaving while working toward her mathematics degree in college. The influences of her weaving are evident in the textures and color combinations in her sweater designs. In addition to her work as the customer service director and senior pattern editor at Classic Elite, Susan also manages her own small weaving business and shows her work at craft fairs.

DEBORAH NEWTON

The author of *Designing Knitwear* (Taunton, Newtown, CT, 1992), Deborah Newton has designed sweaters for many publications, written pattern instructions, and designed knitted fabrics for the garment industry. She is one of *Vogue Knitting's* Master Knitters of the '90s, and today she conducts design workshops across the country and co-owns an educational map business.

CATHY PAYSON

Cathy Payson began knitting while in college and later started designing for herself and for friends' children. In 1989, she joined Classic Elite Yarns, where she quickly developed her signature style of casual, comfortable, easy-to-make knitwear. Cathy is now an assistant knitwear designer at Susan Bristol, a sportswear company in Charlestown, Massachusetts.

LINDA PRATT

While studying business management in college, Linda Pratt perfected her knitting techniques by making sweaters for her boyfriends. In 1986 she joined Classic Elite, where she has created a number of "family sweaters"—designs that work for anyone of any age. These are a direct offshoot of many ill-fated boyfriend sweaters; her philosophy is that knitters should like their projects enough to wear the sweaters themselves if need be.

MICHELE ROSE

Michele Rose is one of America's most prolific knitwear designers. Currently working as a designer for a major retail chain, she also freelances for many yarn companies and knitwear publications. She developed her interest in knitting while studying fine arts and graphic design at Yale and enhanced her design sense while apprenticing at her father's architecture firm.

KATHY ZIMMERMAN

Kathy Zimmerman has been a knitter from the time she was a teenager. She especially enjoys developing unique ribbing patterns and stitch work, and her designs have been published in *McCall's Needlework and Crafts* and *Cast On* magazines. She is a founder of the Laurel Highlands Knitting Guild and the owner of Kathy's Kreations, a yarn store in Ligonier, Pennsylvania.

INDEX